Ergham Bachir, Bernd Vogel
Strategic Contextual Leadership

De Gruyter Transformative Thinking and Practice of Leadership and Its Development

Edited by
Bernd Vogel

Volume 8

Ergham Bachir, Bernd Vogel

Strategic Contextual Leadership

The Blueprint for CEOs and Executives to Master
the Art of Leadership in Dynamic Contexts

DE GRUYTER

ISBN 978-3-11-138120-6
e-ISBN (PDF) 978-3-11-138272-2
e-ISBN (EPUB) 978-3-11-138310-1
ISSN 2701-4002

Library of Congress Control Number: 2025936414

Bibliographic information published by the Deutsche Nationalbibliothek
The Deutsche Nationalbibliothek lists this publication in the Deutsche Nationalbibliografie;
detailed bibliographic data are available on the internet at http://dnb.dnb.de.

Preface

Books allow us to journey into the depths of curiosity and help us move towards change in organizations and more prosperity for all in our societies.

Probably about 25 or so years ago, Ergham started this project, likely not envisioning that a thought-provoking and practical book for current and future senior leaders on Hybrid Strategic Contextual Leadership would be the result. It all started with her practice of helping strategic leaders and respective organizations to wrap their heads around how to deal with multiple contextual demands and making organizations successful and positively embedded in society. This book is hence deeply rooted in practice. However, it also follows the principle that when we combine practice with learning, and exploring and researching our practices, senior level leadership can grow and thrive successfully to new levels and capabilities. With this aim Ergham successfully embarked on her DBA journey at the Henley Business School and the work with the Henley Centre for Leadership. That is where she crossed paths with Bernd.

Bernd could immediately sense Ergham's relentless drive to further advance the quality of strategic leadership which will ultimately benefit society. And this by not only studying and understanding Western organizations but having the main emphasis on businesses in the Middle East which have been overlooked as a source of learning. To the rest of the world, this region was like a black box, yet at the same time one of the most prospering and exciting areas of business. In a hyperconnected world, global learning from global places can assist senior leaders to grow and thrive when facing the dual contextual challenges we set out in this book.

We also passionately believe that learning and developing towards the senior level of an organization starts early. This book is as much for current executives as for those who aim to become senior leaders or who just want to better understand how their top level managers operate, or could operate, to help shape sustainable success of their organizations.

At the heart of this book lies the Hybrid Strategic Contextual Leadership (HSCL) framework, developed by Ergham as the centerpiece of her research, built on the conviction that effective leadership of senior leaders is not generic—it is deeply contextual along multiple layers. Embracing context is not easy, but hard and deeply rewarding leadership work for executives.

In a world shaped by AI, geopolitical fragmentation, shifting generational values, and market volatility, leaders need more than technical skill or charisma. They need strategic contextual intelligence—the ability to interpret, align with, and lead within the specific multiple facets of concrete to ambiguous context they operate in. The HSCL framework is unique in three ways:

- It introduces the Sustainable Success Framework, combining economic performance with cultural and societal legitimacy.
- It builds on years of fieldwork with dynamic global organizations across industries, moving beyond the GLOBE Study and Western-centric models.

https://doi.org/10.1515/9783111382722-202

– It equips leaders with four Strategic Leadership Imperatives—strategic contextual intelligence, integrative communication, strategic financial intelligence, and innovation with agility—to future-proof their organizations and teams.

However, remember, this only comes alive by your reflection and leadership actions in your areas of responsibilities.

A framework for action!
In this book you will read that sustainable success has many nuances and facets. If you apply that logic to your reading of this book and our insights call, you want to ask yourself how much of your intellectual engagement translates into sustainable action and outcomes. We are deeply indebted to you for starting this journey based on our thinking and practice.

Your unique contexts, your stakeholders, network and key allies will benefit greatly from your sharing, working with, and embedding some of the presented insights, which ultimately are the starting point for creating a sustainably successful organization.

Ergham Bachir and Bernd Vogel
UAE; Montreal, Canada; and Henley-on-Thames, United Kingdom
May 2025

Contents

Introduction

Leadership is at an inflection point. The world of leadership is evolving at an unprecedented pace, shaped by geopolitical shifts, market disruptions, and technological advancements. CEOs and top management teams (TMTs) can no longer rely on static strategies or traditional leadership models. The real challenge is not about having a strategy, it's about executing it within a shifting context.

This book introduces hybrid strategic contextual leadership, a powerful framework designed for executives who must operate across multiple realities, aligning internal strategies with external complexities. Backed by five in-depth case studies (2018–2024) of multinational pluralistic organizations, this book offers practical insights, data-driven strategies, and leadership imperatives to help CEOs and top management teams sustain performance in dynamic environments.

If leadership is about making the right decisions at the right time, this book is the executive roadmap to mastering context-driven strategic leadership and ensuring sustainable success in high-stakes environments.

Consider this: What if your biggest leadership challenge isn't your strategy, but your inability to predict and respond to the contextual shifts before they disrupt execution?

Why do some CEOs fail despite having the best strategy on paper?

Why do the most talented executives face unexpected challenge when implementing strategic change?

Why do leadership teams struggle with internal misalignment despite shared objectives?

How do CEOs and top management teams gain the shareholders' trust and support?

The answer lies in context. Leadership failures are no longer just a result of poor strategic planning but of an inability to anticipate, interpret, and integrate contextual factors into strategic direction and execution.

This book introduces *three essential leadership pillars that* define long-term success in pluralistic organizations:

The Context Matrix: A four-dimensional model that enables leaders to decode the external forces shaping their organizations with a special focus on pluralistic organizations:
- Economic and Regulatory Factors (financial markets, investment climates, governance, global policies)
- Cultural and Societal Factors (societal leadership, stakeholder trust, sustainability imperatives)

https://doi.org/10.1515/9783111382722-001

Strategic Imperatives for Leadership: The four critical dynamic capabilities that determine whether leadership teams thrive or fail in complex environments:
- Strategic Contextual Intelligence: The ability to analyze and integrate external contextual factors into decision-making.
- Strategic Financial Intelligence: The capability to drive financial sustainability while navigating economic uncertainty.
- Integrative Communication: The skill to align diverse leadership perspectives, ensuring cohesion in TMT decision-making.
- Innovation and Agility: The strategic foresight to continuously evolve leadership structures to maintain long-term resilience.

Decoding Sustainable Success: True leadership success is not just about performance excellence but the synthesis of economic and cultural resilience.

This book is not just a leadership guide, it's an executive roadmap to mastering strategic contextual leadership and ensuring long-term, sustainable success in high-stakes environments.

Each chapter delivers executive-level insights and practical applications to help leaders navigate complexity:

Chapter 1: Beyond Linearity – The Need for Strategic Contextual Leadership for Sustainable Success in Pluralistic Organizations

Leadership is no longer about linear strategies or singular cultural perspectives. This chapter introduces hybrid strategic contextual leadership (HSCL) as a transformative approach that integrates:

Strategic Leadership – the ability to pivot and realign leadership approaches dynamically.

Contextual Leadership – an acute awareness of external factors influencing leadership decisions. Multicultural and Pluralistic Leadership Mastery – the skill to operate across diverse corporate, national, and geopolitical landscapes.

New Insight: Leadership failures are no longer primarily due to flawed strategies but rather a lack of contextual dexterity. The hybrid strategic contextual framework shifts leadership from a static, prescriptive approach to a dynamic, adaptive, and context-integrated model that aligns strategic execution with external complexities.

Chapter 2: Mastering the Context Matrix in Pluralistic Organizations

Understanding the external context matrix is essential for sustaining leadership effectiveness. This chapter introduces a structured framework for identifying and managing the economic, regulatory, cultural, and societal influences that shape strategic decisions.

Context Matrix: The context matrix provides a four-dimensional framework for analyzing how external contextual factors shape pluralistic organizational success.

Strategic Leadership: Leaders and TMTs must balance all four dimensions to develop holistic strategies that ensure financial sustainability, regulatory compliance, cultural adaptability, and societal alignment.

Pluralistic Organizations: Pluralistic organizations, with their multiplicity of authorities, objectives, logics, and preferences, exemplify the challenges and opportunities that arise when leading in complex, dynamic contexts.

Hybrid Strategic and Contextual Leadership framework: Pluralistic organizations achieve sustainable success by integrating sustainable economic outcomes and sustainable cultural outcomes. These two pillars define an organization's ability to thrive in complex, high-stakes environments while ensuring long-term resilience.

New Insight: The concept of pluralistic organizations is central to the overall theme of this book, which explores the intersection of strategic and contextual leadership in diverse and multicultural environments. Pluralistic organizations demand more than strategy, they require leaders who can anticipate contextual shifts before they disrupt execution.

Chapter 3: TMTs' Driving Performance Excellence through Strategic Contextual Leadership

TMTs are not singular leadership entities; they are complex ecosystems where alignment is critical yet often elusive. This chapter explores TMT composition, structure and process. TMTs dual balancing acts to lead within the organization while managing external pressures.

New Insight: The interplay between external uncertainty and internal misalignment amplifies the strategic risk for organizations, requiring strong TMT alignment to counteract contextual pressures.

Chapter 4: Strategic Contextual Leadership Imperatives for Multicultural and Pluralistic Organizations

To lead effectively, TMTs must develop four critical dynamic capabilities imperatives: Strategic contextual intelligence, integrative communication, strategic financial intelligence, innovation and agility.

New Insight: Strategic contextual intelligence is the compound of knowledge and expertise that enables TMTs to integrate contextual foresight, financial prudence, communication alignment, innovation and agility in pluralistic environments.

Chapter 5: Charting Sustainable Success in Pluralistic Multicultural Organizations
Sustainable success is a synergy of economic and cultural resilience:

Sustainable economic outcomes focus on performance excellence, efficiency of resources and processes, financial sustainability, innovation, and agility.

Sustainable cultural outcomes emphasize societal leadership expectations, stakeholder trust, good governance, continuous learning, and leadership development.

New Insight: This chapter provides a new lens on how economical sustainability, leadership alignment, and cultural sustainability must work in harmony to achieve sustainable success.

Chapter 6: Strategic Contextual Leadership Development A Roadmap to Sustainability
Strategic contextual leadership development advances sustainability leadership development by broadening its scope beyond environmental concerns. It recognizes that true sustainability is a trifecta of economic, cultural, and strategic resilience, considering not only climate imperatives but also the economy, society, organizational culture, and the strategic leadership responsibilities within pluralistic organizations.

This chapter presents a structured roadmap to embedding hybrid strategic contextual leadership into leadership pipelines, ensuring that executives are equipped to navigate complex, dynamic, and multi-stakeholder environments effectively.

New Insight: Leadership development must evolve beyond competency checklists and static theoretical frameworks. Instead, it must be a continuous, context-driven, and dynamic learning process that integrates strategic contextual imperatives into daily decision-making and long-term strategy.

Chapter 7: Looking Ahead – The Urgency for Strategic Contextualized Leadership
Leadership in the future will demand more than just strategic execution; it will require contextual intelligence, financial acumen, and the agility to adapt across global, multicultural environments. This chapter introduces the future strategic leadership imperatives framework, where the imperatives drive the anticipation of and response to economic, geopolitical, and market shifts. It also explores how emerging technologies such as AI, advanced risk mitigation models, and digital integration can be leveraged to achieve a balance between economic performance and cultural sustainability.

New Insight: Leadership failures in the future will not stem from poor strategic planning alone, but from the inability to synchronize leadership execution with external complexities. The future strategic leadership imperatives transition leadership from a reactive model to a proactive, AI-enhanced, and context-driven approach ensuring leaders can thrive in an era of geopolitical shifts, digital transformation, and financial innovation.

Appendix A- Fact Sheets About the Participating Organizations, Participants' Details and Interviews

Appendix B- Introducing the Hybrid Strategic Contextual Leadership Workbook

The workbook is a practical tool that transforms theory into interactive learning experiences. The workbook includes:

Context Mapping Tools: Applying strategic contextual intelligence enabling TMTs identify and interpret external and internal influences.

Scenario-Based Decision: Making Exercises enabling leadership teams to develop contextually aligned strategies.

Strategic Financial Intelligence Training: equipping TMTs to make informed financial decisions in uncertain environments.

Innovation and Agility Assessments: measuring leadership adaptability and innovation readiness.

Balanced Scorecard for Sustainable Success: providing an empirical evaluation model to track leadership effectiveness across performance, efficiency, sustainability, and stakeholder trust.

New Insight: Static training programs are obsolete; in dynamic environments leaders must learn by doing, adapting, and strategically integrating knowledge into execution.

Chapter 1
Beyond Linearity: The Need for Strategic and Contextual Leadership

To set the stage for the hybrid strategic contextual leadership and the strategic leadership skills for CEOs and executives discussed throughout this book, we set out that advanced leadership requires more than traditional management and leadership capabilities. This book argues that CEOs and executives must go beyond linear leadership models and adopt a hybrid approach that integrates strategic intelligence, contextual awareness, and agile decision-making. The Hybrid Strategic Contextual Leadership framework introduced in this book addresses this need by equipping leaders with the ability to synthesize complexity, align strategic execution with external realities, and drive sustainable organizational success. Leadership today requires dynamic capabilities that surpass conventional leadership models (Kartika, 2023). For decades, leadership studies emphasized hierarchical decision-making, goal-setting, and operational efficiency as key components of executive success (Mintzberg, 2009). However, in a world marked by economic volatility, geopolitical uncertainty, digital transformation, artificial intelligence and shifting societal expectations, these skills, though necessary, are insufficient for sustainable success (Teece, Peteraf, and Leih, 2016). Furthermore, recent research underscores the necessity for leaders to develop adaptability, cross-cultural competence, ethical leadership, and strategic foresight to navigate these complexities effectively (Min, 2024; Nair, 2024).

Historically, strategic leadership has been associated with planning, control, and execution, assuming that organizations operate within relatively stable environments (Porter, 1996). However, the reality is far more complex for pluralistic organizations within today's extremely dynamic environments where:

- External forces: Economic, geopolitical, technological, and societal are shifting rapidly.
- Internal challenges: Organizational culture, leadership dynamics, and governance create complexity.
- Traditional strategic planning frameworks fail to accommodate the interconnected nature of modern business challenges.

As organizations become more interconnected across cultures, industries, and regulatory landscapes, CEOs and executives require a hybrid model that blends today's contextual intelligence, strategic foresight, and leadership agility.

Several insightful interviews conducted during our research were with the chairman, CEO and the Chief Human Resources Officer, of Urban Escape, a Middle Eastern real estate company based in UAE.

https://doi.org/10.1515/9783111382722-002

This chapter will present the perspective of Urban Escape CEO who shared his achievements and the business and leadership challenges he faced, offering a transparent and candid account of his leadership journey. He highlighted that leadership today requires more than technical and management skills. "In today's business environment, hierarchies are constantly shifting, and leaders must navigate rapidly changing contexts and strategies, integrate diverse teams, and manage a wide range of stakeholder expectations" (in-person interview communication, December, 2018); he shared his willingness and awareness to reflect on both the successes and the difficulties as a sign of true executive skill, and he also provided a rich, authentic perspective on the complexities of leadership in today's fast-evolving business environment. He emphasized that:

> CEOs cannot embark on the journey of leadership alone. To navigate the complexities of the future, they must cultivate strategic, mutually beneficial partnerships and embrace adaptive leadership models that foster innovation, resilience, and sustainable success. For new CEOs, the key is having the right top management team with you, fostering strong relationships, and continually learning. Leadership is not about individual achievement, it's about collective success and the team that surrounds you. (In-person interview communication, December, 2018)

He referred to the context in terms of significant changes in the economy, evolving local market demands, and, most importantly, the expectations of national leadership. These elements illustrate the multifaceted nature of context, encompassing economic shifts, societal trends, and governance priorities, which collectively shape strategic leadership imperatives.

This perspective aligns seamlessly with the principles of the Hybrid Strategic Contextual Leadership framework introduced in this book. It emphasizes the centrality of strategic leadership, top management team collaboration, and essential leadership skills required for navigating pluralistic, multicultural organizations. As researchers like Osborn, Hunt, and Jauch (2002) have argued, effective leadership is inherently contextual, requiring an adaptive approach that accounts for the dynamic interplay of external and internal factors. Similarly, Johns (2006) highlights that context often serves as the "missing link" in understanding leadership effectiveness, underscoring its role in shaping organizational outcomes. Moreover, the concept of societal leadership expectations finds support in the work of House et al. (2013), who demonstrated that leaders' behaviors are more strongly influenced by societal norms than by cultural archetypes, further emphasizing the pivotal role of context.

Context thus emerges as both the mainframe and the dynamic force shaping these leadership imperatives. By addressing the complexities of an interconnected and ever-evolving environment, leaders can align their strategies with the broader economic, societal, and national expectations that define success in pluralistic organizations.

Urban Escape, established and listed in 2005, was a new development company focusing on the booming markets of real estate development. The CEO recalled:

> I joined when the company was still in its infancy. I was employee number 91, and in just two years, we grew to over 800 employees. This was before the financial crisis hit in 2009. I joined through a structured program that focused on fast-track the nominated national engineers into top management positions. Although I had the technical engineering skills from my education, I had no idea how to apply them at work. (In-person interview communication, December, 2018)

The CEO spoke of his experience with immense enthusiasm:

> I was fortunate to be hired just as the company was launching multi-million-dollar mixed-use development projects. It was a tremendous opportunity for an electrical engineer, like me. I was immediately immersed in a flood of information, rapidly gaining experience by making mistakes, learning quickly, and adapting to the challenges. The knowledge I acquired in just few years was unbelievable. (In-person interview communication, December, 2018)

By 2006, the organization was involved in major development projects, but then the 2008–2009 financial crisis hit. "We had over 50,000 workers when the global financial crisis struck," he explained. "The company faced a massive restructuring everything changed, from the board of directors to the CEO and the management team."

By this time, the Urban Escape CEO had risen to the position of Director of Planning and Infrastructure, responsible for a profit and loss portfolio. "I gained invaluable experience in planning and understanding corporate strategy", he shared. "After the third strategic change in 2011, the new strategic direction was a merger with a major public real estate development company. The merger, which took nine months, was a transformative experience for me as an executive in the management team. It was an intense period of uncertainty, and learning about investments and mergers and acquisitions, as an electrical engineer. The experience I gained was immense," he stated. "Post-merger, I transitioned to learn about the asset management and was nominated by the board to head the asset management team the next year" (in-person interview communication, December, 2018).

In 2016, when the Chief Development Officer left the company, the CEO found himself juggling two roles: Head of Asset Management and Acting Chief Development Officer. Then, in November 2017, another strategic change took place. "I was 'given' the CEO position," he revealed. "It was a challenging transition. I had never been formally trained in a CEO program, and our chairman also left. The lack of top management level development, coaching, and succession planning were not our strengths. It felt like we were going through a systematic change in a state of organized chaos" (in-person interview communication, December, 2018).

As a junior engineer, the CEO of Urban Escape never anticipated the complex leadership journey that lay ahead. His ascent to the top was not a linear path but rather an unplanned evolution, shaped by the need to continuously adapt and develop new skills. Throughout his career, he faced a series of high-stakes challenges, from navigating financial crises to leading major mergers and restructuring efforts. These experiences reinforced a critical lesson: Leadership in today's volatile and interconnected world demands far more than technical expertise or traditional management approaches.

Reflecting on his journey, the Urban Escape CEO underscored the necessity of hybrid strategic contextual leadership, a dynamic approach that blends strategic foresight, high-performance execution, cultural intelligence, and stakeholder engagement. "In today's business landscape, hierarchies are constantly shifting, and success is no longer driven by rigid structures but by the ability to adapt, integrate, and innovate," he explained. "Future CEOs must master the art of navigating complex and evolving contexts by creating mutual-benefit partnerships and embracing new models of engagement that foster collaboration across industries, disciplines, and cultures" (in-person interview communication, December, 2018).

For emerging leaders and new CEOs, his advice is clear: contextual awareness is the key to effective leadership. "The ability to decode shifting environments, build diverse teams, and align stakeholder interests is what separates truly transformative leaders from the rest," he emphasized. "Leadership is not just about personal achievement it is about empowering the people around me, fostering resilience, and driving collective success in an era of constant change" (in-person interview communication, December, 2018).

The CEO of Urban Escape reflected that his engineering background, cultural familiarity, and prior experience within the company were not sufficient to lead effectively. Despite his deep understanding of the business and its operational landscape, he recognized that navigating a multicultural, pluralistic organization with headquarters in the Middle East and global operations required a broader skill set. To lead with impact, he had to upskill himself in finance, investments, and technology areas critical to making informed strategic decisions, securing sustainable growth, and aligning the organization with the complexities of international markets. His journey highlights the necessity for top executives to continuously expand their expertise beyond their core discipline to successfully steer global organizations in an era of rapid change.

1.1 A Blueprint for Hybrid Strategic Contextual Leadership

The Urban Escape CEO's story exemplifies the journey of a strategic leader navigating complex and evolving context, adapting to rapid changes, and learning continuously. His insights provide a compelling introduction to the principles of strategic contextual leadership (SCL) that this book offers – a blueprint for CEOs and TMTs to achieve sustainable success in an interconnected changing world.

In this book, we discover how hybrid strategic contextual leadership is the deliberate fusion of strategic leadership with an acute awareness of and action on contextual variables and developments. It recognizes that effective leadership by CEOs and executives is not just about making the right strategic choices but about understanding, adapting to, and at times proactively influencing the unique environmental conditions that shape those choices. This approach moves beyond traditional models that often view strategic leadership in isolation. Successful CEOs and executives, instead, acknowledge that the internal, business, and wider societal context in which leadership operates is a powerful determinant of its success.

An example from Urban Escape illustrates this principle. During a year when the company's performance faltered due to geopolitical and economic turbulence, the CEO and the management team focused on creating a positive impact by fostering stronger community ties and enhancing the organization's reputation as a socially responsible business. They launched initiatives such as employee volunteering programs and partnerships with local businesses to drive mutual growth, which not only mitigated the short-term effects of the downturn but also reinforced the company's long-term resilience. This proactive effort to influence the context demonstrates how hybrid strategic contextual leadership can turn challenges into opportunities for sustainable success.

1.1.1 Hybrid Strategic Contextual Leadership

The hybrid strategic contextual leadership has several drivers. Firstly, it fills a critical void in traditional leadership studies and some practices of strategic leaders, which often overlook the profound influence of contextual factors on leadership actions and results. Secondly, this approach recognizes that the relationship between leadership actions and their outcomes is not linear and simple. It is significantly shaped by the elements in the layers of the surrounding context. Thirdly, many businesses have, knowingly or unknowingly, evolved into what is known as pluralistic organizations, entities characterized by diverse and often competing objectives, stakeholders, and operational environments (Brès, Raufflet and Boghossian, 2018).

We found these organizations in various sectors, including healthcare, academia, innovation and technology, investments, real estate, and more. They are marked by complex governance structures and a multitude of internal and external stakeholders with often conflicting interests and expectations that ultimately senior leaders need to successfully to navigate. Fourthly, strategic contextual leadership in those pluralistic organizations asks to look differently at success and to focus on sustainable organizational performance. Fifth, we assert that the context in which senior leaders operate is a powerful entity itself, setting the stage and defining the parameters for leadership effectiveness, and hence needs substantial unpacking and understanding by the CEO and his/her executive action. Finally, often business and research endeavors expect senior leaders to have all those requirements we outlined by default. Instead, as strongly emphasized by the Urban Escape CEO, strategic contextual leadership development requires self-guided and assisted leadership, learning and development at the top of an organization.

In this book, we reveal the complex nonlinear relationship between leadership and context, introducing two novel concepts: the *hybrid model of strategic contextual leadership* and the *context dynamics* matrix. These concepts aim to demystify what is traditionally known as the "black box" in strategic leadership. By doing so, we assist strategic leaders in their practice, enabling them to make informed decisions that are both contextually aware and strategically sound.

In our quest to deepen the understanding of strategic leadership among senior managers and its critical consequences within pluralistic organizations, we focus on blending industry-specific and broader external contexts. This endeavor aims to formulate a sophisticated framework based on a hybrid theoretical lens, blending strategic leadership and contextual leadership theories to acknowledge the multifaceted nature of leadership and transcend traditional linear models. By integrating these perspectives, the framework (Figure 1.1) offers a more nuanced approach to leadership within pluralistic organizations, addressing the dynamic interplay of strategic imperatives and contextual variables (Al Bachir, 2022).

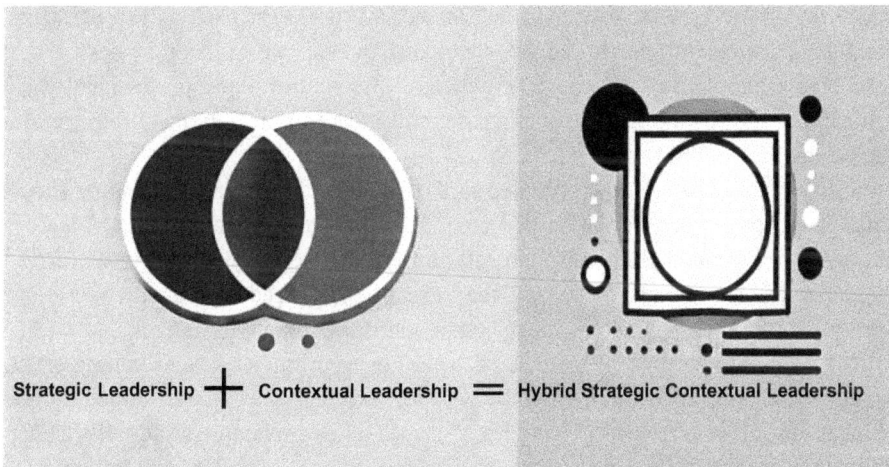

Figure 1.1: Strategic Contextual Theoretical Amalgamation.
The integration of strategic leadership and contextual leadership highlights their convergence into a hybrid approach known as Strategic Contextual Leadership, which emerges from the interplay between the two domains.

Figure 1.1 shows the aim for the book to study the relationship between the first circle representing the strategic leadership and the second circle representing the contextual leadership marrying strategic leaders' experiences and research to produce the hybrid strategic contextual leadership represented in the figure as a circle inside a square. In doing so this book offers fresh perspectives, fostering deeper understanding, and offering alternative explanations, insights and practices. The reader sees the importance of factoring in contextual influences with strategic leadership to foster specific sustainable leadership outcomes and behaviors.

We learned that an organizational maze is never linear. There are often turns and bends, hallmarked by unexpected events. Recognizing the influence of these events, we highlight how leadership often manifests differently depending on how the external and internal context pluralistically operates.

Context plays a dual role in the realm of leadership and organizational strategy. Internally, it serves as the backdrop for individuals within organizations, guiding senior leaders as they navigate critical priorities such as fostering top management team alignment, enhancing organizational culture, and building resilience against internal uncertainties.

For example, in the Urban Escape case, the CEO had to address the need to gain the support of the community and the societal leadership by optimizing the top management team performance and enhancing their communication and engagement with the community using executive training programs and workshops that facilitated execution, communication and collaboration. Similarly, the programs focused on leadership that resembles the national leadership practices such as respect, trust, good governance and people-centric leadership. By such programs they ensure that the TMTs' leadership practices address their diverse cultural and professional backgrounds, ensure cohesion, shared purpose, and most importantly meet the expectation of the societal leadership expectations.

Externally, Urban Escape operated in a broader environment, compelling executives to either adapt to or influence factors such as geopolitical shifts, regulatory changes, and societal leadership expectations. For instance, during a downturn in global trade, the CEO and TMTs of Urban Escape prioritized sustainable operations and invested in environmental construction and development initiatives, showcasing a proactive approach to influencing external perceptions and maintaining stakeholder trust. The need for financial savvy for an electric engineer, and the Chief Human Resources officer of Urban Escape is also a great example of how the leadership team integrated financial reporting transparency and sustainability initiatives to align with shareholder and societal demands, ultimately reinforcing the company's reputation and securing long-term viability.

The different facets of context encompass stimuli and phenomena that exist both within and beyond the immediate organizational environment. These factors, as described by one of our interviewees, *"envelop"* senior executives in their leadership actions, shaping decisions and strategies in profound ways. The ability to identify, interpret, and respond to these contextual elements is a hallmark of strategic contextual leadership, enabling leaders to not only react but also shape their environments for sustainable success.

Our recent study on strategic leadership underscores the profound impact of context on various dimensions of organizational performance. This book challenges the tendency to overlook context or use external factors as an excuse for underperformance at the senior leadership level. Instead, it aligns with research that highlights the consequences of strategic leadership for organizational outcomes and the necessity of contextualizing the roles of CEOs and top management teams (Hambrick et al., 1996). The growing body of literature on strategic leadership emphasizes how CEO characteristics, decision-making processes, and the broader contextual environment shape firm performance (Chatterjee and Hambrick, 2007; Crossland and Hambrick, 2007). Furthermore, the strategic leadership field has increasingly recognized the importance of integrating context into leadership theory, particularly in relation to CEO-TMT alignment and its impact on sustainable success (Hambrick and Chen, 2008; Quigley and Hambrick, 2015).

Our academic and practical studies further illuminate the substantial influence of context on organizational performance, particularly in pluralistic organizations, those operating within environments characterized by multiple reporting authorities, diverse stakeholders, competing objectives, and complex decision-making structures (Denis, Langley, and Rouleau, 2007). Unlike traditional hierarchical organizations, pluralistic organizations must balance often conflicting demands from various power centers, requiring leaders to demonstrate exceptional contextual intelligence, strategic agility, and stakeholder management skills (Jarzabkowski and Fenton, 2006).

A prime example is Urban Escape, which simultaneously reports to the Ministry of Planning, financial regulatory bodies, and an array of public and private stakeholders. The organization must navigate shifting priorities, stringent financial oversight, and competing stakeholder expectations, making leadership effectiveness deeply context dependent. As industries become more volatile and regulatory frameworks more stringent, leaders must develop the ability to decode their environment, anticipate change, and align multiple competing interests to drive sustainable success (Tushman and O'Reilly, 2007).

As the selection of a CEO is one of the most consequential decisions an organization can make, studies by Quigley and Hambrick (2015) found that CEO selection alone can influence up to 25% of an organization's overall performance, underscoring the profound impact of leadership choices. In pluralistic organizations, this influence is even greater, as CEOs must operate in environments where authority is dispersed, decision-making is contested, and success depends on aligning diverse and sometimes opposing interests (Denis, Dompierre, Langley, and Rouleau, 2011). Unlike in traditional corporate settings, where CEOs often have greater unilateral decision-making power, leaders in pluralistic organizations must act as strategic integrators, brokering consensus, and balancing short-term pressures with long-term institutional goals (Bryson, Crosby, and Bloomberg, 2014). In pluralistic organizations, where competing logics and fragmented authority structures shape decision-making, the ability of CEOs and their top management teams to accurately interpret and respond to external shifts is crucial in determining whether the organization thrives or struggles. This complexity demands a more adaptive and integrated leadership approach—one that goes beyond traditional strategic planning. CEOs and TMTs must blend strategic vision with active community engagement and a deep understanding of societal leadership expectations. By doing so, they can effectively navigate their organization's unique challenges, align diverse stakeholder interests, and drive sustainable success in an increasingly dynamic and pluralistic environment.

Thus, contextual leadership skills are not just a desirable trait, they are an essential capability for CEOs operating in pluralistic organizations. In sum, context matters profoundly in leadership effectiveness, and in pluralistic organizations, CEO selection plays an even more critical role in shaping performance. As organizations like Urban Escape illustrate, leaders must not only execute strategic plans but also skillfully manage a diverse network of stakeholders, competing interests, and regulatory demands. This reinforces the importance of a leadership model that prioritizes contextual awareness, stakeholder collaboration, and adaptive decision-making as essential capabilities for CEOs navigating the modern organizational landscape.

This insight pivots our focus towards a holistic appreciation of the context matrix (introduced in the following chapter) to encapsulate the full spectrum of external influences impacting CEO and TMT effectiveness. By leveraging the dynamics of pluralistic organizations, the context matrix provides a framework for understanding how leaders can align internal strategies with external pressures to drive sustainable success.

The different facets of context encompass stimuli and phenomena that exist both within and beyond the immediate organizational environment. These factors, as described by one of our interviewees, "envelop" senior executives in their leadership actions, shaping decisions and strategies in profound ways. The ability to identify, interpret, and respond to these contextual elements is a hallmark of strategic contextual leadership, enabling leaders to not only react but also shape their environments for sustainable success.

The importance of context becomes even more pronounced in pluralistic organizations[1] because their operations are inherently complex, involving multiple layers of influence and competing interests. For example, consider how Urban Escape is expanding into development operations in the United Kingdom where the regulations, community expectations, and varying investor priorities vary. The CEO and the management team must navigate not only the regulatory framework but also ensure the organization's environmental initiatives resonate with local communities while addressing shareholders' demands for profitability.

In this situation, the leadership team might decide to establish a localized sustainability initiative, integrating community involvement into their operations. For instance, they hired engineers from the United Kingdom and partnered with local suppliers. They also launched in both countries, United Arab Emirates and United Kingdom, tailored environmental education programs to community schools to foster goodwill. While these efforts align with societal and regulatory expectations, they also provide a competitive edge by differentiating the organization as a socially responsible entity in the eyes of both communities.

---

1 Pluralistic organization is defined and explained in detail in Chapter 2.

Such initiatives demonstrate how leaders in pluralistic organizations cannot rely solely on generic strategies but must leverage a deep understanding of their unique context. The interplay of diverse shareholder demands highlights that context is not merely an operational factor but a strategic imperative. Leaders must actively interpret and influence these dynamics, ensuring that their strategies are both locally relevant and globally competitive, thus showcasing the critical role context plays in achieving long-term success in pluralistic organizations.

By introducing these frameworks, we aim to provide strategic leaders (top management teams, senior managers, CEOs, directors on boards, and shareholders) with the thinking and tools they need to navigate the complexities of pluralistic organizations, ensuring that their leadership not only achieves strategic objectives but also resonates with the unique contextual realities of their changing environments. The context matrix (see Chapter 2) is a practical tool and an academically rooted concept vital in navigating the complexities of organizational management and leadership. It underscores how various forms of context critically shape, direct, and sometimes redefine leadership trajectories. Despite its importance, leaders at the helm of pluralistic organizations often overlook a thorough understanding of these contextual layers.

The Hybrid Strategic Contextual Leadership framework aims to bridge exactly that gap in leadership thinking and practice. By integrating these nuances into strategic leadership practice, we can enhance decision-making, align strategies with contextual realities, and foster more effective leadership. These concepts aim to offer fresh perspectives in the study of strategic leadership, emphasizing the multi-interest, non-linear, and contextually rich landscape in which today's leaders operate.

1.2 What Is Strategic Leadership and Why Does It Matter?

Strategic leadership is a first main block of our hybrid strategic contextual leadership approach. Child's radical work in 1972 laid the foundation for the upper echelons theory. This theory, a cornerstone in understanding strategic leadership, centers on "strategic direction" – the conscious, impactful decisions that shape an organization's structure, goals, technology, and human resources. Child aptly noted that prevailing theories often overlooked the pivotal role of those wielding the power to initiate structural and strategic changes. Strategic direction, he emphasized, intertwines a political process with constraints and opportunities, all orchestrated by decision-makers in positions of power. Child's concept of the dominant coalition unveils a dynamic picture. It's the executives' minds that forge an organization's strategic choices. These minds, encompassing board directors, executives, investors, and skilled professionals, interact to shape the organizational path.

Hambrick and Mason's inquiry in 1984 echoed in the field of executives' behavior: "Why do organizations act as they do?" Their exploration laid bare the link between executive prestige, social status, and organizational performance. This is the echelon where power resides, the domain of the board, the CEO, and the top management teams. They hold not only the highest formal leadership roles but also the authority and required skill set to mold structures, set priorities, and direct the organization toward its multifaceted goals (Hambrick and Mason, 1984). Understanding executives' characteristics has become pivotal in decoding their impact. The study of these individuals, their selection, their unique composition, and their influence on organizational strategies within specific contexts, constitutes a significant area of strategic leadership research and subsequent practice. Within this complex entanglement, the unseen mechanisms within and between senior leaders in context at play are striking – often referred to as the "black box" that facilitates the connection between executives' characteristics and organizational outcomes.

The "black box" concept refers to the unobservable psychological processes and dynamics that translate between top executives' characteristics and organizational outcomes. The theory posits that the background, experiences, values, and personalities of top executives influence their perceptions, judgments, and decision-making. These cognitive processes, in turn, affect the strategic choices and actions they take, consequently impacting the organization's performance.

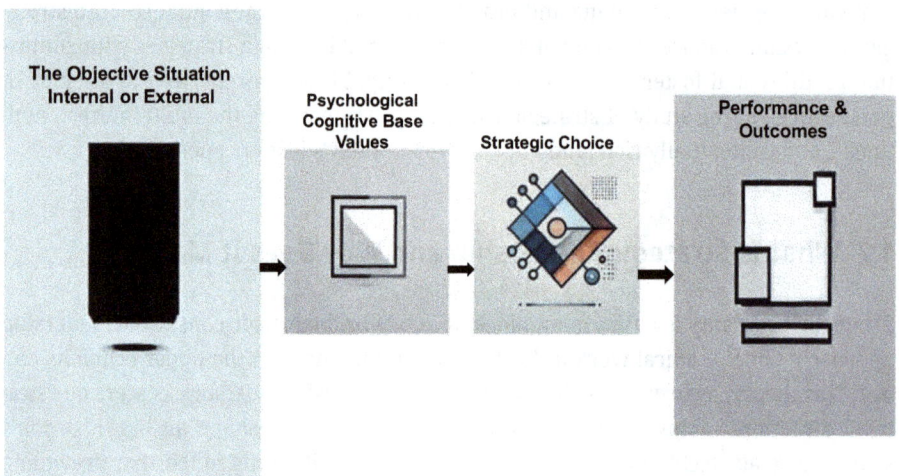

Figure 1.2: An Illustration of Hambrick's Black Box.
Hambrick's black box model illustrates how internal and external objective situations, along with psychological and cognitive factors, shape strategic choices and ultimately influence performance outcomes.

However, to truly understand strategic leadership and provide recommendation, we must address the limitations of the "black box" the concept itself has as an overly linear model (Figure 1.2). While the theory emphasizes the importance of executive characteristics, it falls short in accounting for the dynamic and non-linear impact of the context—both internal and external—that influences these leaders and their organizations. The linearity of the "black box" model oversimplifies the relationship between executive attributes and organizational outcomes, ignoring the complex interplay of contextual factors and may impact the quality of strategic decisions made by leadership.

Our perspective is that context is not a static backdrop but a dynamic force that continuously interacts with executives' leadership and decision-making. For instance, Osborn et al. (2002) argue that context plays a pivotal role in shaping leadership effectiveness, while Crossland and Hambrick (2007) demonstrate how national context influences CEOs' behaviors and the strategic choices they make. However, these studies, often resembling a "black box," lack a detailed exploration of the contextual dimensions and how strategic leaders actively respond to contextual influences. This gap results in an incomplete understanding of how strategic leadership operates in complex, real-world pluralistic environments.

Moreover, the "black box" approach fails to provide what we call a three-dimensional (3D) view of leadership, context, and organizational outcomes. It treats these elements as separate and linear rather than interconnected and dynamic. This limitation becomes particularly evident in pluralistic organizations, where diverse and complex environments are critical yet often overlooked.

This book addresses this gap by advocating for a hybrid strategic contextual leadership approach. This framework recognizes that leadership is not confined to isolated decision-makers but is instead an intricate orchestration of minds, decisions, and contexts. Together, these elements shape an organization's trajectory, emphasizing the need for a more integrated and dynamic understanding of leadership in pluralistic environments. Our view is that context is not a static backdrop but a dynamic force that continuously interacts with executives' leadership and action taking. For example, Osborn et al. (2002) argue that context significantly influences leadership effectiveness, while Crossland and Hambrick (2007) demonstrate how national context can shape CEOs' behaviors and the strategic choices they make. But these studies like the "black box" lack not only the contextual dimension, but how the strategic leaders responded to the contextual influences, leading to an incomplete understanding of how strategic leadership operates in real-world, pluralistic environments.

Moreover, the "black box" also fails to provide what we call a 3D vision of view on leadership, context, and organizational outcomes. It treats these elements as separate and linear, rather than as interconnected and dynamic. In pluralistic organizations, where diverse and complex environments are often overlooked, this limitation is particularly glaring.

This book argues that to bridge this gap, we must adopt a hybrid strategic contextual leadership approach. This approach acknowledges that leadership is not confined to isolated decision-makers but is an intricate orchestration of minds, decisions, and contexts that together mold an organization's fate.

This chapter, and indeed this book, serves as a reminder that while we can observe executives' characteristics and organizational outcomes, we provide a more comprehensive and realistic framework for studying and practicing strategic leadership in pluralistic organizations. In this pursuit, we created a rich mosaic of perspectives within the context of multiple organizations. The organizations were carefully selected to represent the diverse range of challenges faced by multicultural pluralistic organizations across different countries

The discovery voyage through the complex landscapes of pluralistic organizations across different countries yielded a treasure trove of both expected and unanticipated findings and insights. These insights shifted our focus to understand how and why external context marked by economic shifts and cultural diversity, exerted a profound influence on the internal workings of these organizations.

1.3 Understanding Contextual Leadership: Illuminating Organizational Dynamics

Contextual leadership is a second main block of our hybrid strategic contextual leadership approach. In the field of present business, leadership is not about individuals at the helm. It's about steering the organization through uncharted strategic changes, contextual intricacies, and dynamic challenges. This book investigates why strategic and contextual leadership is imperative for shaping the trajectory of sustainable success for pluralistic organizations.

Consider a multinational corporation, a juggernaut in its industry, with teams spread across continents, navigating the complexities of today's globalized business landscape. At first glance, it appears to be a beacon of success, with a strong top management team at the helm. However, as we investigate the organization's intricacies, a complex web of challenges begins to emerge. The CEO, a seasoned leader renowned for his strategic acumen, finds himself in unfamiliar territory as he grapples with divergent leadership styles within the top management team. The head of the company's Asian division has a vastly different approach compared to its European counterpart. The African team, on the other hand, is dealing with unique market dynamics, further adding to the leadership puzzle.

The organization's external environment is equally diverse and dynamic. Economic fluctuations, geopolitical tensions, and shifting stakeholders' preferences are just a few of the contextual factors constantly shaping the leadership landscape. The challenge becomes clear: How can this CEO and their top management team effectively lead and steer a pluralistic, multi-objective organization towards success in such a multifaceted and ever-changing context?

This is where contextual leadership steps onto the stage. It's not merely a theoretical concept; it's a practical necessity. We recognize that understanding the impact of context on leadership outcomes is paramount. It's not a one-size-fits-all scenario; leadership is deeply intertwined with the context in which it operates.

Contextual leadership, with its multifaceted approaches, acknowledges that leadership is not a uniform entity but rather a dynamic interplay between leaders and their surroundings. Whether leadership is nested within the changing organizational structures and decision-making processes, universally embedded in social systems or a hybrid of both, it brings forth a method to observe, measure, and ultimately enhance leadership within a given context.

Our ambition is therefore to unravel the triggers and outcomes of CEO and top management team leadership effectiveness within pluralistic organizations. We don't stop at the organizational level; we extend our gaze to industry and country-level contexts to construct a robust framework that accounts for these diverse contexts and leverages them as catalysts for organizational success.

In essence, contextual leadership is a practical imperative for strategic leaders (top management team members and CEOs), that *integrated* with the practice of strategic leadership helps them navigate the complex, globalized, and ever-evolving landscape of modern business. It's the key to unlocking a holistic comprehension of how leadership's impact is moulded by its surroundings, and our journey begins now.

1.3.1 The Emergence of Contextual Influence in Organizational Leadership

Leadership thinking and practice have not ignored the question of context. Yet, it focussed often on one single area of what is happening in the external and internal layers of the form. For example, path-goal theory investigated how leadership styles interact with situational elements (House, 1997) to influence followers' motivation and satisfaction. This theory investigated the complex interplay between leader attributes, follower dynamics, and contextual factors like task structure and workgroup norms.

In response to the situational leadership studies, strategic management scholars aptly addressed the limitations of contextual influences and their profound implications for leadership. By discerning a set of contextual factors, they charted the course for how these factors subtly shape an organization's openness to leadership (Pettigrew, 2012). Contextual dimensions dictate the reception of leadership efforts, where varying levels of receptivity necessitate distinct transformational leadership strategies. Built on strategic management analysis the study of the organizational internal and external context was recommended. Pettigrew, a global thinker in strategic management, formalized the results of his case study, which he conducted for more than 20 years, by carving a niche for understanding leadership within the multi-level strategic context.

Context encompasses the social, political, and economic environment where an organizational leader operates. The content of senior leader activities includes strat-

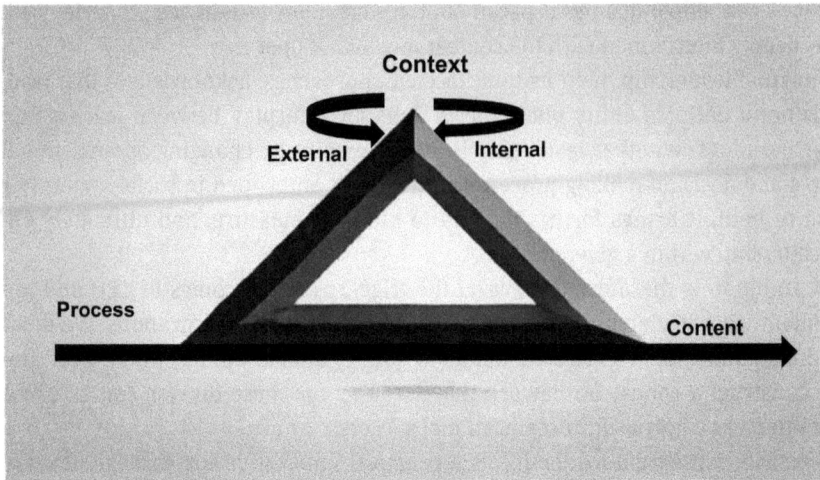

Figure 1.3: The Context, Process, and Content.
Pettigrew's Context, Process, and Content framework emphasizes the dynamic interplay between contextual factors, organizational processes, and the evolving content of strategic change (Pettigrew's, 1987).

egy and objectives, while the *processes* encapsulate operational modes, technology, human capital, products, positioning, and corporate culture (Figure 1.3).

We shift the focus from leaders as standalone entities to leadership as a process within the organizational context used to disseminate the strategic direction and produce outcomes. However, the role of the leaders in strategic management is downplayed in the multi-level perspective. The process framework prioritizes the examination of leadership process which influences actions, interactions, relationships, ideas, and attitudes in the internal context of organizations.

1.3.2 A Cross-Cultural and National Expectations Lens on Context in Leadership

The leadership journey of the CEO of a national industrial development company (NID) offers a profound lens into the interplay of national culture, cross-cultural dynamics, and leadership expectations within the context of the United Arab Emirates. NID[2] is 100 % owned by Echo Capital and was established in 2009 with a mission to construct and manage master developments. Its portfolio spans infrastructure, mixed-use projects, industrial warehousing, and logistics, reflecting its critical role in supporting the country industrial and economic diversification agenda. Under CEO leadership, the company has grown to focus on diversifying its client base, creating innovative solutions for local or-

---

2 An information sheet on National Industrial Development is available in Appendix A.

ganizations, and serving manufacturing and logistics players, aligning with the country's vision of a knowledge-based economy.

The NID CEO brings over 21 years of experience in construction, design management, and real estate development, having held senior positions in notable organizations, including Urban Escape. His academic credentials complement his professional accomplishments. Recognized for his academic excellence with a national award in 1997, the NID CEO exemplifies a leader who integrates technical expertise, cross-cultural experiences, and a deep understanding of local context into his leadership style.

The NID CEO's leadership is deeply rooted in his understanding of the national cultural and economic context. He acknowledges that the geopolitical and economic realities directly impact his company's growth. The fluctuations in oil prices, for instance, have driven the country's economic diversification, creating both challenges and opportunities for companies like National Industrial Development which he is leading. This contextual awareness allows him to navigate external uncertainties effectively, ensuring the company's strategic direction remains aligned with national priorities.

In line with the national cultural values, the NID CEO emphasizes loyalty, respect, and empathy from strategic leaders. His analogy of leadership to parenting illustrates a culturally grounded approach where authority is balanced with empathy. He describes his leadership style as hybrid, combining elements of partnership, authority, and mentorship. This blend reflects the societal expectation of leaders to be both effective leaders and nurturing mentors, guiding their teams with respect and empathy. His practice of engaging personally with his employees, whether through morning check-ins, sharing meals, or knowing their families reinforces his commitment to relational leadership.

Cross-Cultural Dynamics and Pluralistic Organizations

Operating within a pluralistic organizational environment, NID faces the complexities of managing diverse stakeholder preferences, distributed authority, and multiple organizational logics. The NID CEO approach to leadership reflects a nuanced understanding of these dynamics.

The CEO's narrative reveals the intricate interplay between national culture and societal expectations in shaping leadership. While national culture provides a foundational framework of values, societal expectations impose a more immediate and intense influence, demanding perfection and resilience. This case highlights the evolving complexities of leadership in pluralistic and high-expectation environments, where leaders must master the art of navigating societal pressures alongside organizational challenges.

Such insights reinforce the significant rise in studies linking culture to leadership, driven by the increasing globalization of business and the need for leaders to navigate cross-cultural and multicultural environments effectively (Bass, 2019; House et al., 2004). This growing body of research underscores the importance of understanding how cultural contexts shape leadership behaviors and expectations – a relationship extensively examined through the GLOBE study.

The GLOBE project consists of a series of studies (2002, 2004, 2007, and 2013) conducted by a consortium of 170 researchers spanning 62 nations, including the Middle East cluster within its extensive cross-cultural leadership study. It involved over 17,000 managers across 900 organizations in three diverse industries. The study synthesizes concepts from implicit leadership theory, Hofstede's (2003) cultural value belief theory, and the structural contingency theory of organizational effectiveness, forging links between socio-cultural values, leadership behavior, and societal phenomena (House, Javidan, Hanges, and Dorfman, 2004).

1.3.3 The Relationship Between Strategic Leadership and National Culture

National culture encompasses the deeply embedded values, beliefs, and social norms within a society, influencing leadership styles, communication patterns, and decision-making processes. Early results from the GLOBE study demonstrated that socio-cultural values and practices significantly shape leadership expectations and effectiveness. Reflecting on culturally endorsed leadership theory (CLT) and implicit leadership behavior, the study provided detailed country-specific analyses, emphasizing the importance of cultural values and practices in defining cross-cultural leadership expectations (House et al., 2004; Hofstede, 2006; Javidan et al., 2006).

However, later studies, particularly House, Dorfman, Javidan, Hanges and De Luque, (2013), introduced a more nuanced understanding of the interplay between leadership and national culture. In their empirical assessment of CEO leadership across 24 countries, they explored the role of strategic leadership within the framework of globalization and evolving societal dynamics. The study collected data from 1,000 CEOs and over 5,000 TMT members from various industries and revealed pivotal insights into the role of societal expectations versus cultural values in shaping leadership behaviors.

1.3.4 National (Societal) Leadership Expectations Versus Cultural Values

The two CEOs and the chairmen of two major development organizations, Urban Escape and NID, offered a candid reflection on the immense pressure of meeting societal expectations in their leadership roles. Backed by strong support from the shareholders and the national leadership, the CEOs recognized the privilege and responsibility of leading pioneering companies tasked with developing innovative solutions in a dynamic environment. Yet, the weight of societal leadership expectations often outweighed the challenges of the business itself.

The NID CEO explained that in his context, neither he nor his executive team had the luxury of learning through trial and error. "Mistakes are not seen as opportunities to grow," he said. "They are considered a mark of shame" (in-person interview communication, October 2019). He went on to describe how societal expectations extend beyond the organization to his personal and professional identity. "Society leadership expects us to be right in every decision, no matter how complex or unprecedented the challenge. Even as we develop cutting-edge warehousing units in the middle of the desert an innovation that has no blueprint are not allowed to falter" (in-person interview communication, October 2019). This relentless expectation of effectiveness, rooted in societal norms, is distinct from the pressures of national culture. While national culture provides the foundational values of respect, loyalty, and community, societal leadership expectations impose a more immediate, unyielding demand for consistent success.

The CEO contrasted this experience with global leadership norms. "In some contexts, failure is seen as a stepping stone to success an indicator of innovation and risk-taking. Here, the stakes are not just professional but deeply personal. Disappointing societal leadership expectations is not an option; it's a responsibility that lingers and overshadow all other achievements" (in-person interview communication, October 2019).

The narrative of the multiple case studies illustrates the growing influence of societal expectations on strategic leadership, aligning with findings from recent research. The latest GLOBE study by House et al. (2013) highlighted a critical shift in understanding leadership effectiveness. While earlier theories suggested that leaders' behaviors are primarily shaped by the cultural values of their societies (Hofstede, 2006), two groundbreaking insights emerged from our research and the empirical findings of House et al. (2013), pointing to different conclusions:

Limited Influence of Cultural Values: The results, based on nine predefined cultural dimensions, showed no significant relationship between national cultural values and primary leadership behaviors. Contrary to intuitive assumptions, leaders did not merely act as reflections of their cultural environment.

Dominance of Societal Leadership Expectations: The study found a strong relationship between societal leadership expectations and leaders' behaviors. These expectations, deeply ingrained in societal norms, were far more predictive of leadership effectiveness than cultural values. Leaders who aligned their behaviors with these societal expectations were more likely to be perceived as effective, resonating with the norms defining acceptable and desirable leadership within their societies.

1.3.5 Implications for Strategic Leadership

Our findings and House et al.'s (2013) findings challenge traditional views of leadership as a direct outcome of cultural values and emphasize the dynamic role of societal expectations. Societal leadership expectations act as a broader contextual force, shaping leaders' actions and effectiveness beyond cultural boundaries. This is particularly critical in the context of globalization, where dominant paradigms such as Western education and MBA programs have reduced the variability in leadership behaviors across cultures, further emphasizing societal norms over traditional cultural values (House et al., 2013).

Visualizing the Relationship: National Culture and Societal Expectations
This model highlights how societal norms serve as a mediating factor, influencing the way leaders interpret and respond to their cultural environment. By focusing on societal expectations, leaders can achieve greater strategic alignment and effectiveness, particularly in diverse and globalized settings.

This evolution of leadership studies from cultural determinism to a focus on societal expectations marks a significant advancement in understanding strategic leadership. While national culture remains an important contextual factor, it is the societal norms and expectations that play a more decisive role in shaping leadership effectiveness. This insight is essential for leaders operating in today's interconnected world, where the ability to navigate societal expectations is critical for achieving sustainable success in multicultural and pluralistic organizations.

It highlights a critical and often-debated contrast: the paramount role of executive leadership in a company's success or failure. At the center of this debate is the CEO who occupies the highest position of influence, shaping organizational priorities, cultivating processes, attracting talent, and steering the strategic direction. However, it is important to recognize that even the CEO's decisions are influenced by the broader governance structures, such as the boards of directors and other hierarchical powers, indicating a more complex interplay of leadership and oversight.

Leaders who align their behaviors with these ingrained expectations are more likely to be seen as effective, as they resonate with the societal norms that define what is acceptable and desirable in leadership. This alignment between leadership behaviors and societal expectations is essential for achieving strategic leadership success in diverse cultural environments. Their finding challenges the traditional view of leadership as a mere reflection of cultural values and emphasizes the powerful role of societal expectations in defining effective leadership in a global context.

Figure 1.4, embedded in House et al.'s (2013) study, vividly illustrates the link between national culture, societal leadership expectations, and leader's behavior, painting a vivid picture of how context molds leadership dynamics.

Figure 1.4: The Impact of Culture on Leadership.
Adapted from House et al. (2013), this figure illustrates how societal leadership expectations and national culture influence leadership behavior within pluralistic organizations in a global context.

In Chapter 2 we explain how societal expectations create a lasting impact on leadership. The societal expectations play a crucial role in shaping strategic direction, influencing board decisions, guiding top management teams, and ultimately affecting organizational outcomes. By recognizing these societal influences, we highlight how cultural norms and values are integral to determining leadership effectiveness within different contexts.

As we step further into this exploration of contextual leadership, our focus moves beyond individual leadership personalities to encompass the broader influence of their surroundings. By prioritizing the examination of the context itself, we establish the groundwork for decoding the details of strategic leadership within that context.

1.4 Our Knowledge, Evidence and Insights Fundamentals

Our knowledge and experience as practitioners and academics in the field of strategic (top management team) leadership development are deeply intertwined with our identities, our commitment to truthfulness, and the relevance of our work.[3] We found parallels in our knowledge and experience. In our research and practice, we focus on top management teams (TMTs), where strategic decisions wield significant influence over organizational performance and outcomes. Another primary focus is a shift towards the internal pluralistic organizational context, encompassing organizational structure, culture, size, category, industry, organizational resources, and processes. Building also on an extensive review of academic and practice literature and guidance, we embarked on a multiple-case study to bridge the gap between knowledge and practice perspectives. Our selection of the cases was driven by a deliberate focus

---

3 We followed an exhaustive and comprehensive leadership review spanning organizational science, strategic management, strategic leadership, and cross-cultural leadership, which bolsters the foundation of our multiple case study. It underscores our commitment to providing a holistic understanding of how context profoundly influences strategic leadership practice in today's complex and dynamic organizational landscape.

on contextual conditions, recognizing the high relevance of diverse environments for understanding strategic contextual leadership and developing guidance for strategic leaders. Pluralistic organizations, defined by pursuing diverse objectives and facing diverse and changing demands, align perfectly with our criteria for inclusion. The cases were carefully chosen to investigate CEOs and top management teams (TMTs) within pluralistic organizations specifically.

Our guiding questions and the overarching challenges we addressed were instrumental in shaping our strategic approach to case selection, data collection, and subsequent analysis. Recognizing the rapid growth of pluralistic organizations across sectors such as healthcare, financial services, and real estate development, we strategically chose to engage with organizations that exemplify these trends. These sectors are particularly complex due to their multiple, often competing objectives, and their operation in knowledge-based contexts adds another layer of intricacy.

We selected a set of case studies representing diverse industries and geographical footprints. These organizations operate within dynamic contexts, with headquarters in the United Arab Emirates (UAE) and offices or operations spanning multiple countries, including the United Kingdom, the United States, and beyond. Each case study highlights the intricate relationship between local and global operations. Urban Escape, headquartered in the United Arab Emirates, has offices and operations in the United Kingdom. Medi Care is managed from the United States while operating in the United Arab Emirates. Echo Capital maintains branches and investments in the United Kingdom and the Netherlands. DP World, with offices across 103 countries, exemplifies the complexities of global leadership. Collectively, these cases illustrate the distinct challenges and strategic strengths required to navigate pluralistic and multicultural environments.

The United Arab Emirates, home to several of the case organizations, offers a particularly dynamic context. As a global hub of commerce, innovation, and cultural diversity, the UAE hosts multinational teams representing over 50 nationalities (Al Bachir, 2022). This diversity fosters innovation but also requires exceptional leadership to harmonize varied perspectives, cultural norms, and strategic priorities.

To ensure our findings would resonate with a broad spectrum of strategic leaders, we prioritized cases that exhibited significant variation within the realm of pluralistic organizations. This variation encompasses factors such as organizational size, industry type, cultural composition, governance structures, and strategic objectives. For example, Medi Care, a healthcare provider, navigates the intricate regulatory environment of the US while maintaining operational excellence. Echo Capital operates across different legal and economic frameworks in the UK and the Netherlands, requiring compliance and strategy. Urban Escape balances the expectations of a sophisticated urban clientele in the UK with its commitment to sustainable development. Meanwhile, the UAE-based organizations leverage their geographic position to bridge Eastern and Western markets, often navigating political, economic, and cultural intersections with strategic agility.

This deliberate selection strategy enabled us to capture a rich tapestry of experiences and identify contextual factors that significantly influence these organizations. By analyzing cases from such varied and dynamic environments, we uncover practical insights for strategic leaders facing similar challenges. The findings offer a roadmap for navigating complexities such as aligning multinational teams, integrating diverse cultural norms, and adapting to fluctuating economic and regulatory landscapes.

Our approach was intentional and rigorous, designed to provide readers with both a conceptual framework and actionable strategies. The aim is not just to understand the theoretical underpinnings of SCL but to equip leaders with tools they can apply to achieve sustainable success in pluralistic and complex environments. By grounding our analysis in these carefully chosen cases, we provide a robust foundation for understanding the specific elements that contribute to strategic leadership challenges and opportunities, ensuring the relevance and applicability of our insights to a global audience.

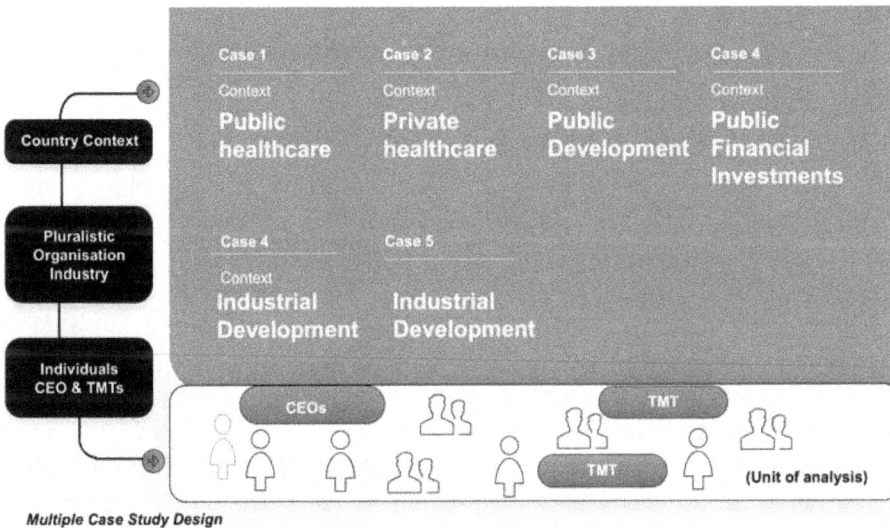

Figure 1.5: Multiple Case Study in Pluralistic Organizations.
The multiple case study design includes five pluralistic organizations across diverse sectors. The framework highlights the layered relationship between country context, organizational level, and the unit of analysis, focusing on CEOs and Top Management Team (TMT) members as key participants in the study.

Figure 1.5 illustrates the multiple case study research design, highlighting five diverse pluralistic organizations across sectors. It emphasizes the layered analysis across country context, organizational complexity, and leadership levels focusing on top management teams and CEOs as the primary unit of analysis to explore strategic contextual leadership in action.

Case 1 – Public Healthcare
Explores leadership dynamics in a government-run healthcare organization.

Case 2 – Private Healthcare

Focuses on strategic leadership within a privately owned hospital group.

Case 3 – Public Financial Services and Investment

Examines contextual leadership in a state-owned investment and finance institution.

Case 4 – Public Development

Analyzes strategic leadership in a government real estate and infrastructure development entity.

Case 5 – Public Industrial Development

Investigates leadership in a national industrial and logistics development organization.

Country Context

National cultural and institutional environment framing organizational behavior.

Pluralistic Organizations

Organizations with diverse stakeholders, conflicting interests, and complex governance.

Units of Analysis: TMTs and CEOs

Top Management Teams and Chief Executive Officers as focal points for leadership investigation.

In summary, our motivation for writing this book stems from our unique position and curiosity. It is driven by our commitment to authenticity, relevance, and the integration of theory and practice, resulting in a comprehensive exploration of the leadership complexities in modern multicultural pluralistic organizations where diverse stakeholders and dynamic contexts demand a leadership style that is both strategic and contextually conscious.

1.5 Conclusion

As we conclude Chapter 1, we've positioned the foundational building blocks for understanding the complexities of modern leadership in a globalized, interconnected and dynamic world. We've explored the limitations of traditional, linear approaches to leadership and highlighted the need for a deeper and complex understanding—one that incorporates both strategic foresight and contextual awareness. By dissecting the concept of strategic leadership and juxtaposing it with the dynamic nature of contextual leadership in pluralistic organizations, we've illuminated the critical role that societal expectations, cultural norms, and organizational dynamics play in shaping strategic leadership.

This chapter has also traced the evolution of context leadership, showcasing how cross-cultural dimensions add layers of complexity that leaders must navigate. The introduction of the theoretical amalgamation of the hybrid strategic contextual leadership to build a framework for strategic leaders within pluralistic organizations is given in Figure 1.6.

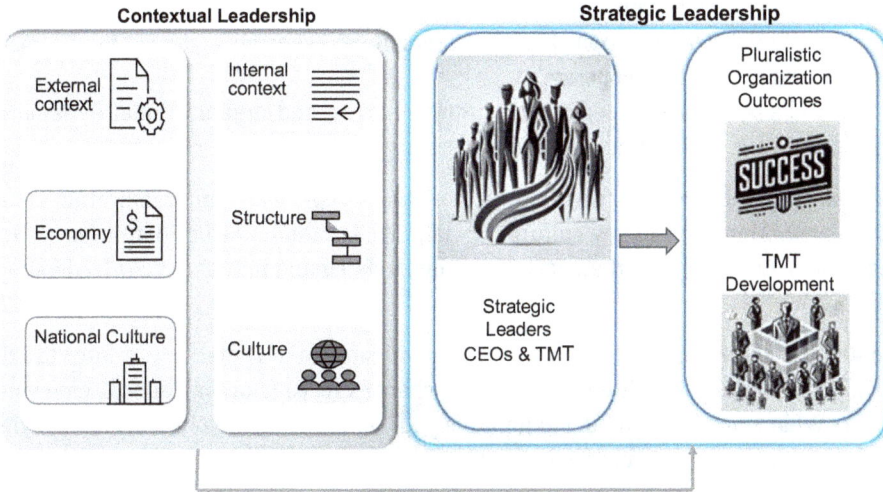

Contextual Leadership   **Strategic Leadership**

External context
Economy
National Culture
Internal context
Structure
Culture
Strategic Leaders CEOs & TMT
Pluralistic Organization Outcomes
SUCCESS
TMT Development

Figure 1.6: Initial Strategic Contextual Framework in Pluralistic Organizations.
This figure presents the integration of contextual and strategic leadership in shaping outcomes within pluralistic organizations. It emphasizes the influence of external and internal contextual factors on strategic leadership by CEOs and Top Management Teams (TMTs), ultimately leading to organizational success and leadership development.

The figure includes the external context elements, the pluralistic organization internal context, and strategic leadership, which includes the CEO and the top management teams (TMTs). The figure shows how the external context impacts the internal context of the organizations in a direct way; it encompasses strategic leadership on different levels, the board, the CEOs and TMT and the pluralistic organization's outcomes, success and TMT development.[4]

As we move forward, these concepts will serve as the cornerstone for the deeper exploration of leadership in multicultural and pluralistic environments. The stage is set for a more comprehensive understanding of how strategic and contextual leadership can be harmonized to achieve sustainable organizational success.

---

4 In Chapter 2 we introduce the hybrid strategic contextual leadership framework, including the pluralistic organizational outcomes.

1.6 Learning/Reflection Activity

1.6.1 Reflection Activity: Understanding Contextual Strategic Leadership in Pluralistic Leadership

Contextual Leadership: Reflecting on Your Leadership Context
Self-Assessment: Reflect on your leadership role within your organization.

Identify three ways in which your leadership style has been shaped by the specific context in which you operate.

How have societal expectations, cultural norms, and organizational dynamics influenced your decision-making and leadership approach?

Context Mapping: Create a "context map" to visually represent your organization's environment. Map out the key cultural, social, and economic factors that affect your leadership. Consider how these factors are interrelated and influence your leadership effectiveness.

Contextual Reflection: Reflect on the concept of contextual leadership as introduced in this chapter. How well do you adapt to changes in your organizational environment? What steps can you take to improve your ability to align your leadership style with your organization's unique context?

1.6.2 Strategic Leadership: Bridging Context and Vision

Strategic Reflection: Evaluate your role in making strategic decisions within your organization. How do you integrate contextual factors into your strategic thinking? Identify three examples of decisions where you had to balance short-term performance goals with long-term sustainability in your strategic planning.

Alignment Assessment: Consider how well your strategic vision aligns with your organization's cultural and societal expectations. What challenges have you faced in ensuring alignment between your strategies and the broader organizational context?

Vision Mapping: Develop a "strategic vision map" to align your leadership decisions with your organization's long-term goals. Include contextual factors that influence this vision, such as market trends, stakeholder needs, and emerging opportunities. Reflect on how your strategic leadership has been impacted by these considerations.

Pluralistic Organizations: In the context of your organization, explore the defining features of pluralistic organizations:

Multiplicity of Preferences: Identify diverse stakeholder preferences and how they influence your leadership decisions. How do you balance competing priorities or conflicting goals?

Multiplicity of Authority: Reflect on the various sources of authority within your organization. How do you navigate power dynamics, shared decision-making, or distributed leadership structures?

Multiplicity of Logic: Consider how different organizational logics (e.g., financial goals, societal impact, operational efficiency) intersect in your decision-making. How do you align these logics to create cohesive strategies?

Collaborative Dialogue: Engage with peers to discuss how they navigate the complexities of pluralistic organizations. Share insights about common challenges and successful strategies for managing multiplicity. What lessons can you apply to your own leadership context?

Introducing Hybrid Strategic Contextual Leadership
Conclude the activity by synthesizing insights from your reflections on hybrid contextual leadership, strategic leadership, and pluralistic organizations.

Reflect on the concept of hybrid strategic contextual leadership introduced in this chapter.

Key Questions to Consider:
- How does understanding the interaction between context, strategy, and multiplicity improve your leadership effectiveness?
- What steps can you take to identify how your leadership approach can be aligned with the demands of pluralistic organizations?
- How can the Hybrid Strategic Contextual Leadership framework help you lead more effectively in complex, dynamic, and diverse environments?

By completing this activity, you will gain a deeper understanding of the interplay between leadership, strategy, and pluralistic organizational contexts, preparing you to embrace and apply the principles of hybrid strategic contextual leadership effectively.

Chapter 2
Mastering the Context Matrix in Pluralistic Multicultural Organizations

In pluralistic organizations, effective strategic leadership requires more than just knowledge and expertise; it demands an understanding of the diverse and dynamic contexts in which decisions are made. This chapter explores the concept of the "context matrix," a framework for understanding the multi-layered environments that shape leadership effectiveness in pluralistic organizations. We will define what is a pluralistic organization and examine how the context matrix impacts the pluralistic organization internal context. We will also investigate how strategic leaders (TMTs and CEOs) navigate the internal dynamics and their interactions with boards of directors, while simultaneously managing external factors like regulatory changes, market shifts, and stakeholder expectations.

2.1 Introducing the Context Matrix

This book introduces the "context matrix" (Figure 2.1), which represents the multifaceted and dynamic contextual external factors that impact organizations on multiple levels, the organization internal context, the strategic direction, the TMTs and CEOs and the organizational outcomes.

Table 2.1 presents the four dimensions of the Context Matrix – dynamic economy, industry regulations, country culture, and societal leadership expectations – each shaping strategic leadership in unique ways. It illustrates how leaders must develop financial intelligence, navigate regulatory complexity, adapt to national cultures, and align with evolving societal expectations for responsible and contextually relevant leadership.

The context matrix underscores that the contextual environment, encompassing external condition such as the country economy, the national culture, the industry regulations and societal expectations, are as significant as, if not more than, individual characteristics in determining leadership effectiveness.

This model underscores that no strategic decision is made in isolation, leaders must continuously interpret, adapt, and align their strategies within the dynamic interplay of these contextual forces.

In the following section we will show how the four areas of these external contextual factors interplay and influence decision-making, strategic direction, and overall organizational success.

By viewing leadership through the contextual matrix, we emphasize the necessity of understanding and integrating these complex contextual dimensions to achieve sus-

https://doi.org/10.1515/9783111382722-003

Context Matrix

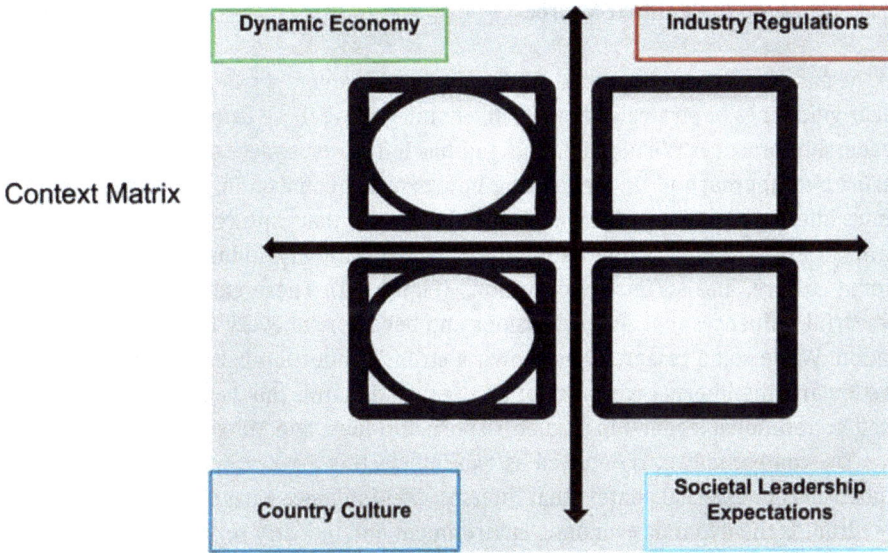

Figure 2.1: The Context Matrix.
The Context Matrix highlights how external contextual dimensions such as a dynamic economy, industry regulations, country culture, and societal leadership expectations play a critical role in shaping leadership effectiveness, potentially influencing outcomes as significantly as individual leader traits.

Table 2.1: Differentiating the Four Dimensions.

Dimension	Focus Area	Impact on Leadership and Strategy
Dynamic Economy	Market volatility, globalization, technological shifts	Requires financial intelligence, risk management, and resource optimization.
Industry Regulation	Legal frameworks, compliance, sector-specific policies	Requires governance expertise, regulatory foresight, and strategic compliance.
Country Culture	National values, work ethics	Requires cultural adaptability and identification of national leadership values.
Societal Leadership Expectation	Public trust, ESG, ethical governance	Identifying and implementing national leadership expectations, shareholders' engagement, transparency, and sustainable leadership.

tainable success in pluralistic and multicultural organizations. This approach broadens the scope of leadership analysis and enriches our comprehension of the complex realities faced by TMTs and CEOs in today's rapidly evolving business landscape.

2.1.1 Decoding the Context Matrix

In the past, studies on contextual leadership have frequently fallen short in providing clear guidelines or strategies for effectively integrating these external influences into leadership practices (Yukl, 2013). This gap has left many leaders and teams without a structured approach to understanding how external contexts impact their organization's internal dynamics. The context matrix is a tool that captures a set of four quadrants of external factors: the national and global economy, industry regulations, national culture, and societal expectations (Figure 2.1). These external elements are powerful influences that shape decisions and behaviors at every level of your organization. While some research has shown a strong connection between these external factors and the internal workings of an organization, this link is often underappreciated in traditional leadership studies (Osborn, Uhl-Bien, and Milosevic, 2014).

The context matrix is depicted as two intersecting arrows, symbolizing the multi dimensions of external context that intersect and influence each other. The upper left quadrant is the dynamic economic environment and industry regulations factors that fluctuate over time and require organizations to be agile and responsive. This quadrant reminds managers that economic conditions and regulatory landscapes are not static; they evolve and must be continuously monitored and managed to maintain organizational alignment with external realities.

Below the horizontal axis are the cultural and societal leadership expectations quadrants, the more stable yet profoundly influential factors that shape organizational culture and leadership practices. The national culture and societal leadership expectations highlight the importance of grounding strategic decisions in a deep understanding of national culture and social norms, ensuring that the organization's leadership approach is both contextually relevant and sustainable.

The intersection of the matrix axes serves as a reminder that strategic leadership requires balancing the immediate demands of the business with a deep understanding of the cultural and societal context in which the organization operates. This balance is crucial for navigating the complexities of a pluralistic, multicultural business environment and ensuring long-term success.

2.1.2 Dynamic Economy

The upper left quadrant of the context matrix represents the dynamic economic environment, a constantly evolving external factor that exerts direct and indirect influences on organizational strategy, investment decisions, and operational resilience. Unlike static economic conditions, a dynamic economy is characterized by fluctuations in market demand, inflation rates, trade policies, interest rates, technological advancements, and financial market stability (Dunning, 2009). These factors create a complex landscape that requires organizations to remain agile, adaptive, and strategically responsive (Barney, Wright, and Ketchen, 2001).

At the national level, a country's economic health, industrial policies, workforce productivity, and fiscal policies shape the operating environment for organizations. Gross domestic product (GDP) growth, labor market conditions, taxation structures, and inflationary trends determine the cost of capital, consumer purchasing power, and overall business climate (North, 1990). For instance, high economic growth rates create expansion opportunities, enabling companies to invest in innovation, infrastructure, and talent development, whereas economic recessions constrain corporate spending and force strategic realignments (Porter, 1990).

A notable example is the United Arab Emirates (UAE), which has implemented strategic initiatives to reduce its reliance on oil and gas revenues. The UAE Vision 2021 emphasizes the development of a competitive knowledge economy by fostering innovation, research and development, and strengthening the regulatory framework for key industries (Al-Suwaidi, 2021). The establishment of Dubai Internet City, Masdar City, and Abu Dhabi's AI and digital transformation initiatives exemplifies the nation's commitment to becoming a regional leader in technology and sustainable development (Forstenlechner and Rutledge, 2010).

Similarly, Saudi Arabia's Vision 2030 aims to diversify the national economy by investing in healthcare, education, digital infrastructure, tourism, and green energy (Ramady, 2018). A key component of this vision is the enhancement of digital capabilities and investment in high-tech industries to prepare a future-ready workforce (Alqahtani, Rajkhan, and Al-Ajlan, 2021). Initiatives such as the Neom Smart City project and the Saudi Green Initiative illustrate Saudi Arabia's push toward sustainable and technology-driven economic transformation (Al-Tamimi, 2022).

On a global scale, South Africa exemplifies a dynamic economy through its strategic efforts to transition from a resource-based model to a knowledge-driven economy. Recognizing the limitations of relying solely on natural resources, the South African government has introduced initiatives to foster innovation, digital transformation, and human capital development (Kruss, McGrath, and Petersen, 2015). These efforts aim to enhance economic resilience, global competitiveness, and long-term sustainability (OECD, 2022).

A pivotal step in this direction was the introduction of the Ten-Year Innovation Plan (2008–2018) by the Department of Science and Technology (DST). This plan aimed to transform South Africa into a knowledge-based economy by prioritizing biotechnology, space science, and energy security (Department of Science and Innovation, 2018). The plan emphasized the importance of research and development (R&D) and set ambitious targets for increasing R&D expenditure as a percentage of GDP, with the goal of enhancing technological innovation and industry growth (Mouton, Gaillard, and Ani, 2015).

In recent years, South Africa has accelerated its digital economy transformation. In 2024, a report by Naspers and the Mapungubwe Institute for Strategic Reflection

(MISTRA) highlighted the need for regulatory sandboxes to spur innovation in South Africa's digital platform sector. These controlled testing environments would enable businesses to experiment with new services within a regulatory framework, thereby fostering growth in e-commerce, fintech, and digital entrepreneurship (MISTRA, 2024).

Moreover, in 2025, Microsoft launched an initiative to train 1 million South Africans in artificial intelligence (AI) and cybersecurity by 2026. This program targets companies, government entities, and youth, aiming to equip them with essential digital skills for the evolving global economy (Microsoft South Africa, 2025). By developing a digitally skilled workforce, South Africa seeks to bridge the digital divide, increase employment opportunities, and drive economic inclusion (OECD, 2022).

These initiatives underscore South Africa's commitment to fostering a dynamic economy that leverages knowledge, digital transformation, and innovation as key drivers of sustainable growth. By investing in digital infrastructure, skills development, and supportive regulatory frameworks, South Africa aims to enhance its global economic standing, attract foreign investment, and improve industrial productivity (Kruss et al., 2015).

Globally, organizations operate within a complex interdependent system shaped by international trade agreements, global financial markets, supply chain stability, and geopolitical factors (Dunning, 2009). Exchange rate fluctuations, commodity price volatility, foreign direct investment (FDI) flows, and the competitiveness of national industries dictate how organizations navigate cross-border investments and supply chain networks (Ghemawat, 2016). Companies in sectors such as technology, financial services, and industrial development are particularly vulnerable to shifts in global trade dynamics, monetary policies of major economies, and regional economic blocs like the European Union or ASEAN (Rugman and Verbeke, 2001).

From a strategic leadership perspective, operating within a dynamic economy demands continuous environmental scanning, scenario planning, and economic risk mitigation strategies (Teece, 2018). Organizational leaders must be adept at interpreting economic indicators such as interest rates, government spending, and business cycle trends, ensuring that decision-making aligns with both short-term financial realities and long-term economic forecasts (Barney et al., 2001). This requires a blend of financial intelligence, strategic contextual intelligence, and macroeconomic awareness, allowing firms to anticipate disruptions, seize emerging opportunities, and remain competitive in volatile market conditions (Ghemawat, 2016).

2.1.3 Industry Regulations

The upper right quadrant is industry regulations which establish the framework within which organizations operate, influencing strategic decisions, compliance requirements, and operational adjustments. These regulations vary across industries and regions and are often driven by economic shifts, technological advancements, and public policy changes. Adapting to evolving regulations necessitates a comprehensive understanding of industry standards and regulatory frameworks to maintain competitiveness while ensuring compliance (Teece, 2018). The context matrix underscores the importance of strategic foresight in navigating regulatory landscapes, enabling organizations to anticipate changes, leverage opportunities, and align operations with new legal frameworks (Fenwick,, Vermeulen, and Compagnucci, 2024).

In countries transitioning toward knowledge-based economies, significant regulatory changes have been implemented to facilitate this shift. For example, the United Arab Emirates implemented several regulatory reforms to support its move toward a knowledge-driven economy. Several Federal Decree Laws were issued to regulate financial development and technology-driven industries to enhance economic diversification and sustainability (State Department, 2023). Additionally, the UAE has focused on regulating emerging technologies, particularly artificial intelligence (AI) and digital transformation. The financial regulations have been updated to include the data protection laws to governing artificial intelligent deployment, ensuring compliance with global standards while fostering technological innovation (White and Case, 2023). These changes in industry regulations reflect the need for establishing a new regulatory framework to facilitate technological leadership and digital transformation (Al-Suwaidi, 2021).

Another example is Saudi Arabia's Vision 2030 initiative aiming to introduce business-friendly regulatory changes to attract foreign investment and achieve economic diversification. In September 2023, the government approved the regulatory frameworks in renewable energy, digital finance, and artificial intelligence-driven governance to align economic priorities with global investment trends (Ramady, 2018).

As regulatory landscapes evolve, organizations must stay ahead of industry compliance requirements while leveraging new opportunities in digital transformation and economic policy reforms. The context matrix highlights the necessity of proactive leadership, ensuring that business models remain adaptable and aligned with regulatory changes and technological shifts (Ghemawat, 2016).

2.1.4 Country Culture

The left lower quadrant of the context matrix introduces national culture as a fundamental factor that shapes the internal culture of an organization. National culture profoundly influences the internal dynamics of pluralistic organizations. Comprehensive frameworks, such as those developed by Hofstede and the GLOBE study, offer valuable insights into these cultural dimensions. Geert Hofstede's model identifies six dimensions that elucidate how cultural values impact organizational behavior. For example, the power distance index (PDI), introduced by Hofstede (1980, 2011), primarily refers to the extent to which less powerful members of a society (such as employees, citizens, or subordinates) accept and expect power to be distributed unequally. It is a societal and cultural characteristic, rather than an individual leadership behavior.

As we conducted several of our cases study in the UAE, we examined a cultural dimensions power distance and collectivism which both significantly influence organizational behavior and leadership styles. However, one size does not fit all when analyzing cultural impact, even within the same geographical region. While the UAE is often classified as part of the Middle East, its cultural, social, and organizational dynamics differ significantly from other Arab countries like Egypt.

Hofstede's cultural dimensions study did not include the UAE in its original dataset. However, later studies have generalized cultural scores for the UAE based on its economic model, governance structure, and business practices. Similarly, the GLOBE study did not survey all countries directly. Instead, it grouped them into the Middle East cultural cluster (House et al., 2004, 2013). Such assumptions fail to recognize the distinct cultural evolution, particularly in the business environment and leadership expectations.

National culture impacts leadership in pluralistic organizations by shaping the holistic context. For example, in contrast to Egypt and other Middle Eastern nations, where bureaucratic state influence remains high, wealthier countries such as the UAE and Saudi Arabia foster a hybrid leadership approach that balances hierarchical structures with progressive, innovation-driven governance. The e-government systems in both countries impact the effectiveness of strategic leaders, who are expected to uphold respect for hierarchy while actively engaging in transformational and innovative leadership practices aligned with Vision 2030 and Vision 2050 initiatives (Al-Suwaidi, 2021).

Similarly, collectivism emphasizes historical social structures and state-driven nationalism; however, some countries are corporate-driven, fostering a multiethnic business community with globalized values. The diversity of these countries' workforce (in the UAE, over 85% expatriates) challenges traditional in-group collectivism models. Instead, corporate loyalty often replaces national cultural loyalty as organizations operate with international talent and leadership styles (Davidson, 2018).

It is flawed to assume that cultural frameworks used to describe Egypt's leadership model, which remains state-influenced and public sector-driven, where bureaucracy plays a significant role in decision-making (Abdalla, 2017), apply universally. The UAE, on the other hand, has embraced a "government-as-a-business" model, where leaders are expected to drive innovation, economic reform, and global partnerships, making it more aligned with high-performing economies rather than regional political traditions (Al Bachir, 2022; Davidson, 2018). In cultures with high power distance, there is an expectation for leaders to exhibit authority and provide clear direction. Conversely, in societies that value collectivism, there is an emphasis on teamwork and participative decision-making. Strategic leaders must navigate these expectations, aligning organizational strategies with cultural norms to ensure effectiveness and social legitimacy.

This book builds on these findings by directly connecting culture to organizational context and strategy. Our recent qualitative and onsite case studies reveal that the international education of TMT members significantly reduces the impact of national culture within multicultural teams. This exposure to diverse educational backgrounds acts as a unifying factor, bridging cultural gaps and fostering a more cohesive and effective leadership team.

2.1.5 Societal Leadership Expectations

The fourth lower right quadrant of the context matrix focuses on societal leadership expectations, a concept extensively examined in the GLOBE study. This dimension refers to the specific expectations and demands that society places on organizations' leaders, encompassing aspects such as ethical governance, social responsibility, and alignment with prevailing societal values (House et al., 2013). These societal imperatives are not merely passive cultural norms but constitute active pressures that significantly influence leadership decisions and organizational strategies.

Research indicates that societal expectations profoundly shape leadership behavior and strategic outcomes. For instance, a study by Smith et al. (2020) found that leaders who align their strategies with societal values tend to achieve better organizational performance and enhanced public trust. Similarly, Jones and Taylor (2019) demonstrated that societal demands for ethical governance compel leaders to adopt more transparent and accountable practices, which in turn positively affect organizational reputation and stakeholder engagement.

In the case study, the impact of societal expectations on CEOs and TMTs was evident across all cases. In the healthcare sector, a hospital CEO reported feeling pressured to meet societal expectations, even when the hospital lacked the necessary medical equipment to accommodate specific patient needs. This scenario underscores the tension leaders often face between societal demands and organizational capabilities.

The case study highlighted challenges faced by a newly appointed Group CEO who was not familiar with the local societal expectations. This lack of cultural alignment led to insufficient support from the TMT and the board during the implementation of new strategic initiatives. This example illustrates the critical importance of cultural competence and sensitivity to societal expectations in leadership roles.

Similar dynamics have been observed in other parts of the world. Over a five-year period of interviewing candidates, a prominent theme emerged: Societal expectations significantly influence strategic leadership and directly impact organizational outcomes. Notably, the development of leaders surfaced as a major societal expectation. This aligns with findings from the GLOBE project, which posits that societal culture values shape both leadership expectations and behaviors, thereby affecting organizational performance (House et al., 2014).

Furthermore, the way business decisions are implemented, particularly during restructuring or terminations, is critical. Handling these processes with care and empathy is essential. Our case study the CEOs and TMTs demonstrated that empathy enhances trust and collaboration within teams, leading to improved organizational outcomes. Additionally, managing dismissals with empathy and professionalism helps maintain a positive company culture and minimizes the emotional impact on employees (Psico Smart, 2024).

These examples underscore the critical importance for leaders to be acutely aware of and responsive to societal expectations. By aligning organizational strategies with societal values, leaders can enhance organizational performance, build public trust, and ensure long-term sustainability.

The Dual Balancing of External and Internal Pressures

After decoding the context matrix four quadrants; country economy, industry regulations, national culture, and societal leadership expectations; it becomes evident that strategic leadership in pluralistic organizations is defined by the intersection of the external contextual influences and internal organizational demands and pressures. This intersection represents a dual balancing act, requiring CEOs and TMTs to navigate both immediate market demands, and enduring cultural and societal contexts as shown in Figure 2.2.

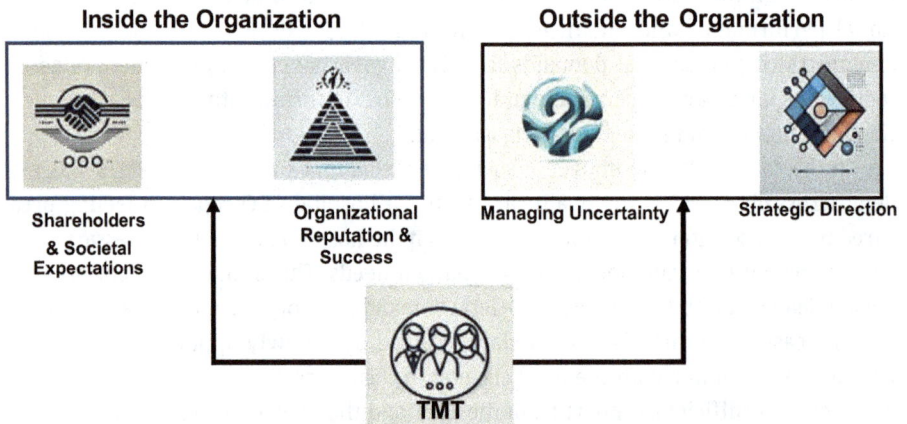

Inside the Organization   **Outside the Organization**

Shareholders & Societal Expectations | Organizational Reputation & Success | Managing Uncertainty | Strategic Direction

TMT

Figure 2.2: TMTs Balancing Organization Internal and External Demands.
This figure illustrates the dual balancing act faced by CEOs and Top Management Teams in pluralistic organizations. Positioned between external influences such as uncertainty and strategic direction, and internal pressures including stakeholder expectations and organizational reputation, the TMT navigates complex demands. It reflects how strategic leadership is shaped by the interaction of external context and internal organizational dynamics.

By visualizing the context matrix, CEOs and TMTs gain a structured perspective on the multiple external pressures they must address. Economic and regulatory factors dictate strategic redirection, market adaptability, financial sustainability, and compliance requirements. Culture and societal expectations shape organization culture,

CEOs and TMTs authority, stakeholder engagement, and long-term reputation management. The intersection of these axes serves as a powerful reminder that successful strategic leadership is not just about responding to economic or regulatory forces it also requires deep contextual intelligence and alignment with the societal expectations (House et al., 2013; Hofstede, 2011).

Navigating this intersection demands a nuanced approach, where leaders must balance competing priorities such as innovation, regulatory compliance, global strategies, local cultural norms, and short-term financial performance with a due regard for the long-term social impact. Failure to address this complexity holistically can lead to strategic misalignment, loss of stakeholder trust, and reduced organizational effectiveness (Smith et al., 2020).

2.2 Pluralistic Organization

Pluralism in the context of organizational and management studies has evolved and gained increasing attention over the past few decades. While the term was mentioned sporadically over decades, it has become more clearly defined in recent years.

Pluralistic organizations operate in environments characterized by multiple authorities, diverse objectives, and varying preferences (Denis, Langley, and Rouleau, 2007). These organizations function within complex institutional logics where professionals, managers, and external stakeholders interact dynamically, often with competing priorities (Raffaelli and Glynn, 2014). They are commonly found in healthcare, education, technology, development, industrial development, logistic and supply chain sectors, where decentralized authority, diverse goals, and multidisciplinary collaboration are fundamental to their structure.

Pluralistic organizations exhibit several key characteristics that make them outstanding, with predominantly diverse objectives and fragmented power dynamics among different professionals and management. These characteristics present complex challenges when it comes to understanding the connections between contextual changes and organizational leadership dynamics (Morrison and Milliken, 2000). Studies across various industries identified the relative balance or imbalance within pluralistic organizations (Raffaelli and Glynn, 2014).

Figure 2.3 shows that the structure and context of pluralistic organizations are influenced by the multiplicity of objectives, logics, preferences and authority level (Denis, Langley, and Rouleau, 2007). This coexistence of diverse and often competing elements within a single organizational framework can be understood through three key dimensions:

Multiplicity of Authorities: This dimension refers to the presence of various actors, such as professionals and stakeholders, who operate within the organization without a formal hierarchical structure. In pluralistic organizations, authority is not central-

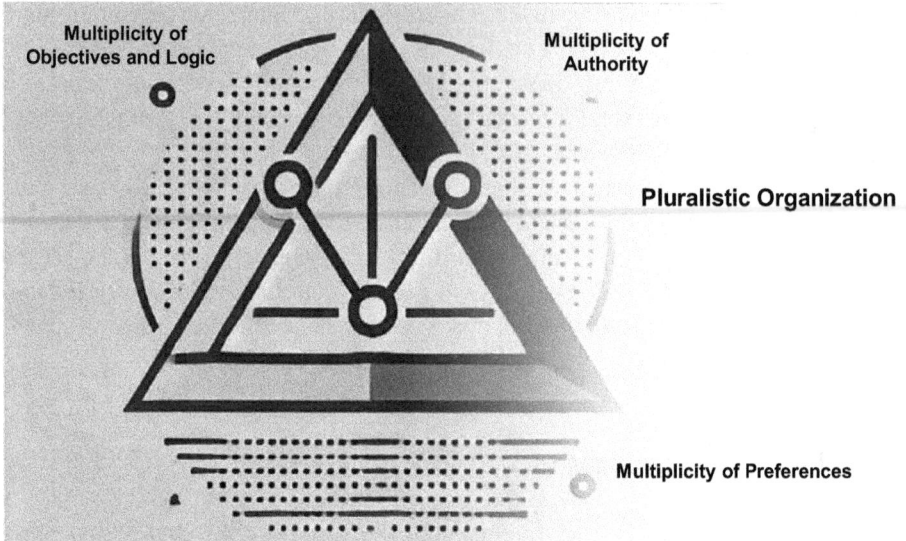

Figure 2.3: Pluralistic Organization.
This figure conveys the concept of a pluralistic organization, emphasizing the coexistence of multiple logics, authorities, and preferences. It highlights the complexity leaders face in navigating and reconciling diverse goals, power structures, and stakeholder interests.

ized but is distributed across different groups, each with its own influence and decision-making power. This can lead to a more collaborative environment, but it also creates challenges in aligning different interests and ensuring cohesive leadership.

Multiplicity of Objectives and Logics: The second dimension involves the existence of multiple missions, objectives, and values among the organization's members. Different groups within the organization may have varying priorities and perspectives, which can lead to divergent interests and conflicting goals. This diversity of logics can result in inconsistent organizational missions and challenges in achieving unified strategic outcomes (Denis et al., 2007).

Multiplicity of Preferences: The third dimension focuses on the preferences in how pluralistic organizations interact with their external context. Unlike traditional organizations that adhere to standardized efficiency and formal rules, pluralistic organizations often operate with more flexibility and adaptability with their external context. They may lack a comprehensive rulebook, yet this allows them to respond to diverse external demands and navigate complex environments more effectively.

The internal context of a pluralistic organization consists of interrelated elements that define its structure, strategic leadership, and operational framework. These elements shape decision-making, stakeholder expectations, and the readiness of the organization to external challenges.

2.2.1 Pluralistic Organization's Internal Context

The internal context of a pluralistic organization consists of several interrelated elements that define its structure, strategic leadership, and operational framework. These elements shape decision-making, stakeholder expectations, and the adaptability of the organization to external challenges. The context matrix interacts with these elements, influencing the strategic direction and leadership effectiveness within the organization (Figure 2.4).

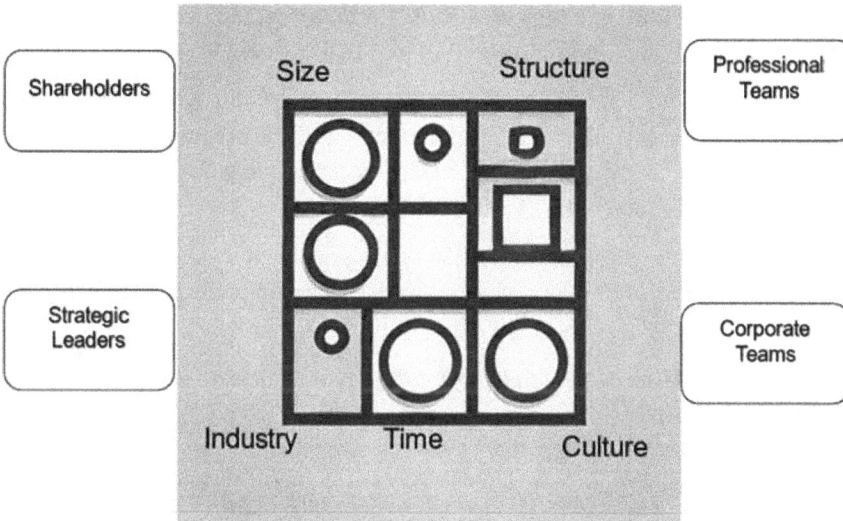

Figure 2.4: Pluralistic Organizational Internal Context.
This figure presents the internal context of a pluralistic organization by emphasizing interrelated dimensions such as size, structure, industry, time, and culture. These internal factors interact with key stakeholder groups and influence decision making, leadership approaches, and the organization's ability to adapt and perform effectively.

Structure

In pluralistic organizations, the term "structure" refers to the organizational frameworks that facilitate collaboration among actors possessing diffuse power and divergent perspectives (Brès and Raufflet, 2013). Unlike traditional hierarchical structures, where decision-making authority is centralized, pluralistic organizations often adopt more complex and decentralized configurations. These structures are designed to enable cooperation on substantive issues by accommodating a variety of viewpoints and distributing power more evenly across the organization. This approach allows for greater flexibility and inclusivity in decision-making processes, which is essential in environments where multiple stakeholders with differing objectives must work together effectively.

Status: The organization's standing within its industry or sector can be influenced by its pluralistic nature and the diverse interests it represents.

Size: The scale of pluralistic organizations can vary, but their complexity often increases with size due to the multiplicity of stakeholders and interests involved.

Industry: Pluralistic organizations operate across various industries, and their internal contexts are shaped by the specific dynamics and demands of their respective sectors.

Culture: A defining feature of pluralistic organizations is their cultural diversity, stemming from the inclusion of multiple groups with unique ideologies and values working collaboratively.

Time: The historical development and evolution of pluralistic organizations influence their current structures and processes, reflecting the accumulation of diverse perspectives over time.

Shareholders: In pluralistic organizations, stakeholders may include a broad array of interest groups beyond traditional shareholders, each exerting influence on organizational decisions.

Strategic Leaders (CEOs and TMTs): Leadership in pluralistic organizations involves navigating and integrating diverse perspectives, requiring skills in managing complexity and fostering collaboration among varied stakeholders.

Professional and Corporate Teams: These teams must work together within the pluralistic framework, balancing professional expertise with the need to address the interests of diverse stakeholder groups.

While the pluralistic organization framework defines the structural, leadership, and cultural complexities inherent in such entities, its application varies significantly across industries due to differences in regulatory environments, stakeholder expectations, and operational demands (Denis, Langley and Rouleau, 2007).

2.3 The Practical Understanding of Pluralistic Organizations

By presenting case examples from different industries, we can bridge the gap between theoretical constructs and their practical implications, offering a contextualized analysis of how pluralistic organizations operate under diverse conditions (Greenwood, Raynard, Kodeih, Micelotta and Lounsbury, 2011). Industries such as healthcare, financial services, real estate development, and international trade demonstrate distinct pluralistic dynamics, making it necessary to contextualize leadership challenges, structural adaptations, and strategic decision-making (Finkelstein, Hambrick and Cannella, 2009).

2.3.1 Healthcare: Multiplicity of Professional Authorities and Institutional Logics

Healthcare organizations are highly pluralistic due to their reliance on medical professionals, administrators, insurers, regulatory agencies, and policymakers, all operating under different goals. The complexity arises from the intersection of clinical expertise, patient care, financial management, and regulatory compliance (Denis et al., 2015).

Example: Medi Care and Vita Care
Pluralistic Structure: Healthcare organizations share leadership in a complex, multistakeholder healthcare system. These organizations integrate medical professionals, researchers, and administrators in a collaborative governance model, ensuring a balance between medical autonomy and administrative efficiency (Lockett et al., 2014).

Multiplicities in Action: Physicians have professional autonomy, yet administrative leadership ensures cost control and operational efficiency. Patient-centered care is prioritized while aligning with financial sustainability.

Challenges in Healthcare:
Healthcare organizations face complex challenges due to competing institutional logics, regulatory requirements, and professional autonomy (Ferlie, Fitzgerald, and Ashburner, 2005). One of the key challenges is *balancing medical decision-making with cost-efficiency mandates* imposed by governments and insurance providers (Denis, Langley, and Rouleau, 2015). Physicians and medical professionals prioritize patient care and ethical medical practices, while administrators focus on financial sustainability, operational efficiency, and regulatory compliance (Checkland, Harrison, and Marshall, 2007). Additionally, technological advancements and digital health integration require adaptation, creating tensions between innovation adoption and maintaining standardized, evidence-based practices (Lockett et al., 2014). Furthermore, public trust and patient satisfaction play critical roles, as healthcare organizations must balance cost control with quality service delivery under public scrutiny (Dopson and Fitzgerald, 2006).

2.3.2 Development Organization

Commercial, residential and industrial development organizations operate within highly pluralistic environments, balancing urban planning regulations, real estate investment strategies, environmental sustainability, and community expectations (D'Arcy and Keogh, 1999). These organizations engage with governments, urban planners, real estate investors, construction firms, environmental agencies, and local communities, each bringing diverse objectives, economic considerations, and social responsibilities (Healey, 2006).

Example: Urban Escape (UAE)

Pluralistic Structure: Urban Escape Properties, a global real estate developer headquartered in United Arab Emirates, exemplifies pluralism in large-scale commercial and residential development. The company balances government-driven urban expansion policies, foreign investor expectations, and sustainable development goals (Davidson, 2021).

Multiplicity of Authorities: Urban Escape collaborates with government regulators (Dubai Municipality), investors, property owners, and international business partners, ensuring that projects align with national development strategies and international real estate trends (Balchin, 2020).

Multiplicity of Objectives and Logics: The company operates in luxury residential, hospitality, retail, and industrial real estate sectors, requiring leadership to balance high financial returns with long-term community development initiatives (Davidson, 2021). While investors prioritize profitability and market growth, urban planners emphasize livability, infrastructure, and sustainability.

Multiplicity of Preferences: Urban Escape's developments include Burj Khalifa and Downtown Dubai, which attract international investors, while its affordable housing projects align with government social housing policies. The organization must navigate regional economic shifts, global investment trends, and sustainability regulations (Balchin, 2020).

Challenges in Development Organizations

Development organizations, including real estate, commercial, residential, and mixed-use infrastructure projects, face challenges due to urban planning constraints, social impact considerations, and environmental policies (Healey, 2006). The primary challenge is balancing economic returns with social responsibility and sustainability (Davidson, 2021). Governments and urban planners push for smart cities and sustainable construction, while real estate developers seek rapid expansion and financial returns (Gyourko, 2021). Additionally, the housing market volatility creates further complexities (D'Arcy and Keogh, 1999). Developers must also navigate fluctuating interest rates, real estate market cycles, and foreign investment policies, which affect long-term project feasibility (Balchin, 2020).

2.3.3 Industrial Development: Balancing Economic Growth, Sustainability, and Regulation

Industrial development organizations operate within a highly pluralistic ecosystem, integrating government policies, environmental regulations, international trade agreements, private sector investments, and community development initiatives (Barney, Wright, and Ketchen, 2001). These organizations must balance economic expansion with sustainability mandates and stakeholder expectations, often managing conflicting interests from global supply chains, regulatory authorities, and commercial clients (Dunning, 2009).

Example: Dubai Ports World (DP World-UAE) and National Industrial Development Company

Pluralistic Structure: DP World, one of the largest global port operators, exemplifies pluralistic leadership in industrial logistics and international trade. With operations spanning more than 60 countries, DP World balances global trade facilitation, infrastructure development, regulatory compliance, and environmental sustainability (Cahill, 2018).

Multiplicity of Authorities: DP World must coordinate with international shipping firms, host governments, customs and regulatory bodies, and private sector investors. The company operates under the jurisdiction of UAE national policies, while simultaneously adhering to World Trade Organization (WTO) regulations and regional trade agreements (Cahill, 2018).

Multiplicity of Objectives and Logics: The firm operates at the intersection of economic growth, logistics efficiency, and environmental sustainability. While investors prioritize revenue generation and trade expansion, regulatory agencies enforce compliance with maritime security laws, carbon footprint reduction, and worker safety protocols (Notteboom and Winkelmans, 2014). DP World's logistics hubs must also align with host countries' national economic development goals, further complicating its strategic planning.

Multiplicity of Preferences: DP World serves diverse stakeholders, including shipping companies, supply chain managers, industrial firms, and global policymakers. The company must ensure that supply chain efficiencies are maintained, while simultaneously investing in sustainable port infrastructure, digital logistics solutions, and workforce development (Ng and Liu, 2014). Its expansion into free trade zones (Jebel Ali Free Zone) and inland logistics hubs reflects the need to diversify beyond traditional port operations and cater to regional industrial needs (Cahill, 2018).

Challenges in Industrial Development Organizations

Industrial development firms operate at the intersection of economic growth, environmental sustainability, and regulatory governance, facing conflicting stakeholder expectations (Barney, Wright, and Ketchen, 2001). One major challenge is managing infrastructure expansion while adhering to environmental policies and labor regulations (Dunning, 2009). Governments and urban planners seek long-term industrial resilience and sustainability, whereas private sector stakeholders prioritize cost reduction and rapid project execution (Notteboom and Winkelmans, 2014). Additionally, global supply chain disruptions, geopolitical risks, and regulatory compliance issues create uncertainties that impact industrial investments (Ng and Liu, 2014). Industrial firms must also navigate the transition toward digitalization and automation, balancing workforce retention with emerging technology implementation (Cahill, 2018).

2.3.4 Financial and Investment Sector: Balancing Risk, Return, and Stakeholder Interests

Investment organizations, financial services firms, asset management companies, financial brokers, and specialized investment entities exemplify pluralism through their diverse investment strategies, multi-stakeholder engagement, and regulatory compliance obligations (Fichtner, Heemskerk and Garcia-Bernardo, 2017). These organizations operate within complex financial ecosystems, balancing the interests of institutional investors, governments, corporate clients, and individual stakeholders (Davis and Kim, 2015). Their decision-making is influenced by macroeconomic conditions, legal frameworks, sustainability mandates, and global capital flows (Zingales, 2015).

Pluralism in asset management firms is evident in how they allocate capital across multiple sectors, geographies, and asset classes while adhering to fiduciary duties and sustainability commitments (Eccles and Klimenko, 2019). For example, alternative investments have emerged as powerful pluralistic entities, shaping corporate governance by integrating environmental, social, and governance (ESG) criteria into investment decisions (Fichtner et al., 2017). Similarly, financial brokers and hedge funds must reconcile risk-taking strategies with regulatory scrutiny, adapting to shifts in investor sentiment and market conditions (Lazonick and Shin, 2020). Investment and financial organizations strategically invest in technology, infrastructure, and sustainable energy projects, aligning financial growth with national development objectives (Callen, Cherif and Hasanov, 2022). Furthermore, investment banks and private equity firms navigate pluralistic tensions by balancing short-term deal-making incentives with long-term value creation, requiring them to manage multiple authorities and financial interests (Gompers et al., 2016).

Pluralistic Nature: These financial institutions demonstrate pluralistic complexity by engaging with diverse stakeholders, managing competing financial logics, and adapting to regulatory shifts and economic volatility. Their leadership structures necessitate strategic contextual intelligence to reconcile profitability, ethical investment standards, and dynamic market forces (Freeman, Harrison and Zyglidopoulos, 2018).

Pluralistic Logic and Objectives: Financial institutions and investment firms operate in highly pluralistic environments, where they must balance profitability, regulatory compliance, investor expectations, and broader economic stability (Zingales, 2015). These organizations engage with governments, central banks, institutional investors,

corporate clients, and individual consumers, each with distinct objectives, risk toler-
ances, and return expectations (Davis and Kim, 2015).

Challenges for Financial and Investment Pluralistic Organizations
Financial and investment pluralistic organizations face significant challenges due to
their multi-stakeholder environments, regulatory complexities, and evolving market
dynamics (Zingales, 2015). One of the primary challenges is balancing profitability
with regulatory compliance. Investment firms must navigate stringent financial regulations, such as Basel III for banking stability (BCBS, 2017) and ESG reporting requirements, while ensuring competitive returns for investors (Eccles and Klimenko, 2019).

Another key challenge is managing competing stakeholder interests, where institutional investors, sovereign funds, and retail clients often have divergent investment
goals. For example, asset managers must integrate short-term profit maximization
with long-term sustainability mandates, as seen in BlackRock's climate-focused investment strategy (Fichtner, Heemskerk and Garcia-Bernardo, 2017). Similarly, sovereign
wealth funds like Saudi PIF must align national economic objectives with global market opportunities and risk diversification (Callen, Cherif and Hasanov, 2022).

Moreover, geopolitical and macroeconomic instability poses a persistent risk to
financial pluralism. Organizations must adapt to fluctuating interest rates, currency
volatility, and trade restrictions, impacting investment decisions and cross-border
capital flows (Davis and Kim, 2015). Additionally, the rise of technological disruptions
in fintech and decentralized finance (DeFi) introduces operational and cybersecurity
risks, requiring firms to continuously innovate while maintaining regulatory oversight (Arner, Barberis and Buckley, 2016).

Finally, corporate governance and ethical dilemmas present another layer of
complexity. With increasing pressure from activist investors and global institutions,
financial organizations must enhance transparency, adopt responsible investment
strategies, and align with stakeholder capitalism (Freeman, Harrison and Zyglidopoulos, 2018). However, conflicts arise between profit-driven motives and ethical investment principles, making strategic decision-making increasingly complex.

2.4 Industry-Specific Pluralism in Action

Pluralistic organizations require advanced leadership approaches due to their multiple authorities, competing objectives, and external pressures (Denis, Langley, and
Rouleau, 2007). Leaders must balance stakeholder interests, regulatory demands, and
financial sustainability while ensuring long-term viability, innovation, and ethical
governance. The challenge for leadership is integrating diverse logics across professional, regulatory, financial, and social dimensions to drive sustainable success. Each
industry presents unique pluralistic challenges, requiring contextual intelligence,

strategic adaptability, and multi-stakeholder collaboration. For example, healthcare organizations must balance medical ethics and cost efficiency, while financial services firms navigate profitability, regulation, and investor expectations (Table 2.2).

Table 2.2: Examples of Pluralistic Organizations in Different Industries.

Industry	Pluralistic Organization	Key Challenges
Healthcare	Medi Care and Vita Care	Medical autonomy versus administrative efficiency
Development	Urban Escape	Economic versus social responsibility and sustainability Volatile market
Industrial Development	DP World (UAE)	Economic growth versus environmental sustainability
Financial Services and Investment	Echo Capital (UAE), BlackRock (USA), Saudi PIF (Saudi Arabia)	Shareholder returns versus regulatory and ESG compliance
Development	Urban Escape, Emaar Properties (UAE), Brookfield Asset Management (Canada)	Urban expansion versus environmental and social responsibility

Pluralistic organizations operate in multi-dimensional environments where authority, objectives, and preferences are decentralized. Strategic leadership in these contexts requires navigating ambiguity, integrating diverse stakeholder interests, and ensuring long-term financial, regulatory, and ethical sustainability. Understanding pluralism in healthcare, education, technology, financial services, industrial development, and multi-use real estate will equip leaders to drive innovation, achieve sustainable outcomes, and build resilient organizations in an evolving global landscape. In such organizations, traditional leadership models often fall short because they fail to account for the diverse and competing elements that define these entities.

Rather than examining the entire internal context, the emphasis here is on the aspects that directly shape decision-making, governance, and alignment within pluralistic organizations. Organizational structure shapes the distribution of authority, responsibilities; strategic leadership determines how CEOs and TMTs interpret and respond to contextual pressures; and organizational culture influences organization and people dynamics (Finkelstein, Hambrick and Cannella, 2009; Schein, 2010).

2.5 Impact of Context Matrix on Pluralistic Organizational Internal Context

The following section focuses on three critical internal components: structure, strategic leadership (CEOs and TMTs), and organizational culture. These elements are most susceptible to external pressures and play a defining role in how organizations adapt to shifting demands, align leadership priorities, and sustain strategic coherence (Denis, Langley and Rouleau, 2007) (Table 2.3).

Table 2.3: Elements of Pluralistic Organization's Internal Context.

Pluralistic organization structure	**The organization structure that outlines how tasks are divided, grouped, and coordinated within the organization.**
CEOs and Top Management Team	The upper echelons of the organization
Culture	The set of shared values, beliefs, and norms that influence the behaviour and practices of the organization's members.

Each of these elements interacts with the components of a pluralistic organization's internal context in the following ways (Figure 2.5):

Economic and Regulatory Context Impact

Structure: Economic policies and regulations can necessitate changes in organizational structure to ensure compliance and optimize performance.

Cultural and Societal Leadership: Societal leadership expectations and national cultural norms influence organizational culture, affecting internal cohesion and stakeholder engagement.

Shareholders: Social leadership expectations can shape stakeholder priorities, influencing organizational goals and strategies.

Context Impact on Pluralistic Organization's Structure

The external context plays a crucial role in shaping organizational hierarchies, roles, and responsibilities. For instance, economic downturns may prompt restructuring efforts focused on cost reduction, while regulatory changes can lead to the establishment of new compliance departments.

The four cases presented in this book predominantly feature organic public structures (Figure 2.6), involving industry regulations, public shareholders, regulatory bodies, and boards of directors. Within these organizations, an organic hierarchy exists where both corporate and professional TMTs report directly to their CEOs. However,

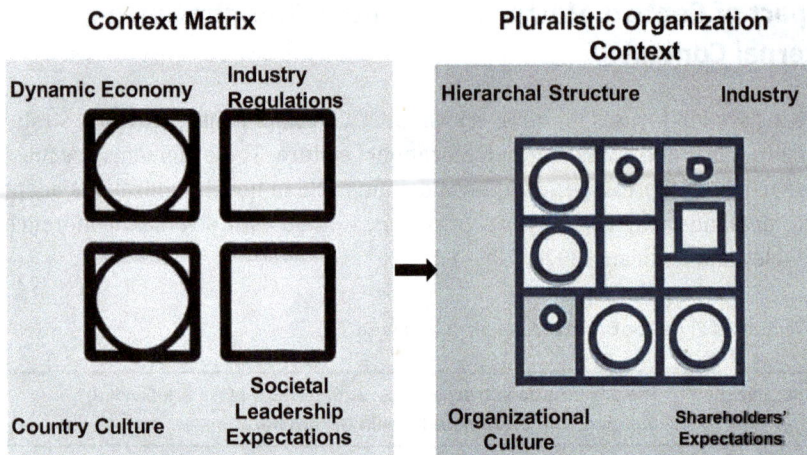

Figure 2.5: The Context Matrix Impact on the Internal Organizational Context.
This figure shows how the external context including dynamic economy, industry regulations, country culture, and societal leadership expectations influences the internal context of pluralistic organizations. These external dimensions shape organizational structures, industry responses, internal culture, and shareholder expectations, highlighting the interaction between broader contextual forces and internal organizational behavior.

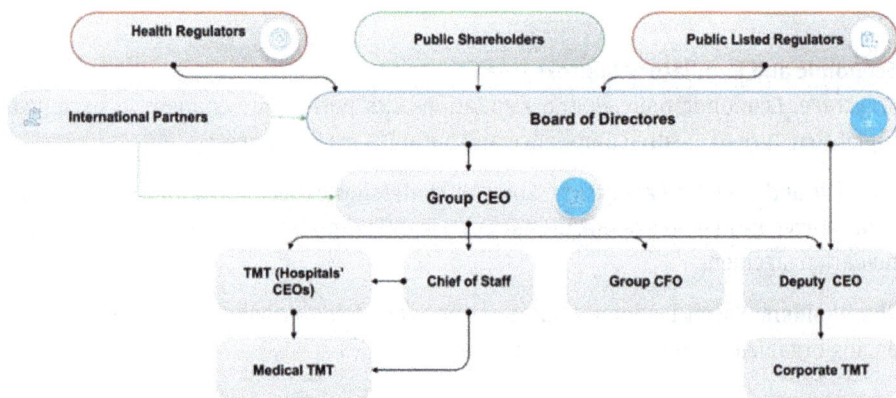

Figure 2.6: The Pluralistic Organizational Hierarchical Structure.
This figure outlines the governance structure in which the Board of Directors oversees the Group CEO, who works with both corporate and professional Top Management Teams. It highlights how direct reporting lines from certain team members to the board can impact the CEO's authority and the overall alignment within the organization.

in all cases, certain TMT members maintain direct reporting relationships with the board of directors, which significantly influences the level of support provided to their CEOs.

Building on the examination of organizational structures, it is crucial to understand how the context matrix influences the individual.

2.6 Context Matrix Impact on TMTs and CEOs in Pluralistic Organizations

The context matrix is a powerful tool for understanding the external factors that impact strategic leadership within pluralistic organizations, particularly focusing on the roles of TMTs and CEOs. These elements influence how leaders navigate organizational transformations, make strategic decisions, and maintain effective communication and networking both internally and externally. Additionally, the context matrix, with its multifaceted external factors, impacts TMTs by shaping their alignment, effectiveness, and interactions with both the CEO and the board. The interplay between these relationships is critical in navigating strategic directions and achieving organizational success (Figure 2.7).

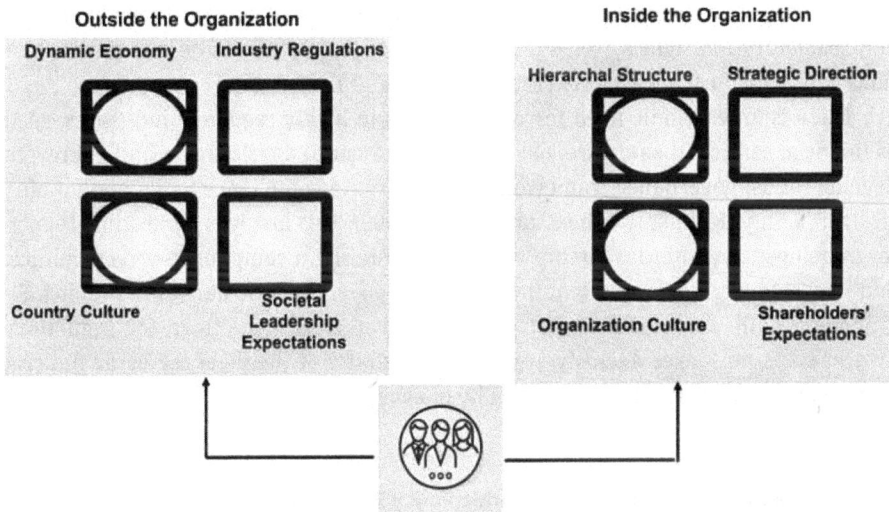

Figure 2.7: Context Matrix Impact on Strategic Leadership.
This figure explains how the context matrix influences strategic leadership within and beyond organizational boundaries. External contextual forces such as a dynamic economy, industry regulations, country culture, and societal leadership expectations interact with internal organizational elements including hierarchical structure, strategic direction, organizational culture, and shareholder expectations. The top management team is positioned at the intersection of these domains, navigating complex demands in pluralistic organizations.

Dynamic Economy and Industry Regulations Impact on TMTs and CEOs
One of the significant external factors highlighted by the context matrix is the influence of economic conditions and industry regulations on organizational governance,

reporting, and hierarchical structures (Hitt, Ireland, and Hoskisson, 2020). In pluralistic organizations operating across multiple jurisdictions, economic shifts can have profound implications for leadership decision-making, requiring top management teams and CEOs to exercise strategic contextual intelligence to ensure alignment with the evolving regulatory and financial landscape

Economic volatility, such as financial crises, inflationary pressures and global supply chain disruptions, can destabilize organizations, necessitating rapid strategic recalibration (Van Essen, Otten, and Carberry, 2015). Regulatory bodies often respond to these economic fluctuations by introducing new compliance requirements, reporting standards, and governance mandates, further complicating the strategic decision-making process for TMTs (Aguilera, Desender, Bednar, and Lee, 2015). TMTs who fail to anticipate and adapt to these regulatory shifts risk legal penalties, reputational damage, and loss of stakeholder confidence (Judge, Fainshmidt, and Brown, 2020).

For TMTs and CEOs, navigating these challenges requires a high level of contextual awareness and ability to integrate economic, regulatory, and market signals into strategic planning (Osborn, Jauch, Martin, and Glueck, 2022). CEOs and executive teams are expected to cultivate foresight by leveraging technology, future planning, and regulatory foresight systems to mitigate risks associated with economic fluctuations and regulatory uncertainty (Teece, Peteraf, and Leih, 2016).

There is an emphatic need for organizations in highly regulated industries, such as financial services, healthcare, development, industrial development and energy, to develop robust governance frameworks and to ensure compliance while maintaining strategic agility (Hillman, Withers, and Collins, 2009). This involves embedding regulatory intelligence within leadership structures, fostering a compliance-driven culture, and integrating risk management into corporate governance strategies (Cumming, Filatotchev, Knill, Reeb, and Senbet, 2017). In other words, the need for regulatory awareness is no longer exclusively the responsibility of the legal teams or the risk management teams. It is the responsibility of every TMT member.

2.6.1 Strategic Leadership and Economic Policy Responses

Public policies, such as funding, tariffs, taxation policies, and labor laws, also shape the strategic flexibility of organizations. The regulatory burden varies significantly across countries, with emerging economies often experiencing more unpredictable policy shifts compared to established economies (Khanna and Palepu, 2010). In such environments, CEOs and TMTs must proactively engage with regulatory bodies, participate in industry forums, and develop contingency strategies to safeguard organizational sustainability (Peng, Sun, Pinkham, and Chen, 2009).

Organizations that successfully navigate economic and regulatory changes often exhibit strong strategic and contextual leadership, proactive risk management, and adaptive governance structures (Filatotchev and Wright, 2011). The interplay between economic conditions and regulatory changes presents a dual challenge for TMTs and CEOs operating in pluralistic organizations. While economic shifts create uncertainty and volatility, regulatory transformations demand compliance and strategic adaptability. Leaders who cultivate strategic contextual intelligence and develop proactive governance frameworks are better positioned to navigate economic fluctuations, regulatory complexities, and market uncertainties, ensuring organizational stability, sustainable success, and long-term stakeholder confidence.

Building on our examination of pluralistic organizational context, it becomes clear that the context matrix plays a crucial role in shaping how TMTs and CEOs navigate contextual uncertainty. The volatile business environment, external economic conditions, frequent strategic redirections, historical organizational challenges, and the high turnover rate of CEOs have created a climate of persistent uncertainty (Hitt, Ireland, and Hoskisson, 2020). These disruptions demand continuous strategic change, requiring TMTs to balance stability and agility within an ever-changing operational context.

We found that the key challenge for TMTs in pluralistic organizations is maintaining strategic alignment despite frequent shifts in economic and regulatory landscapes. Economic downturns, inflationary pressures, geopolitical tensions, and technological disruptions introduce unpredictability, compelling leadership teams to reconfigure their strategic priorities (Barney, 2020). These factors have impaired leadership instability, with CEO tenure decreasing globally, creating further disruptions in TMT alignment and decision-making continuity (Van Essen, Otten, and Carberry, 2015). Studies suggest that frequent CEO changes correlate with declining organizational performance if not managed strategically, as leadership transitions often introduce misaligned strategic priorities and cultural discontinuities (Osborn, Jauch, Martin, and Glueck, 2022).

Despite these structural and environmental challenges, our study revealed a strong commitment from TMT members, as evidenced by their extended tenure and sustained engagement with their organizations. This dedication to organizational sustainability suggests that while uncertainty poses challenges, it also solidifies team alignment and resilience in leadership (Judge, Fainshmidt, and Brown, 2020). The ability of TMTs to navigate these complexities effectively is directly linked to their capacity to apply hybrid strategic contextual leadership principles, which include contextual intelligence, integrative communication, strategic financial intelligence, and innovation agility.

The Hybrid Strategic Contextual Leadership framework, which is introduced in the following section, provides a structured approach to enhancing TMT resilience, adaptability, and strategic foresight within uncertain economic and organizational contexts. This framework integrates strategic agility and contextual intelligence to mitigate the adverse effects of frequent strategic redirections. By embedding context-driven strategic leadership within TMT structures, pluralistic organizations can improve strategic alignment, decision-making continuity, and long-term sustainability.

2.6.2 Influence of Cultural Diversity and Social Leadership Expectations on TMT

Another critical aspect of the context matrix is the cultural diversity within TMTs, particularly in pluralistic organizations. The TMTs in our case study represent a wide array of cultural backgrounds, with executives from 31 different nationalities. While this diversity brings a wealth of perspectives and insights, it also introduces challenges related to alignment, performance, and innovation. The cultural dynamics within these teams are significant in shaping organizational strategies and ensuring that diverse viewpoints are harmonized to drive the organization forward.

Our study findings confirm that the presence of multiple cultural perspectives within TMTs fosters dynamic strategic capabilities, as pluralistic organizations with diverse leadership structures display greater agility in responding to market changes and regulatory shifts. However, cultural diversity also requires careful leadership orchestration to bridge differing viewpoints and avoid fragmentation in strategic decision-making (Meyer and Xin, 2020). Cultural variations in power distance, risk tolerance, and decision-making styles often lead to misalignment in leadership expectations, which, if not addressed, can result in internal conflict and delays in strategic execution (Hofstede, 2001).

Additionally, the educational background of TMT members further influences leadership dynamics. Our study revealed that 68% of TMT members were educated in the United States, which significantly impacts how they approach professional challenges, structure organizational priorities, and implement strategic frameworks. Western educational paradigms, particularly those emphasizing individualistic leadership, competitive market strategies, and data-driven decision-making, shape how these executives operate within their multicultural teams (Northouse, 2021; Meyer, 2017). While Western-trained executives often introduce globally recognized best practices, a direct application of Western management models in non-Western business environments can create misinterpretations of local business norms and lead to cultural friction within leadership teams (House, Hanges, Javidan, Dorfman, and Gupta, 2004).

To leverage cultural diversity while mitigating its challenges, organizations must adopt a leadership approach which integrates cultural diversity and contextual strategic agility (Heifetz, Grashow, and Linsky, 2009). Such a framework enables TMTs to align strategic priorities while accommodating diverse cultural perspectives, ensuring collaborative decision-making and sustainable leadership performance (Pearce and Conger, 2003). Organizations that successfully implement integrative leadership models and context-sensitive governance structures can harness diversity as a competitive advantage, enabling long-term organizational sustainability in an increasingly complex and pluralistic global environment (Teece, 2018).

By embedding context-driven leadership mechanisms into their organizational framework, TMTs can enhance strategic coherence, improve cross-cultural collaboration, and drive sustainable success, ensuring that diverse perspectives become a strength rather than a barrier. In this way, pluralistic organizations can transform cultural diversity from a leadership challenge into a powerful asset, positioning themselves for long-term resilience and growth in an increasingly interconnected world.

2.7 Context Matrix Influence on Pluralistic Organizational Culture

Strategic leadership in pluralistic organizations is shaped by an intricate interplay of national culture and societal leadership expectations, both of which significantly influence organizational culture and leadership effectiveness. The study by House et al. (2013), examining strategic leadership effectiveness across 24 countries, emphasized that national cultural norms shape leadership styles, decision-making processes, and stakeholder interactions, but with a crucial distinction – societal leadership expectations have a more substantial impact on shaping leadership behaviors than national cultural values alone.

The Influence of National Culture on Organizational Culture: A Partial but Significant Foundation

Organizational culture is deeply embedded in the broader national culture, shaping leadership styles, workplace norms, and stakeholder interactions. National cultural values influence how authority is perceived, how decisions are made, and how employees engage within organizations. As reflected in Figure 2.8, participants in our study attributed 40% of organizational culture to national culture, emphasizing its role in shaping internal structures and leadership dynamics.

Hofstede's (2006) cultural dimensions theory provides a useful lens for understanding this impact. For example, in high-power-distance cultures, such as in parts of the Middle East and Asia, hierarchical leadership structures are reinforced, and decision-making authority is concentrated at the top. This contrasts with low-power-distance cultures, such as those in Scandinavia, where leadership is often more participatory and consensus-driven. Similarly, individualistic cultures, such as those in the United States and the United Kingdom, encourage decentralized decision-making and personal accountability, while collectivist cultures, including many in the Middle East and East Asia, prioritize group harmony and consensus-driven leadership.

In the context of pluralistic organizations, the national culture sets the foundation for workplace interactions, leadership expectations, and governance practices. However, as participants highlighted, national culture alone does not fully define organizational culture. They emphasized that societal leadership expectations exert an even greater influence, accounting for 60% of the impact on organizational culture, a distinction that will be explored in the following section.

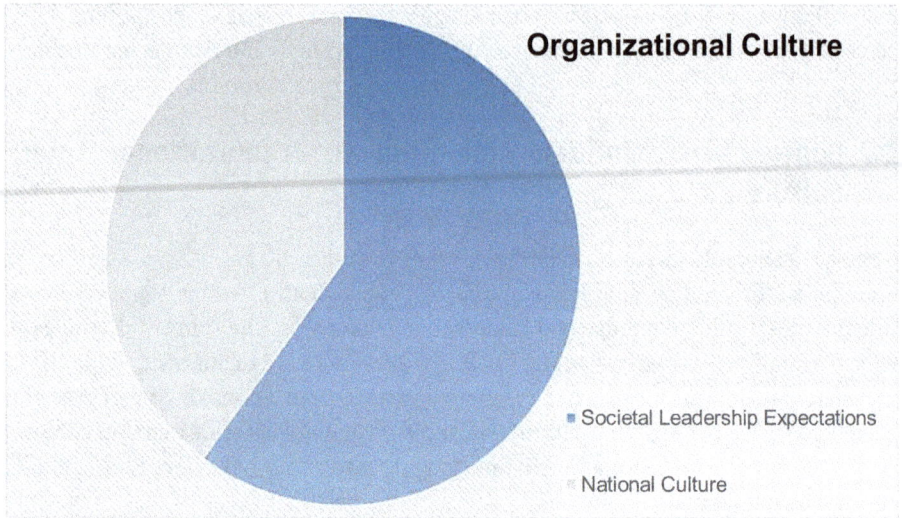

Figure 2.8: Context Influences on Pluralistic Organizational Culture.
This figure illustrates participants' views on the relative influence of contextual factors on organizational culture in pluralistic organizations. While national culture lays the foundation for workplace norms and practices, societal leadership expectations are perceived to have a stronger influence accounting for approximately 60% of the overall impact on organizational culture.

Societal Leadership Expectations as a Stronger Determinant of Organizational Culture

While earlier studies suggested that leaders primarily reflect their cultural environment, House et al.'s (2013) research presented a paradigm shift, revealing that societal leadership expectations exert a greater influence on leadership behaviors than national cultural values alone. Our case studies reinforce this finding, demonstrating that leaders who align with societal expectations are more likely to be viewed as effective and gain stakeholder trust.

The chairman, CEO, and TMTs of Urban Escape recognized that effective leadership requires alignment not only with national cultural values but also with deeply ingrained societal leadership expectations that prioritize stability, trust, and a long-term vision. The TMT attributed their long tenure to their ability to sustain organizational stability, which in turn fostered strong shareholder trust and enabled the pursuit of long-term strategic objectives.

While their country national culture is characterized by high power distance and collectivism, the broader societal expectations of business leaders demanded a balance between hierarchical authority and consultative decision-making. This approach was essential for securing stakeholder buy-in, reinforcing leadership legitimacy, and ensuring organizational resilience in an evolving economic and regulatory landscape

Similarly, in Echo Capital, despite operating in a regulatory environment influenced by Western financial principles, societal expectations in the region demand a leadership approach that prioritizes transparency, relationship-driven decision-making, and ethical responsibility. The CEO's ability to meet these expectations played a crucial role in shaping the company's governance structure and stakeholder relations.

Across these cases, leaders were actively navigating the more dominant societal leadership expectations that define their legitimacy and effectiveness. This distinction underscores why societal expectations accounted for 60% of organizational cultural influence in Figure 2.8, compared to 40% from national culture. Leaders who failed to adapt to these expectations struggled to gain credibility, align their teams, or sustain long-term success.

By incorporating these practical insights, our study moves beyond theoretical debates and demonstrates how societal leadership expectations play a decisive role in shaping pluralistic organizations, their internal cultures, and their strategic leadership approaches.

2.7.1 Contextual Variations in Societal Leadership Expectations

Building on our analysis of how societal leadership expectations exert a stronger influence than national culture on organizational culture, our study further highlights the contextual variations in these expectations across different regions. These variations are particularly pronounced within pluralistic organizations, where top management teams must balance competing stakeholder priorities, steer diverse cultural landscapes, and respond to evolving societal demands.

In the Middle East, for example, TMT members consistently emphasized that organizational values must align with national societal expectations to ensure long-term legitimacy and stakeholder trust. Leaders are expected to demonstrate respect, generosity, family cohesion, tolerance, and solidarity, values deeply embedded in the region's cultural ethos (Hofstede, 2001). Unlike in Western contexts, where professional and personal spheres are more distinctly separated, Middle Eastern leaders often face heightened personal stakes, as failure impacts not just their professional standing but also their societal and familial reputations (Schein, 2010).

The case studies provide practical evidence of these dynamics in action. At Medi Care, for instance, societal expectations shaped internal leadership dynamics, particularly in executive decision-making regarding talent retention. When faced with restructuring pressures, the deputy CEO and Middle Eastern TMT members strongly advocated for investing in strategic leadership development rather than terminating senior executives, aligning with national leadership's broader vision of stability and continuity within leadership ranks (House et al., 2004). This perspective often clashed with the expectations of Western CEOs, who prioritized short-term efficiency and operational restructuring over long-term leadership sustainability.

Similarly, at Echo Capital, conflicts emerged between Middle Eastern executives and Western leadership over resource allocation. The Middle Eastern TMT members viewed relationship-driven decision-making, ethical responsibility, and community engagement as integral to the company's success, whereas Western executives initially prioritized immediate financial performance and restructuring. These competing perspectives required strategic contextual intelligence to align leadership approaches with societal expectations while maintaining organizational agility.

These case insights demonstrate that societal leadership expectations are not static; they vary across contexts and industries, shaping how leaders must adapt their strategies. This growing recognition of context-driven leadership imperatives sets the stage for the Hybrid Strategic Contextual Leadership framework (Al Bachir, 2022).

By synthesizing the findings from the case studies, Figure 2.9 presents the emergent Hybrid Strategic Contextual Leadership framework, integrating cultural and societal dynamics into a broader strategic leadership model (Al Bachir, 2022). This framework provides a roadmap for CEOs and TMTs navigating pluralistic and multicultural organizations, equipping them with the tools to balance societal expectations, organizational strategic direction, and sustainable performance outcomes.

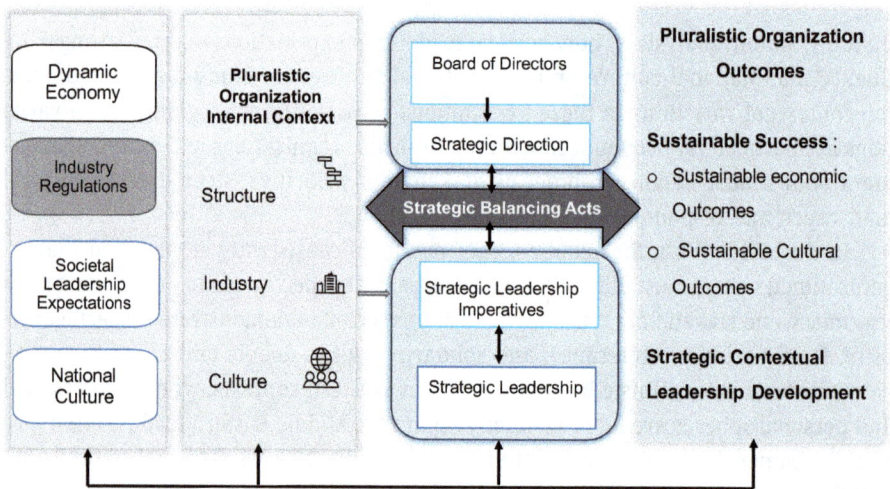

Figure 2.9: Hybrid Strategic Contextual Leadership Framework.
The Hybrid Strategic Contextual Leadership Framework synthesizes findings from multiple case studies, showing how external and internal contextual factors influence strategic leadership. It emphasizes the dual role of CEOs and top management teams in aligning with board direction while shaping and executing leadership strategies that contribute to sustainable organizational outcomes and leadership development in pluralistic environments.

The Hybrid Strategic Contextual Leadership framework provides a structured approach for strategic leaders and their teams to navigate the complexities of external influences while driving sustainable success, and strategic contextual leadership development within pluralistic organizations. By integrating insights from the context matrix, the framework ensures that both strategic and contextual leadership practices are aligned with the evolving internal and external landscape.

This framework outlines how contextual elements ranging from economic conditions and industry regulations to national culture and societal leadership expectations shape an organization's internal context, strategic leadership decisions, and overall outcomes.

Dynamic Economy and Industry Regulations

A dynamic economic environment and evolving industry regulations create external pressures that shape an organization's strategic leadership approach and long-term sustainability.

National and global economic fluctuations directly impact market conditions, governance structures, financial stability, and strategic decision-making. Leaders must anticipate economic trends, adjust investment strategies, and ensure financial resilience to sustain organizational growth.

The regulatory frameworks define the legal and operational boundaries within which organizations must function. Strategic leaders must anticipate policy shifts, adapt compliance measures, and navigate evolving governance requirements to remain competitive and ensure sustainable results. In this rapidly changing environment, leaders who proactively manage economic uncertainties and regulatory changes strengthen their organization's ability to innovate, maintain financial stability, and align with compliance mandates while driving long-term success.

Societal Leadership Expectations and National Culture

Organizational leadership does not operate in isolation, it is deeply influenced by societal leadership expectations and national culture.

National culture shapes leadership styles, decision-making processes, and organizational behavior. In pluralistic organizations, leaders must navigate cultural diversity within and beyond their headquarters, ensuring alignment with various national and corporate cultures.

While national culture provides a foundational framework, societal leadership expectations exert a greater influence on organizational leadership (as discussed in Figure 2.8). Leaders are expected to demonstrate credibility, long-term vision, good governance, and social engagement, ensuring that their leadership aligns with stakeholder expectations, including employees, customers, and shareholders.

Strategic and contextual awareness is essential for CEOs and TMTs to integrate societal leadership expectations into organizational culture, fostering alignment between internal leadership practices and external societal demands. This ensures that organizational strategies resonate with both employees and external stakeholders, leading to sustainable performance and leadership effectiveness.

Strategic Leadership

The Hybrid Strategic Contextual Leadership framework demonstrates how effective leadership is shaped by the dynamic interaction between the internal dynamics of strategic direction changes, and the external cultural and societal expectations that leaders must navigate. CEOs and TMTs focus on the impact of shifts in strategic direction within an organization. These changes driven by market disruptions, regulatory shifts, or internal decisions and restructuring create uncertainty. To effectively respond, leaders must be contextually aware, agile and capable of balancing short-term responses with long-term planning. The need for strategic leadership imperatives allows leaders to maintain effectiveness amid constant flux, handle the contextual impacts, and drive their organizations toward sustainability and growth.

Conversely, the national culture and societal expectations shape leadership. Different cultural contexts dictate what is perceived as effective leadership, influencing decision-making styles, communication practices, and interpersonal dynamics. Societal leadership expectations shape the values and behaviors expected by key stakeholders including employees, customers, and shareholders. This axis illustrates the complex landscape leaders must navigate, where their effectiveness in aligning with diverse cultural norms and societal demands are essential for success.

The context elements impacts emphasize the necessity for a comprehensive set of strategic leadership imperatives that enable leaders to navigate both internal complexities and external pressures effectively. Mastery of these imperatives requires balancing their strategic acts inside and outside their organizations. This dual capability is vital for achieving sustainable success in pluralistic multicultural organizations.

Strategic Leadership Imperatives: Balancing External and Internal Pressures

Strategic leaders face significant challenges due to strategic direction changes and external pressures. This context demands strategic leadership imperatives that equip leaders to navigate both internal and external uncertainties. TMTs and senior managers must balance immediate responses to strategic direction change with the pursuit of long-term objectives, effectively integrating these elements into their organizational strategies. This strategic leadership dynamic capability allows leaders to synthesize and balance external pressures with the internal needs of the organization. It enhances the ability to understand, interpret, and act upon the interplay between external cultural and societal expectations and the internal dynamics at play. By leveraging context, leaders can craft strategies that align with the external environment while being effectively executed within the organizational context, ultimately driving performance excellence, sustainability, and leadership development (in Chapter 3 the two balancing acts are discussed in greater detail).

Pluralistic Organizations Outcomes in the Strategic Contextual Leadership Framework

Within the Hybrid Strategic and Contextual Leadership framework, pluralistic organizations pursue sustainable success, which is achieved through sustainable economic outcomes and sustainable cultural outcomes. These interconnected dimensions serve as key indicators of an organization's ability to thrive in complex and dynamic environments while maintaining long-term viability.

Sustainable Success (Explored in Detail in Chapter 5)

Sustainable success is not merely about financial performance; it is about securing an organization's long-term resilience by integrating economic and cultural sustainability. This ensures that organizations maintain their social license to operate while navigating pluralistic and evolving business landscapes.

Sustainable Economic Outcomes

Strategic leaders must go beyond profitability to optimize processes, drive performance excellence, and leverage innovation and technology as enablers of financial sustainability. Organizations must embed efficiency into their operational frameworks, ensuring effective resource utilization, streamlined processes, and strategic financial intelligence that foster both stability and agility.

Performance Excellence: Ensuring operational efficiency and continuous improvement in financial and organizational performance.

Efficiency of Resources and Processes: Driving cost-effectiveness, productivity, and agility in execution.

Financial Sustainability: Utilizing advanced financial strategies and risk management to ensure long-term financial stability.

Innovation and Agility: Leveraging technological advancements and digital transformation to enhance financial resilience and competitive advantage.

These elements are essential for navigating complex economic landscapes while maintaining a strong competitive edge in a rapidly evolving business environment.

Sustainable Cultural Outcomes

Pluralistic organizations must align their strategies with societal expectations, fostering trust through governance, stakeholder engagement, and ethical leadership. This requires a deep understanding of national and organizational culture, societal leadership expectations, and governance models that drive long-term success.

Societal Leadership Expectations: Aligning leadership strategies with national and societal norms that shape stakeholder expectations.

Stakeholders' Support and Trust: Building credibility and transparency through ethical decision-making and stakeholder collaboration.

Growth and Good Governance: Establishing governance structures that balance financial success with ethical, sustainable business practices.

Continuous Learning: Embedding a learning-driven culture that fosters adaptability, innovation, and strategic foresight.

Strategic Contextual Leadership Development – The Way to Achieve Sustainability (Chapter 6)

The Strategic Contextual Leadership framework emphasizes that leadership development cannot be one-size-fits-all; it must be grounded in a nuanced understanding of the broader cultural and contextual norms that drive organizational success. The framework by equipping strategic leaders with four critical imperatives: strategic contextual intelligence, integrative communication, strategic financial innovation, and Innovation and agility. These imperatives prepare leaders to navigate the complexities of pluralistic environments with agility and foresight. The effectiveness of strategic contextual leadership development depends on the leaders' ability to align with societal expectations, thereby enhancing their relevance and long-term impact. Cultivating leaders who are contextually aware and strategically adept allows forward-thinking organizations to not only achieve performance excellence but also ensure sustained success amid evolving challenges. This approach fosters a new generation of leaders who can guide their organizations through uncertainty, leveraging context as a strategic asset, and maintaining resilience in a rapidly changing world.

Given its strategic importance for strategic contextual leadership development, we have dedicated Chapter 6 to an in-depth exploration of how organizations can embed strategic contextual leadership into their leadership development pipelines. This ensures that sustainable success is not just an aspiration but a practical, measurable, and strategic reality.

2.8 Conclusion

As we conclude our exploration of the Strategic Contextual Leadership framework, it is evident that the framework intricately captures how external forces ranging from macroeconomic changes to leadership transitions shape organizational internal contexts. These external factors profoundly influence leadership practices, the structural and operational dynamics of TMTs, and the broader organizational culture. These insights set the stage for the deeper exploration in Chapter 3. We will dive into the specific competencies required for effective strategic contextual leadership. We examine how performance excellence, strategic leadership imperatives, and sustainable success are driven by the adept application of strategic contextual framework, further building on the foundational concepts discussed in this chapter.

2.9 Interactive Learning and Reflection Section: Engaging with the Context Matrix

To fully grasp the complexities of strategic leadership in pluralistic organizations, it is essential to actively engage with the context matrix and reflect on real-world applications within your own leadership context. The following exercises will guide you through an interactive learning process, helping you apply the context matrix, assess internal and external contextual strategic factors, and reflect on the challenges of leading in pluralistic organizations.

2.9.1 Understanding and Applying the Context Matrix

The context matrix is a strategic tool that helps TMTs identify, assess, and navigate key contextual factors influencing leadership and decision-making. It consists of four interdependent areas, each representing a critical aspect of an organization's external and internal environment Table 2.4.

Table 2.4: Four Areas of the Context Matrix.

Contextual Area	Key Indicators
Economic and Regulatory Context	Country economic conditions Industry regulations and compliance requirements Tax policies and legal frameworks Market trends and competitive landscape
Cultural and Social Context	Societal leadership expectations Cultural diversity within TMT and workforce Public perception and reputation Social and ethical responsibilities
Technological and Industry Context	Disruptive innovations and emerging technologies Industry-specific regulatory changes Digital transformation strategies Cybersecurity risks and data governance Research and development (R&D) investments

Table 2.4 (continued)

Contextual Area	Key Indicators
Organizational and Strategic Context	Internal governance structures
	Decision-making processes
	Strategic priorities and long-term vision
	Leadership and succession planning
	Financial health and operational efficiency

2.9.1.1 Exercise: Mapping Your Organization's Context

1. List key strategic internal and external factors affecting your TMT's decision-making.
2. Categorize each factor into one of the four areas of the context matrix.
3. **Reflect:**
   - How does your organization currently respond to these contextual elements?
   - Where are the biggest gaps in your TMT's strategic awareness?
   - Which areas require greater focus to enhance decision-making and adaptability?

2.9.2 Deep Dive into Pluralistic Organizations

Pluralistic organizations are characterized by multiple authorities, objectives, and stakeholder preferences. These organizations often pursue diverse goals while facing complex, shifting demands from various internal and external actors.

To ensure effective leadership in a pluralistic setting, TMTs must navigate:

- Multiplicity of Authorities: Various stakeholders with decision-making power (e.g., board members, regulatory bodies, investor groups).
- Multiplicity of Objectives and Logics: Conflicting or complementary strategic priorities (e.g., financial profitability versus social responsibility).
- Multiplicity of Preferences: Diverse interests and expectations from employees, customers, and external stakeholders.

2.9.2.1 Exercise: Identifying Key Pluralistic Challenges in Your Organization

1. Identify the key authorities in your TMT and stakeholder network:
   - Who has the power to influence strategic decisions?
   - Are there competing leadership voices or power struggles?
2. Recognize multiple objectives and logics within your organization:
   - What are the core business goals, and do they align with stakeholder expectations?

- Are there tensions between financial, social, and operational priorities?
3. Analyze the range of stakeholder preferences:
    - What are the dominant values and priorities among different stakeholder groups?
    - How do customers, employees, and investors view the organization's leadership approach?
4. **Reflect**:
    - Where do contradictions exist in your organization's objectives and leadership structure?
    - How can you balance competing demands while maintaining strategic focus?

2.9.3 Driving Impact: Strategic Stakeholder Engagement in Action

Effective leadership in a pluralistic organization requires active engagement with key stakeholders.
1. Reach out to a mentor or a trusted member of your personal sounding board:
    - Share your reflections on contextual factors and pluralistic challenges.
    - Ask for feedback on how you are navigating multiple stakeholder expectations.
2. Develop an engagement strategy:
    - Identify a network of individuals within and outside your organization whom you need to engage with.
    - What actions can you take to align with multiple authorities and priorities?
3. Plan for strategic alignment:
    - How can you create structured dialogue between competing stakeholder interests?
    - Are there forums, councils, or meetings that can facilitate cross-functional collaboration?
4. Anticipate resistance and manage change:
    - How can you use adaptive leadership to address stakeholder concerns?
    - What communication strategies can bridge diverse perspectives within your leadership team?

2.9.4 Implementing the Hybrid Strategic Contextual Leadership Framework

To integrate the context matrix insights and pluralistic organization realities into leadership practice, TMTs can adopt the Hybrid Strategic Contextual Leadership framework. This framework focuses on:
- Building contextual intelligence: Strengthening awareness of economic, cultural, technological, and organizational shifts.

- Enhancing integrative communication: Developing mechanisms for cross-functional and cross-cultural dialogue.
- Applying strategic financial intelligence: Ensuring that financial decisions align with broader strategic objectives.
- Fostering innovation and agility: Encouraging adaptive strategies in response to external market shifts.

2.9.5 Action Plan: Bringing Hybrid Strategic Contextual Leadership Framework Into Your Organization

1. Identify three key leadership actions you can take in the next 90 days to improve context-driven decision-making.
2. Develop a stakeholder engagement plan to enhance collaborative decision-making.
3. Initiate a strategic review within your TMT to assess current contextual adaptability and pluralistic leadership effectiveness.
4. Seek feedback and refine by engaging with mentors, external advisors, and industry peers to adjust and refine your strategic leadership approach.

2.10 Final Reflection

After completing these exercises, take a moment to reflect:
- What new insights did you gain about your organization's context and pluralistic dynamics?
- How will you adjust your leadership approach to improve alignment and adaptability?
- What concrete steps will you take to integrate the context matrix and HSCL framework into your strategic leadership practice?

Leadership in pluralistic organizations is not static, it requires continuous learning, engagement, and growth. By actively analyzing contextual factors, engaging with diverse stakeholders, and implementing hybrid leadership models, you can enhance strategic decision-making and drive sustainable success in a complex and evolving business landscape.

Chapter 3
TMT's Driving Performance Excellence Through Strategic Contextual Leadership

The previous chapter meticulously identified the strategic leadership imperatives needed in today's pluralistic, contemporary organizations.

Most of the strategic leadership studies draw attention to leaders' demographic aspects, personalities, and values, particularly when assessing the relationship between leadership and organizational performance. *However, a gap remains in the need to understand where and when TMTs and CEOs exert their leadership.* Instead of focusing on the TMTs' demographics and personality traits, we investigate how the composition, structure and process of the TMT amplify or limit their role and impact inside and outside their organizations. On the one hand, TMTs provide leadership within the organization and shape the environment in which individual members operate. On the other hand, they navigate the broader external landscape that influences organizational direction and strategy.

We presented the context matrix as a complex, multifaceted entity, comprising external factors that affect both individual leaders and the organization, requiring TMTs to adapt and respond effectively at multiple levels. In this chapter we reveal *how and when* TMTs and CEOs exert their strategic contextual leadership while balancing their two strategic acts: (1) interplay between TMTs inside their organization, interface with boards, relationships between TMTs and CEOs, and internal interactions within TMTs themselves. (2) TMT acts outside their organizations. This narrative disentangles the multi-layered and complex roles TMTs play in guiding organizations through strategic changes and leadership challenges, showcasing how these teams navigate leadership terrain and drive organizational outcomes.

We also expand the definition of strategic leadership by showing a critical dichotomy: *the perceived versus the actual importance of strategic leadership in driving organizational outcomes.* While the widespread belief is that CEOs and senior executives are the primary architects of an organization's direction, we argue that this view oversimplifies the complexities involved. Typically, when discussing strategic decisions, the focus is on the choices made by these strategic leaders. However, *this narrow perspective overlooks the broader contextual factors that influence both the strategists and their strategies.* We challenge the assertion made by Finkelstein (2009) that *"if we want to understand strategy, we must understand the strategist."* Our position goes further to contend that truly understanding an organization's strategy requires a comprehensive grasp of the context in which both the strategist and the strategy operate. It is this context—encompassing cultural, economic, political, and social dimensions—that shapes the decisions and actions of those at the helm, influencing not just the minds behind the strategy *but the strategic direction itself.* Therefore, to fully com-

https://doi.org/10.1515/9783111382722-004

prehend strategic leadership, one must consider the complex interplay between the leaders' decisions and the contexts that drive or constrain those decisions.

An intriguing aspect of our approach challenges the conventional wisdom that tends to elevate CEOs as the primary drivers of organizational success. While many strategic leadership books and studies often group CEOs with their executive teams, we found that CEOs do not always carry an outsized influence over their organizations' direction and character. Instead, the influence of the TMTs was far more tangible and impactful. In contemporary organizations strategic leadership should be understood as a collective endeavor rather than attributing organizational outcomes solely to CEOs (Hambrick, Humphrey, and Gupta, 2015; Ling, Wei, and Simsek, 2022). Our view advances this narrative from portraying CEOs as the singular architects of success to recognizing the collective leadership power of TMTs, especially within pluralistic organizations. When TMTs embody strategic and contextual leadership imperatives, they drive alignment, resilience, sustainable success and often outperform the leadership impact of CEOs alone, leveraging their collective capabilities to navigate complexity and accelerate organizational growth.

This claim is reinforced by findings from our four case studies, where TMTs highlighted that they have witnessed frequent CEO turnovers, yet the organizations remained operationally stable and strategically adaptive due to the TMTs' sustained leadership and vertical ascent. At Urban Escape, the organization saw six different CEOs, while Medi Care experienced four, and Echo Capital had three CEOs in just three years. Despite these leadership transitions, the TMTs' vertical ascent leading upward through strategic foresight, contextual intelligence, and collective decision-making ensured continuity, mitigated disruptions, and upheld their performance. Their ability to rise beyond hierarchical dependencies demonstrates that in pluralistic organizations, sustained leadership excellence can be anchored in the ascent of TMTs.

The need for TMT alignment was particularly evident in the case of Medi Care, a healthcare organization that experienced three CEO transitions, two board changes, and a significant strategic shift from a public company to a privately owned company. During interviews with the TMT members, all of whom had been with the organization for over five years, it became clear how vital their role was in managing these transitions. The TMT was composed of corporate executives (70%) and medical professionals (30%), a mix that presented both opportunities and challenges in aligning diverse perspectives and expertise.

One notable example was the deputy CEO, who had been promoted by the chairman of the board from an administrative position and found himself responsible for securing buy-in and support from other TMT members for the new strategic direction set by the incoming Group CEO. As he explained, "My first responsibility was to advance internal operations during the strategic transition from a government-funded to a public joint stocks company".[1] In this new scenario, the Medi Care CEO and TMT operate under increased accountability and transparency due to public ownership and the new regulatory requirements. Their leadership is influenced by the need to balance shareholder expectations, comply with legal obligations, and achieve sustainable performance, which often requires collective decision-making and strategic alignment to ensure the company's success and maintain shareholders' confidence. His second challenging task was to align the newly appointed Group CEO, who brought in three new TMT members, with the expectations of the new public shareholders—a process that required constant negotiation and adjustment to ensure strategic alignment between the different parties. The third critical responsibility was to enhance the effectiveness and timeliness of communication within the TMT during this strategic shift. Despite implementing advanced communication technology under the leadership of the Chief Technology Officer, the deputy CEO lamented, *"The result is we have too much technology, with very little communication amongst the TMT."*

This narrative sets the stage for understanding who the TMTs are, why they matter, and how their structure, composition, and processes directly impact their ability to lead strategically. In the next section, we explain the three pillars of TMTs—structure, composition, and process—within pluralistic organizations, linking these elements to the principles of strategic and contextual leadership.

3.1 Three Pillars of Top Management Teams: Structure, Composition and Process

The term "top management team" is a misnomer. Rather than a cohesive unit, it represents a dynamic group of strategic leaders, each wielding individual power and influence within the organization that can be aligned or not.

The spectrum of TMT structures is not fixed. Depending on the strategic challenges at hand, different members might take center stage, giving the TMT its fluid composition. Power and authority underscore the executive world. In the TMT context, power finds its roots in several areas: structural positions, social networks, ownership, and specialized expertise. Yet not all power dynamics have equal influence. Some TMT members naturally hold more sway, making it essential to understand these authority gradients. Distinct studies have shown significant power disparities within TMTs, which influence strategic outcomes.

Moreover, TMTs in pluralistic organizations aren't always harmonious groups; they comprise individuals with diverse objectives. Their decision-making often wades

---

1 A public joint-stock company (PJSC) allows shareholders to participate in management and limits their liability to the value of their shares, with shares being publicly traded and potentially exceeding their nominal value if the company is successful.

by their conflicting and diverse objectives and preferences. TMT has its unique dynamics. For instance, how engaged they are in mutual endeavors, clarity in their organizational roles, and commitment to a collective execution strategy.

These pillars intersect significantly, affecting how TMT members in pluralistic organizations interface with each other and with the CEO (see TMT composition, structure, and process, Figure 3.1.)

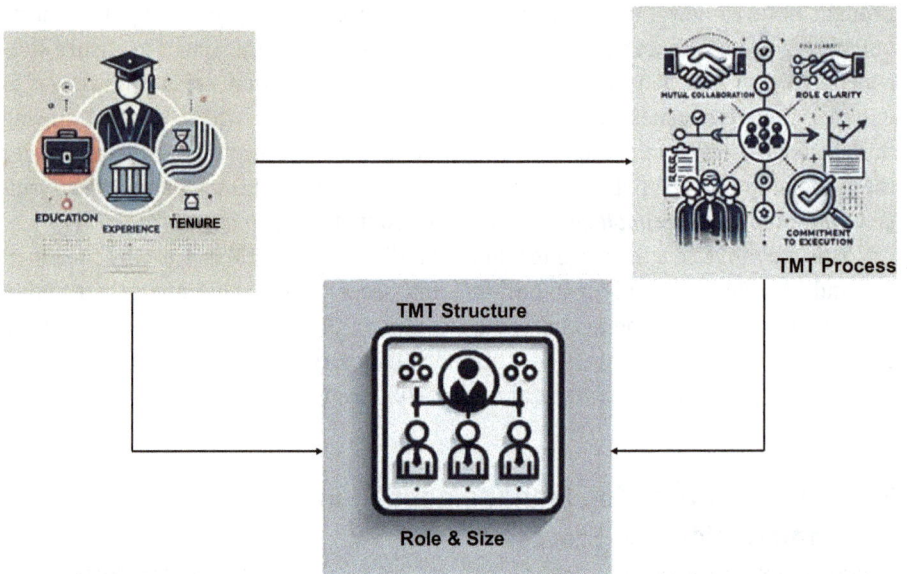

Figure 3.1: Three Pillars of TMT – Composition, Structure and Process.
This figure presents the three interconnected pillars of top management teams in pluralistic organizations: composition, structure, and process. Composition includes members' education, professional experience, and tenure. Structure refers to the team's configuration, roles, and size. Process focuses on internal dynamics such as collaboration, role clarity, and commitment to execution. Together, these elements shape how top management teams engage with each other and with the CEO, influencing decision making and organizational performance.

3.1.1 TMT Composition (Education, Experience and Tenure)

The upper echelon scholars defined top management team (TMT) composition as the collective characteristics of top team members, such as their values, cognitive bases, personalities, and experiences, to conceptualize TMT diversity (Finkelstein et al., 2009: 123). TMT composition encompasses various attributes, including education, professional experiences, values, tenure, and functional backgrounds. These factors provide insights into the essence of a TMT, shaping their strategic decision-making, leadership style, and overall influence on organizational outcomes (Eesley, Hsu, and Roberts, 2014).

While prior studies have examined TMT diversity through individual factors, our research advances the exploration of TMT dynamics by integrating multiple dimensions of experience, tenure, functional background, and educational background into a unified study.

TMT Educational Background

TMT educational background significantly shapes strategic decision-making, leadership style, and organizational adaptability. In pluralistic organization such as healthcare medical education, public health, and preventative medicine, education provides foundational knowledge, strategic skills, and industry-specific expertise, which influence how executives approach corporate challenges (Northouse, 2021).

Our case study revealed that 31% of TMT members were educated in the United States, bringing Western management perspectives, competitive strategy frameworks, and financial modelling expertise to their organizations. However, Western education alone does not determine strategic success; instead, the ability to integrate diverse educational perspectives with contextual insights is key to pluralistic leadership effectiveness (Meyer, 2017). In Medi Care and Vita Care, healthcare leaders with backgrounds in medical sciences, public health, and healthcare administration ensured compliance with global medical standards while integrating regional healthcare policies. In financial services (Echo Capital), executives with degrees in finance, economics, and business administration helped the firm navigate financial risks, develop investment strategies, and align with international regulations. In Urban Escape, a mix of educational backgrounds—including engineering, urban planning, and business development equipped TMTs to balance commercial real estate expansion with sustainable city development goals.

TMTs' Industry-Specific Experience in Pluralistic Organizations

Top management team (TMT) experience is pivotal in shaping strategic leadership effectiveness within pluralistic organizations. The depth and breadth of TMT members' professional experiences significantly influence their capacity to navigate industry-specific challenges and drive organizational success.

In pluralistic organizations, the TMTs' familiarity with industry dynamics allows them to anticipate market shifts, manage risks effectively, and implement strategies that align with organizational goals. Research indicates that TMTs with extensive experience are better equipped to lead organizations through strategic changes, thereby improving performance outcomes (Gharama, Al-Abrrow, and Abdullah, 2020). In our case studies across healthcare, financial services, and urban development, the specific industry contexts underscore the necessity for tailored TMT expertise:

Healthcare (Medi Care and Vita Care): TMTs in healthcare organizations must possess deep knowledge of medical practices, patient care standards, and regulatory compliance. Such expertise ensures the delivery of high-quality healthcare services and adherence to evolving healthcare regulations. Strategic leaders with extensive experience in healthcare can effectively manage the complexities of healthcare delivery, including the integration of new technologies and the implementation of patient-centered care models.

Financial Services (Echo Capital): TMTs in financial services require a comprehensive understanding of financial markets, investment strategies, and risk management. This expertise is crucial for making informed decisions that enhance financial performance and ensure compliance with financial regulations.

With relevant effective experience, strategic leaders in financial services can navigate economic fluctuations, develop innovative financial products, and maintain stakeholder trust through prudent financial management.

Development (Urban Escape): TMTs in urban development need expertise in urban planning, real estate development, and sustainability practices. This knowledge enables them to design and implement projects that meet community needs and regulatory requirements. Strategic leaders with experience in development can effectively manage stakeholder relationships, secure funding, and oversee project execution to foster urban growth and development.

Industrial Development (DP World): A global leader in logistics and port operations, the TMT's extensive experience plays a pivotal role in navigating complex industry challenges and driving organizational success. Experienced TMTs bring industry dynamics to anticipate market shifts, manage risks effectively, and implement strategies that align with organizational goals.

DP World's leadership exemplifies the importance of TMT experience in industrial development: The Group Chairman and CEO, has been instrumental in expanding DP World's global footprint, including the acquisition of P&O for $6.8 billion in 2006, which positioned DP World as a leading global port operator. Their Executive Vice President of International Projects brings over two decades of experience within DP World, specializing in information technology and its application to port management (DP World, 2024).

In pluralistic organizations, the experience of the TMT is integral to strategic leadership effectiveness. The extensive industry experience can drive organizational success, highlighting the critical role of seasoned leadership in navigating the complexities of global logistics and port operations.

Redefining the Role of Long-Tenured TMTs

Another notable finding from our case study is that more than 70% of TMT members have been with their organizations for over 10 years. This longevity is not merely a by-product of hierarchy or stability but is deeply linked to satisfaction with incentives, leadership responsibilities, and continuous growth opportunities within their organizations (Appendix A includes the education, experience and tenure of participating TMTs).

Traditional perspectives often suggest that long-tenured executives may become resistant to strategic change, overly comfortable with the status quo, or hesitant to align with new CEOs' visions (Hambrick and Fukutomi, 1991). The stagnation hypothesis in strategic leadership argues that executives with longer tenure may develop cognitive rigidity, rely on outdated mental models, and become less receptive to new strategic initiatives (Miller, 1991; Wiersema and Bantel, 1992). For instance, Hambrick, Geletkanycz, and Fredrickson (1993) found that long-tenured executives tend to resist external environmental changes, preferring to uphold existing strategies rather than embracing new competitive realities.

A notable case supporting this traditional view is the classic Kodak leadership failure, where long-tenured executives dismissed digital photography as a passing trend, clinging to the film-based business model despite clear industry signals favoring digital transformation (Lucas and Goh, 2009). Similarly, BlackBerry's leadership, despite its dominance in mobile communications, failed to recognize and adapt to the rise of touchscreen smartphones, largely due to the complacency and strategic rigidity of its long-serving leadership team (Yoffie and Baldwin, 2015).

However, our research challenges and expands this perspective, shedding light on what strategic leaders do and how they do it. In Medi Care, Echo Capital, and Vita Care, the long-tenured TMT members were not seen as barriers to change but were instead recognized as strategic enablers—the pillars of their organizations who drive transformation and continuity.

The Medi Care CEO named and described 12 out of the 42 TMT members under his leadership as the "performance champions, the powerhouses,"(Virtual interview communication, June 2020) acknowledging their expertise, resilience, and ability to navigate complex industry challenges. Similarly, at Echo Capital, the chairman referred to long-tenured TMTs as "transformational champions," (Virtual interview communication, June 2020) emphasizing their strategic foresight and adaptability in sustaining organizational performance despite economic volatility, the frequent leadership transitions, and the frequent strategic direction changes. These findings indicate that long-tenured TMT members are not always passive holders of institutional memory but can be active drivers of strategic evolution, contributing to organizational agility, stakeholder trust, and sustainable performance.

Our study further highlights that long-tenured TMTs tend to adhere to industry standards and best practices, integrating their collective experience, education, and tenure into decision-making processes. Their influence extends beyond operational continuity, shaping organizational culture, governance models, and leadership succession planning. Unlike traditional views that link tenure with inertia, our findings suggest that when properly incentivized and engaged, these executives function as strategic stewards, ensuring alignment between past learnings, present challenges, and future aspirations.

By moving beyond traditional examinations of TMT composition, we illuminate the critical role that long-tenured TMT members play in shaping the strategic trajectory of pluralistic organizations. These insights contribute to a more nuanced understanding of TMT effectiveness, reinforcing the need for leadership frameworks that recognize the strategic value of experience, institutional knowledge, and transformational leadership within top teams.

3.1.2 TMT Structure

Understanding the TMT structure in the context of pluralistic organization and its external context provides valuable insights into strategic leadership. It highlights the need for an approach to configuring TMTs that aligns with both the internal organizational needs and the external environment in which the organization operates. TMT structure is defined by the roles of the top management members and the group size. At the core of the TMT, structures set the authority the interdependence different members in a TMT have for strategic decision-making (Hambrick, 2007b). TMTs are mainly heads of departments and functions. The nature of the executive roles and the team's size constitute a fundamental aspect of the TMT structure.

TMT structure is rooted in the individual roles of its members and the overall team size plays a critical role in the formulation of strategic decisions. The beauty and complexity of TMTs lie in the interplay of their members—each of whom typically stands at the helm of separate organizational functions. This interplay shapes the organization's very core, including its status and structure. It's not just about who's on the team, but how they fit together. Expanding on the concept of TMT structure, it's essential to understand how it varies across different organizational structure types and how external contextual factors can influence it.

In our case study, two organizations operated with an organic organizational structure, characterized by combining flexibility with compliance. In these contexts, the TMT structure was notably less hierarchical and more strategically aligned. Each strategic leader was positioned with clear intent, fully aware of their role, objectives, and future trajectory within the organization. It was evident that these leaders were not just occupying positions but were strategically placed to achieve specific outcomes, with a clear roadmap for where they aimed to steer the organization. The roles of TMT members might still intentionally overlap, emphasizing fluidity over fixed functions. The decision-making process is often decentralized, allowing for quicker responses to changing external factors.

The other two organizations had mechanistic organizational structures. Contrarily, in mechanistic or traditional structures, TMTs roles are usually more rigidly defined. Roles are delineated, and the hierarchy is more pronounced. Decision-making tends to be centralized at the top, with a focus on efficiency and stability.

It is critical to explore how TMT structures uniquely exhibited in pluralistic organizations compared to standard unitary organizations.

Complexity of TMT Structure in Pluralistic Organizations

Pluralistic organizations, like those in healthcare and financial services, often have a range of stakeholders with diverse interests. This necessitates a TMT structure that is adept at balancing and addressing these diverse needs (Denis et al., 2007). The multifaceted strategic decisions in such settings are typically more complex due to the multitude of factors influencing the organization, including regulatory requirements, ethical considerations, and public health impacts.

One of the most important and critical characteristics of the TMT lies within their interdisciplinary or interdepartmental collaboration. TMT structures in pluralistic organizations often consist of members from varied professional backgrounds, such as professional experts, administrators, and financial officers. This interdisciplinary nature demands a more collaborative and communicative TMT structure. In this context, the TMT structure must be carefully crafted to handle the intricacies of the industry.

Power and Authority Within TMTs

Understanding the dynamics of power and authority within TMTs is crucial for effective strategic leadership. Vogel's research highlights the role of leadership in mobilizing and maintaining energy within organizations, suggesting that leaders who can effectively manage power dynamics are better equipped to harness the collective energy of their teams (Bruch and Vogel, 2011). A TMT's structure is deeply rooted in the roles of its members and the overall group size, which are crucial for strategic direction and change. The way these roles interact and complement each other can significantly impact the organization's strategic direction. The size of the TMT can influence its functionality. A smaller team might be more agile but could lack diverse perspectives, while a larger team offers a broader viewpoint but may face challenges in coordination and decision-making speed.

Executives within TMTs wield varying levels of power and authority, stemming from structural position, network prestige, ownership stakes, and domain-specific expertise (Cannella, 2001b; Shen, 2003; Ma and Seidl, 2018). These power dynamics create complex interactions, where certain members exert greater influence over strategic decisions. For example, in the case of Echo Capital, shifts in TMT leadership, coupled with the promotion of executives, led to changes in decision-making power, which ultimately impacted the organization's strategic direction and effectiveness. Understanding these dynamics is crucial for TMTs to navigate the dual balancing acts they face internally. They must manage team dynamics to ensure alignment and cohesion, while externally, they need to adapt to broader organizational strategies and respond to uncertainties such as economic conditions, regulatory changes, and societal expectations.

The fluidity of power within TMTs is illustrated in the Echo Capital case (presented in detail in Chapter 4). It influences their ability to manage these dual responsibilities effectively. Shifts in TMT composition or leadership roles can alter power dynamics, directly affecting the team's ability to drive strategic decisions. This reinforces the strategic leadership imperatives discussed in Chapter 4, highlighting the necessity of strategic and contextual leadership advanced skills for navigating these complexities inside and outside pluralistic organizations. TMTs navigating external factors such as market dynamics, regulatory changes, and cultural shifts can significantly influence the TMT structure. For instance, in a rapidly changing market, an organic TMT structure may be more effective to quickly adapt and respond. Conversely, in a stable market or industries with heavy regulation, like healthcare and investments, a mechanistic structure might provide the needed consistency and control.

TMT structure in pluralistic organizations is markedly more complex compared to standard unitary organizations. The key lies in designing a TMT that can efficiently navigate this complexity, manage diverse stakeholder expectations, and make decisions that align with both the organization's mission and the dynamic context.

3.1.3 TMT Process

TMT processes are critical in shaping strategic leadership effectiveness within organizations. These processes, encompassing mutual collaboration, role clarity, and commitment to execution, define how top managers interact during strategic planning and implementation (Finkelstein, Hambrick and Cannella, 2009). Unlike team dynamics at lower organizational levels, TMT interactions determine how strategic decisions are formulated, debated, and enacted.

Our case studies reveal that these processes are shaped by two key dynamics: **the promotion of TMT members to new positions and the pressures of uncertainty**, which can either enhance or undermine the effectiveness of strategic contextual leadership. The interplay between these dynamics emphasizes the need for strategic leadership imperatives we introduce later in Chapter 4, such as strategic contextual intelligence, strategic financial intelligence, integrative communication, innovation, and agility. TMT processes consist of a set of distinct core processes:

Engagement in Mutual and Collaborative Actions: Our findings indicate that promoting TMT members to new positions can significantly enhance their engagement and effectiveness within the team. In the cases of Medi Care and Vita Care, for example, newly promoted TMT members showed increased motivation to participate actively in strategic discussions and align closely with organizational objectives. This aligns with other strategic leadership studies that found promotions foster a greater willingness to collaborate, build trust, and strengthen overall TMT effectiveness (Hambrick, Humphrey, and Gupta, 2015). However, our study also revealed that heightened uncertainty arising from external market pressures or internal changes can lead to increased divergence and disagreements within TMTs in pluralistic organizations. This divergence underscores the necessity of strategic leadership, skills such as strategic contextual intelligence and integrative communication, as outlined in the strategic contextual framework, to maintain cohesion and facilitate mutual engagement in complex contexts.

Clarity of TMT Role and Objectives: The clarity of roles and objectives within the TMT is essential for effective leadership, particularly in uncertain environments. In cases like Urban Escape and Echo Capital, newly promoted TMT members exhibited a stronger sense of ownership and accountability, which helped align their efforts more closely with the organization's strategic goals. Conversely, in times of uncertainty around strategic direction or external pressures, a lack of clear roles exacerbated disagreements among TMT members. The Strategic Contextual Leadership framework presented in Chapter 2 helps address these challenges by ensuring that TMTs use the context matrix to continuously evaluate and adjust their roles in response to both internal and external changes. This adaptive approach maintains strategic alignment, even under fluctuating conditions, reinforcing the importance of clarity and agility.

Commitment to Collective Execution: The commitment of TMT members to execute strategies collectively is vital for achieving strategic goals. For example, in Vita Care, promoting members within the TMT enhanced their commitment to the success of the implementation of the new technologies due to the CFO and the technology team joining forces to the successful collective execution, as they felt more empowered and invested in the organization's strategic direction.

However, during periods of heightened uncertainty, such as leadership transitions or market volatility, this commitment can waver, leading to fragmentation and divergent interests. The Strategic Contextual Leadership framework addresses these challenges by fostering a culture of integrative communication which helps align diverse interests and sustain collective execution even under pressure. This ensures that TMTs remain focused on their strategic objectives while leading change in the dynamic context.

By integrating these three central processes – mutual collaboration, role clarity, and commitment to execution – the strategic contextual framework and context matrix provide a sophisticated, adaptive approach to strategic leadership. They enhance TMT processes by recognizing the dynamic nature of team alignment and promote a proactive, contextually aware response to internal and external challenges within pluralistic organizations.

3.2 TMTs' Dual Frontiers: The Strategic Balancing Acts of TMTs in Pluralistic Organizations

In pluralistic organizations, the role of the TMT extends far beyond routine decision-making. TMTs are tasked with navigating two critical arenas that demand their attention and expertise: the internal dynamics of their organization and the unpredictable external environment. First, inside the organization, TMTs must ensure strategic alignment, foster collaboration, and maintain coherence with the CEO and board of directors. Second, they must also address external challenges, such as market fluctuations, regulatory changes, and other uncertainties that impact the organization's trajectory.

These dual responsibilities form the essence of the TMT balancing act, managing the complexities within their organization while simultaneously responding to the ever-changing external landscape. Balancing these responsibilities means for TMTs accepting, noticing and engaging proactively with the multiple dualities and opposing forces in pluralistic organizations (Lee and Quinn, 2023). This does not mean solving those challenges and elevating or suppressing one powerful context factor, but TMTs must deal with their co-existence.

3.3 TMT Balancing Act 1: Strategically Leading Inside the Pluralistic Organizations

3.3.1 Vertical Ascent: TMT Leading Upward

In pluralistic organizations, the dynamics between the CEO, the board, and the TMT are critical to shaping strategic leadership. As explored earlier, TMT processes, how top managers interact during strategic planning and execution are unique at this level, involving complex decision-making and collaboration that go beyond traditional group dynamics (Finkelstein et al., 2009). The effectiveness of these processes is closely tied to how well the TMT balances internal responsibilities while interfacing with the CEO and board (Figure 3.2).

Our case study shows that the relationship between the CEO, the board, and the TMT is marked by varying expectations. Some chairpersons see themselves as strategic leaders directly involved in shaping and implementing strategy (the chairman of Urban Escape and the chairman of Echo Capital), whereas many CEOs and TMTs believe that strategy development and execution primarily fall within their domain. This divergence reflects the complex power dynamics within the TMT, where authority and influence are not uniformly distributed.

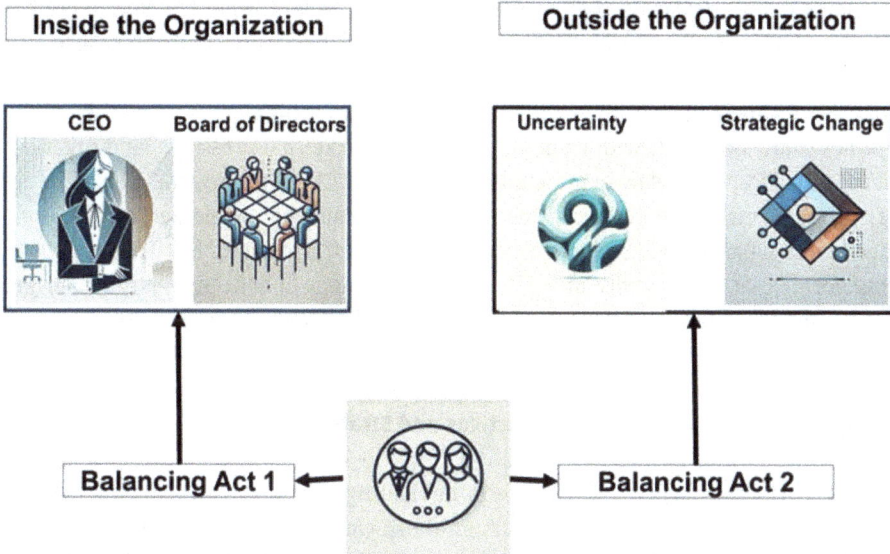

Figure 3.2: TMT Balancing Acts.
This figure illustrates the two strategic balancing acts performed by TMTs in pluralistic organizations. Balancing Act 1 occurs inside the organization, where TMTs must align with the CEO and the Board of Directors. Balancing Act 2 unfolds outside the organization, requiring TMTs to respond to external uncertainty and drive strategic change.

Navigating Power Dynamics Within the CEO-Board-TMT Relationship

Understanding the interplay of TMT power dynamics—how authority and influence are distributed among team members—is essential for navigating the internal balancing act. In our case studies, we observed that power within TMTs is often unequally distributed, affecting decision-making processes. For example, at Echo Capital, the CEO worked closely with the investment TMT, which led to other TMT members having less involvement, thus affecting the team's overall influence. This illustrates that whose perspectives are prioritized can shape the effectiveness of TMT processes and, in turn, strategic leadership.

3.3.2 Balancing Internal Dynamics by Aligning Roles and Actions

The challenge of TMT balancing within pluralistic organizations is, therefore, twofold: managing the internal power dynamics while ensuring effective engagement in strategic processes. Our findings indicate that TMTs are most effective when they achieve a delicate balance between diverse interests, power sources, and collaborative decision-making as effective engagement in strategic processes. This balance enables TMTs to align their roles and actions with broader organizational goals, fostering a cohesive approach to strategic leadership.

For example, learning from past leadership failures has become a critical strategy for some TMTs. A CEO of a Medi Care hospital shared, "I learned a lot from those who failed, like the previous CEO" (in-person interview, May 2020), reflecting a flexible response to changing power dynamics within the TMT. In this context, power dynamics are not static; they shift with changes in leadership, external pressures, and organizational priorities. As we saw in our study, international CEOs with significant experience often faced constrained authority due to cultural mismatches, while national CEOs enjoyed more balanced power and stronger TMT support. This shows how TMT processes collaborative actions, clarity of roles, and commitment to collective execution—are heavily influenced by the distribution and exercise of power within the team.

3.3.3 Navigating Diversity of Perspectives and Strategic Alignment

The TMT process plays a crucial role in navigating this internal balancing act. For TMTs to function effectively, they must establish clear processes for communication, decision-making, and conflict resolution, ensuring that diverse perspectives are integrated into strategic planning. When TMTs engage in mutual and collaborative actions, as described earlier, they can better navigate the complexities of their roles, align with the CEO's strategic vision, and support the broader organizational strategy.

However, these processes are only effective when there is a clear understanding of the power dynamics at play. TMT members must recognize where power is concentrated and how it can be leveraged to achieve strategic objectives. As seen in the case of Echo Capital, the balance between power dynamics and effective processes is critical: When the new CEO marginalized other TMT members by centralizing decision-making with the CFO, it weakened the team's overall alignment and subsequently its effectiveness.

To illustrate the TMT balancing act within their pluralistic organizations, we can draw on empirical insights from our case studies of Echo Capital (Box 3.1). This example demonstrates how TMTs strategically navigate their roles, exert influence, and align organizational goals through collaborative decision-making and feedback mechanisms.

> **Box 3.1 – TMT Strategic Navigation and Influence Within Echo Capital**
> *TMT Vertical Ascent: Driving Strategic Influence Upwards*
> Echo Capital is a high-performing financial services company known for its stringent performance standards, uncompromising execution, and elite talent acquisition strategy. The firm recruits multinational professionals primarily from blue-chip organizations, ensuring that its TMT is composed of top-tier executives with world-class educational backgrounds and extensive industry experience. Within this high-stakes, results-driven environment, errors are neither tolerated nor excused, reinforcing a culture where precision, strategic foresight, and execution excellence are paramount. The expectations placed on Echo Capital's TMT and CEO extend beyond merely achieving corporate targets—they are expected to exceed objectives consistently, sustaining the firm's sterling reputation and shareholder confidence. Shareholders demand unwavering strategic acumen, financial intelligence, and the ability

to navigate volatile market conditions with agility. This intense performance culture means that TMT members must strategically influence upward, ensuring alignment with shareholder expectations while driving innovative and sustainable growth strategies.

At Echo Capital, the firm's strategic direction often determined which TMT member would take the lead, illustrating the flexible and dynamic nature of leadership within the organization. For instance, when the shareholders demanded a shift in the investment strategy, the Chief Investment Officer (CIO) was appointed to spearhead the initiative. In this scenario, all other TMT members, including the COO, CFO, and Chief People Officer, provided their input directly to the CIO rather than the CEO. This allowed the CIO to integrate diverse perspectives, such as financial implications, operational feasibility, and human capital considerations, into a comprehensive investment strategy that addressed shareholder demands. The CEO, in this instance, took on a more facilitative role, allowing the CIO to drive the process while ensuring alignment with the broader organizational goals.

Key Insights and Unpacking the Case
Feedback and Influence
The importance of this TMT-lead approach became evident during strategic review sessions, where the CIO presented the new investment strategy to the board, incorporating the collective insights of the entire TMT. This structure enabled the board to see a more detailed, nuanced plan that had already been vetted by multiple perspectives within the TMT, reinforcing the collaborative and integrated nature of Echo Capital's strategic decision-making process. This model of leadership not only empowered the CIO but also allowed for greater ownership and accountability among the TMT members, ensuring that strategic decisions were well-rounded, thoroughly evaluated and facilitated alignment.

Vertical Integration: Driving Strategy into Execution
Echo Capital TMTs translate strategic directives into organizational action, ensuring that middle management and frontline teams align with top leadership decisions. Just as vertical ascent represents influencing upward to shape strategic decisions, vertical integration represents cascading those decisions downward to drive execution and organizational coherence. This scenario unfolded when Echo Capital introduced a new technology initiative. In this case, the Chief Technology Officer (CTO) was designated as the key leader, responsible for driving the technology transformation across the organization. The CTO received input and support from other TMT members, but they reported directly back to the CEO and the board regarding the progress and challenges of the initiative. This approach streamlined decision-making, allowing the CTO to lead the organization through the technology adoption process with a clear vision and authority. By centralizing leadership around the CTO, Echo Capital ensured that the technological integration was aligned with the company's broader strategic objectives while allowing other TMT members to contribute their expertise where needed.

TMT members emphasized the operational implementation of the strategic initiatives, ensuring that visions set at the top are effectively executed across organizational levels. They ensured that the CEO motto "strategic cascading" was implemented, where all teams' meetings where held to highlight the flow of leadership influence downward, bridging the gap between vision and execution, ensuring alignment across departments and at all levels.

Navigating Hierarchies
These examples from Echo Capital demonstrate the organization's ability to adapt its leadership structure based on strategic needs, highlighting the importance of flexible power dynamics within the TMT. By allowing different TMT members to lead based on the nature of the strategic direction, Echo Capital created an environment where expertise was leveraged effectively, and decision-making was both agile and informed. This approach not only enhanced the TMT's ability to navigate complex organizational challenges but also ensured that the CEO could focus on facilitating alignment and maintaining the overarching strategic vision.

These scenarios from Echo Capital underscore the dynamic role of TMTs in navigating strategic initiatives, showcasing how flexibility, collaboration, and targeted leadership can drive successful outcomes in pluralistic organizations.

Key Takeaways
This case study highlights the dynamic role of TMTs in strategically navigating their organizations. It underscores the importance of collaborative decision-making, clear delegation of responsibilities, and robust feedback mechanisms in aligning the organization's direction with its strategic goals. The experiences of Echo Capital and Urban Escape exemplify how TMTs must balance their internal roles with the broader organizational context to effectively lead within pluralistic environments.

These insights link directly to the broader theme of TMT Balancing Act 1, where the focus is on strategically leading within the organization by managing relationships with the CEO, board, and other internal stakeholders. The lessons learned from these cases provide a practical framework for understanding how TMTs can successfully navigate and influence complex organizational structures, ultimately contributing to their organization's strategic success.

As demonstrated in the case studies of Echo Capital in Box 3.1, the interfacing between the CEO, TMT, and board is fundamental in shaping the strategic direction and overall success of an organization. These examples illustrate how TMTs strategically steer their roles, influence decision-making, and align their organizations with strategic goals through effective collaboration and feedback mechanisms. The success of these internal dynamics directly impacts the organization's ability to execute its strategy and achieve its objectives.

However, the responsibilities of the TMT extend beyond the internal structure of their organization. The second critical balancing act that TMTs must master is strategically leading outside their organizations, where they face the challenge of managing external uncertainties and navigating complex industry landscapes.

In the next section, we will explore how TMTs expand their influence beyond the organization's walls, addressing external challenges such as market volatility, regulatory changes, and competitive pressures. This balancing act is equally essential, as the ability of TMTs to effectively manage external factors can significantly impact the organization's long-term sustainability and success. We will delve into the strategies and approaches that TMTs use to maintain this balance, ensuring that their organizations remain resilient and adaptive in the face of external challenges.

3.4 TMT Balancing Act 2: Strategically Leading Outside Pluralistic Organization

3.4.1 Managing Uncertainties in Strategic Change

The insights from our multiple case studies revealed that external contextual factors frequently triggered strategic changes, such as shifts from public to private funding, reduced budgets, and alterations in the strategic direction of their organizations. These changes often resulted in an internal climate of uncertainty, as reflected in the participants' sentiments: "We need stability. Fast strategic changes created uncertainty." This perspective challenges previous empirical studies that primarily linked uncertainty to organizational structure and resource accessibility (Waldman et al., 1998; Carpenter et al., 2004; Smith, 2014). In other studies researchers associated the TMT uncertainty to the organization's internal context and the ability of TMTs to access resources and information during periods of turbulence and challenges (Antonakis et al., 2003; Gardner et al., 2005).

Even in the Medi Care case, which is a healthcare group of hospitals and clinics, the dynamic and fluctuating economy played a significant role in driving changes in strategic direction, which in turn led to frequent leadership transitions. This constant need to adapt to external economic pressures resulted in the succession of four CEOs during eight years, further amplifying uncertainty among TMT members. All TMT members identified this environment of uncertainty as a major challenge, which was directly linked to the frequent changes in Medi Care strategic direction and the frequent leadership turnover driven by the dynamic economic context.

In 2018, a new chairman was appointed, and he hired a new Group CEO to lead the new strategic direction to privatize Medi Care. The Chief Technology Officer and Chief Operations Officer felt that they were under intense scrutiny and lacked sufficient time to process the transition of leadership before being confronted with yet another strategic shift. This atmosphere of being closely monitored led to feelings of marginalization and hindered the team's ability to function cohesively. The Medi Care case underscores how economic volatility can trigger strategic and leadership changes, disrupting team dynamics and significantly impacting the effectiveness of strategic leadership.

In Vita Care, a private healthcare network of hospitals, clinics and pharmacies was also subject to several accelerated strategic changes which affected the interfacing of the TMT and the shareholder. Vita Care TMTs described their relationships with other TMTs, the CEO, and their shareholders as complex and uncertain. This was largely due to significant budget reductions, headcount cuts, and the transition of two CEOs within eighteen months. These frequent leadership changes and financial constraints created an environment where strategic continuity was nearly impossible, leading to a pervasive sense of instability.

Similarly, in Urban Escape, the feeling of uncertainty was heightened by the frequent succession of CEOs and shifts in strategic direction. This ongoing senior leader turnover increased the level of uncertainty within the TMT and the entire internal organizational context. The constant changes disrupted long-term planning and created a volatile atmosphere, making it difficult for the TMT to maintain a stable and focused approach.

Echo Capital faced its own set of challenges with external context impacting internal stability. TMT members described the organization's context as dynamic and uncertain due to the fluctuating global economy and its effects on the stock market. This economic volatility was compounded by the dismissal of two CEOs in eighteen months, who failed to implement the strategic direction effectively. The economic instability and leadership upheaval contributed to a sense of unpredictability, complicating the TMT's efforts to steer the organization toward its strategic goals.

The primary discovery from these cases is that uncertainty, often driven by frequent leadership changes and shifts in strategic direction, poses a significant challenge for TMTs. This uncertainty can undermine the effectiveness of TMTs by creating an atmosphere of instability and scrutiny, which hampers their ability to function cohesively and make long-term strategic decisions. By understanding these dynamics, strategic leaders and managers can better anticipate the challenges associated with uncertainty and take proactive steps to strengthen their TMTs, ensuring that their organizations can maintain stability and strategic direction in the face of change.

Consequences of Uncertainty:

Leadership Stability is Crucial: Frequent CEO turnovers and changes in strategic direction can severely disrupt the stability of an organization. For strategic leaders, it's essential to recognize the impact of such instability on the TMT's ability to perform effectively. Measured stability in leadership is crucial for maintaining strategic continuity and allowing the TMT to function as a unified, cohesive force.

Context Awareness: Understanding the broader context, whether it's economic volatility or internal organizational dynamics is key to navigating uncertainty. Leaders must be vigilant in assessing how external factors, like the global economy, and internal changes, such as leadership transitions, influence the organization's strategic direction and TMT dynamics.

Building Resilience: In an environment of uncertainty, building resilience, the capability to thrive and grow during adversity, within the TMT is critical. This includes fostering open communication, ensuring that team members feel supported rather than scrutinized, and creating a culture that can adapt to change without losing strategic focus. For readers, this highlights the importance of developing strategies that can buffer the negative effects of uncertainty and enable TMTs to remain effective even in turbulent times.

Strategic Continuity: Ensuring strategic continuity despite leadership changes is vital. This may involve setting long-term goals that transcend individual leaders, thus providing a stable strategic foundation that can endure through periods of leadership transition. Readers should consider implementing mechanisms that safeguard strategic continuity to mitigate the disruptive effects of frequent leadership changes.

These examples illustrate how external contextual factors such as economic conditions, leadership transitions, and strategic changes can significantly impact TMT uncertainty, affecting their ability to lead effectively and achieve desired outcomes

3.4.2 Managing Uncertainty and Organizational Reputation

A key finding from our multiple case studies revealed that the legacy of predecessor CEOs and an organization's financial history play a significant role in shaping TMT uncertainty and effectiveness. Across all cases, TMT members frequently referenced past CEOs, demonstrating how previous leadership decisions and financial performance resulting in damaging the organization's reputation and a decreased stakeholder trust which cast a long shadow over current strategic leadership efforts. This connection between organizational history, frequent leadership transitions, and financial uncertainty had profound implications on TMT alignment, strategic confidence, and execution effectiveness, ultimately influencing the organization's reputation and stakeholder trust.

This was particularly evident at Vita Care, where the newly promoted CEO, previously a senior member of the medical TMT, expressed deep skepticism about his appointment in the wake of organizational turbulence. His promotion occurred amid a structural change, following the abrupt removal of his predecessor and the dismissal of multiple TMT colleagues. Reflecting on his concerns and doubts about his promotion to the CEO position, he shared:

> I am uncertain about this promotion to the CEO position. I just witnessed another structural change, my colleagues in the TMT were sacked, and our former CEO was let go (in-person interview, October 2019).

His statement underscores the psychological and strategic instability that accompanies leadership transitions, particularly when the organization's financial performance has been negative or when prior CEOs depart under unfavorable circumstances. The new strategic direction at Vita Care introduced additional pressure, requiring a 15% reduction in resource costs, increased human resource and process efficiencies, and the urgent need to restore financial stability.

This case highlights a critical insight: While TMT promotions are often strategically aligned with corporate transformation efforts, the lingering impact of past leadership and financial instability creates an internal context of uncertainty that directly affects the confidence, cohesion, and effectiveness of the newly appointed CEO and TMT members. The burden of navigating inherited challenges can undermine alignment, delay strategic execution, and weaken TMT decision-making effectiveness, ultimately affecting the organization's credibility, reputation, and long-term stakeholder trust. This underscores the importance of strategic contextual intelligence and integrative leadership in mitigating uncertainty and ensuring sustainable organizational success.

Our study's findings indicate that the effectiveness of the new CEO and TMT is not solely determined by their actions but is profoundly influenced by the existing internal and external contexts shaped by predecessor leadership and past financial outcomes (Osborn and Marion, 2009). This underscores the idea that TMT promotions, while linked to strategic shifts, require navigating a complex landscape of in-herited uncertainty and organizational reputation, which can significantly impact their ability to drive effective change.

3.4.3 Adapting to Cultural and Societal Expectations

In all four of the in-depth cases, the TMTs demonstrated their ability to navigate strategic changes and frequent CEO transitions by remaining culturally aware and focusing on the external context, particularly societal expectations. This adaptability allowed them to maintain stability and drive organizational success, showing that their effectiveness was closely tied to meeting societal leadership expectations rather than adhering strictly to national cultural values. Furthermore, the case's insights confirmed that leaders' effectiveness is directly linked to societal leadership expectations, echoing the findings of the latest GLOBE study (House et al., 2013). The GLOBE results revealed a strong relationship between TMT and CEO performance and their society's leadership expectations, indicating that leaders' certainty of being effective is driven more by social expectations than by cultural values.

At Medi Care, the more experienced CEO, described as a performance-driven leader by his TMT, lost the support of shareholders and some TMT members. This was attributed to his inability to meet the societal leadership expectations and cultural tones that were critical to the shareholders. People-oriented leadership, which aligns more with national culture and leadership expectations, was found to be a significant determinant of strategic leadership effectiveness. In this case, the leadership expectations were tied to the realization of the strategic leadership development, highlighting the importance of aligning leadership approaches with cultural and societal norms.

In the case of Urban Escape, the rapidly changing context underscored the critical importance of delivering positive financial results, meeting shareholders' expectations, and sustaining performance excellence as key indicators of organizational success. The TMT played a strategic role in balancing these external pressures with the internal demands of the organization. A crucial aspect of this balancing act was the TMT's ability to effectively interface with the board of directors. By engaging closely with the board, the TMT ensured that the organization's strategies were aligned with both internal priorities and external expectations.

The TMT's strategic leadership extended beyond managing day-to-day operations; it involved a nuanced understanding of the external environment and a proactive approach to aligning the organization's internal capabilities with the evolving external context. The TMT's interaction with the board was essential in navigating these complexities, as it allowed for a unified approach to decision-making and ensured that the board's strategic vision was effectively communicated and implemented throughout the organization.

By successfully interfacing with the board and balancing the internal and external forces, the TMT ensured that Urban Escape not only met its immediate financial targets but also laid the groundwork for sustained organizational performance in a dynamic and competitive market (Hambrick and Mason, 1984; Dess and Beard, 1984). This strategic balancing act highlights the pivotal role that TMTs play in steering organizations through the intricacies of both internal dynamics and external pressures, while maintaining a strong alignment with the board's strategic direction).

In conclusion, Chapter 3 highlights the pivotal role of TMTs as the strategic nexus within organizations, emphasizing their ability to navigate two critical balancing acts that shape organizational outcomes. The first balancing act involves managing the dynamics between the TMT, CEO, and board, where TMTs must align with the CEO's vision while simultaneously responding to the board's expectations. The second balancing act requires TMTs to navigate their internal interactions, maintaining cohesion and collaboration among themselves while adapting to external pressures. These dual balancing acts reveal the complexity and criticality of TMTs in influencing strategic direction and driving organizational success. As catalysts and mediators of change, TMTs serve not merely as executive bodies but as central pillars that translate strategic visions into tangible outcomes. They adeptly manage power dynamics, cultural nuances, and leadership challenges, both internally and externally, solidifying their role as essential drivers of sustainable success in complex, pluralistic organizations.

3.5 Embedding Insights and Reflective Practice

This chapter sets the stage for understanding the pivotal role of top management teams. It's vital to recognize the sophisticated dynamics that top management teams steer within pluralistic organizations. The internal balancing acts managing relationships with the CEO and board and the external balancing acts managing uncertainties after frequent CEO transitions, their impact on shareholders, and the organization's reputation are critical to the success of any TMT.

The case studies we explored underscore how these dynamics are often underplayed in organizations. Yet, they significantly influence the TMT's ability to maintain strategic continuity, manage external expectations, and steer the organization through periods of change. The complexities of these balancing acts require a deep understanding of both the internal and external environments in which TMTs operate.

To help you embed these concepts early on and integrate them into your leadership practice, we've designed a series of reflective questions and activities. These tools are intended to encourage you to think critically about the dynamics within your organization and to apply the insights and your individual lessons from this chapter to enhance your leadership effectiveness.

3.5.1 Reflective Questions

Navigating Internal Dynamics: Reflect on the current dynamics between your TMTs, CEO, and board.
    How do these relationships influence decision-making and strategic direction?
    Are there tensions or gaps that need to be addressed to improve cohesion and effectiveness? What are the causes of these tensions or gaps?

Managing External Uncertainty: How does your TMT respond to external uncertainties, such as CEO transitions or shifts in strategic direction?
    What impact do these changes have on shareholder confidence and the organization's reputation?
    How can your team better anticipate and mitigate these challenges?

Strategic Continuity and Reputation Management:
Consider how frequent leadership changes have impacted your organization's strategic continuity and reputation. What steps can your TMT take to ensure that these transitions do not disrupt long-term goals or damage the organization's public image and attractiveness for all stakeholders?

Dynamic Contexts: How well does your TMT understand and adapt to the dynamic contexts in which your organization operates? Are you able to stay ahead of external pressures, or do they often force reactive rather than proactive strategies?

3.5.2 Learning Activities

TMT Dynamics Workshop:
Organize a workshop focused on the internal dynamics of your TMT. Use case studies (available in the empirical section in Appendix B) to analyze how well your team navigates its relationships with the CEO and board. Identify areas where stronger alignment could improve decision-making and strategic outcomes.

Uncertainty Management Strategy:
Develop a strategy for managing external uncertainties, particularly those arising from strategic leaders' transitions and shifts in strategic direction. Consider how your TMT can maintain stability and protect the organization's reputation during periods of change.

Contextual Analysis Session:
Conduct a session with your TMT to map out the dynamic contexts your organization faces. Identify key external factors that could impact your strategic plans and develop proactive strategies to address these challenges before they become critical issues.

Strategic Continuity Plan:

Create a comprehensive strategic continuity plan that ensures your organization's long-term goals remain on track, even during leadership transitions. This plan should include steps to manage both internal dynamics and external pressures effectively.

By engaging with these reflective questions and activities, you and your TMT can reinforce the crucial concepts covered in this chapter, ensuring that they are not just understood but actively applied in your leadership practice. As you move forward in this book, keep these insights at the forefront of your strategic thinking, enabling your TMT to navigate both internal complexities and external uncertainties with greater confidence and success.

Chapter 4
Strategic Contextual Leadership Imperatives for Multicultural and Pluralistic Organizations

In Chapter 3, we delved into the complex dynamics within TMTs and their pivotal role in shaping strategic leadership within multicultural and pluralistic business environments. We examined how the effectiveness of strategic leaders is not only dependent on their ability to drive performance but also on their deep understanding of the contexts in which they operate. TMTs must balance their actions both internally, within their organizations, and externally, in relation to diverse cultural, social, and organizational realities.

Consider the case of Echo Capital in the Middle East, where a newly appointed Chief Operating Officer (COO) was hired to enhance operational excellence and to strengthen the confidence of the shareholders in the organizational performance and effectiveness. Coming from a French corporate culture with a strong focus on performance, efficiency and productivity, the COO swiftly identified inefficiencies in processes and resources. Believing that non-revenue-generating roles should be minimized, he proposed a restructuring plan, which involved reducing highly paid TMT members in non-strategic roles. Redundancy or right structuring, as it is termed by the performance specialists, included the termination of employment of a number of a senior director in the investment team.

However, this decision did not account for the cultural and social sensitivities surrounding termination of employment in some regions in the Middle East. In this region, termination of employment is not just a matter of business; it is deeply intertwined with cultural and religious values, making it a socially sensitive issue. Although employment terminations occur as frequently in the Middle East as in Western countries, the perception and implications of such actions are markedly different. Middle Eastern chairpersons and CEOs often attempt to distance themselves from being directly associated with terminations, recognizing the potential for social backlash.

One of the most controversial decisions the COO made was to terminate a senior director who was part of a national leadership development initiative, and it set off a series of unintended consequences. This action, perceived not merely as a performance measure but as a violation of local cultural and social norms, caused significant concern among shareholders and created internal unrest.

This scenario illustrates the critical importance of contextual awareness in strategic decision-making. While the COO's actions were aligned with his objective of driving productivity, his failure to grasp the local cultural context undermined his effectiveness and caused substantial organizational disruption. The incident at Echo Capital underscores the necessity for leaders to balance strategic actions with a

https://doi.org/10.1515/9783111382722-005

nuanced understanding of both internal and external contexts, ensuring decisions are operationally sound while culturally and socially informed. In this case, he failed to consider the deep cultural and social sensitivities surrounding employment termination in the Middle East (Hofstede, 2001).

Unlike Western corporate environments where performance-based employment termination is an accepted norm in the Middle East, job loss is often intertwined with broader cultural, social, and familial implications (House et al., 2013). In this region:

- Employment is not solely a professional identity but a marker of social standing, family responsibility, and community honor.
- Termination decisions are carefully handled to minimize reputational damage for both the organization and the individual.
- Executives and senior leadership, particularly CEOs and chairpersons, tend to distance themselves from direct involvement in dismissals to avoid social backlash.

The COO's decision had unintended repercussions causing:
- Shareholder dissatisfaction and erosion of confidence in leadership.
- Internal unrest among employees, who viewed the move as a violation of cultural and professional norms.
- Reputational damage, requiring months of crisis management, including legal consultations, stakeholder communication, and public relations efforts.

Instead of strengthening team performance, the decision undermined the COO's credibility, stalled productivity, and forced the company into a prolonged recovery phase.

This chapter introduces four strategic contextual leadership imperatives. We will call them the dynamic capabilities of strategic leadership that are essential for navigating contextual and pluralistic organizations complexities. Figure 4.1 shows the impact of the context elements on each of the four imperatives:

Strategic Contextual Intelligence: The findings from our five case studies reveal that societal leadership expectations have the most significant impact on strategic leadership, with over 40% of participants identifying it as the primary external force shaping executive decision-making (Figure 3.3). This underscores the reality that leaders operate within a broader societal framework, where public trust, governance standards, and evolving leadership models influence strategic direction. Beyond societal expectations, economic dynamism was cited by 25% of participants, reflecting the profound influence of financial volatility, investment climates, and market fluctuations on corporate strategy. The remaining two factors, industry regulations and national culture, were mentioned with equal frequency, highlighting their role in shaping organizational constraints, operational mandates, and leadership behaviors. These insights reinforce the premise that no strategic decision exists in isolation. It is constantly mediated by contextual forces that either enable or constrain leadership action.

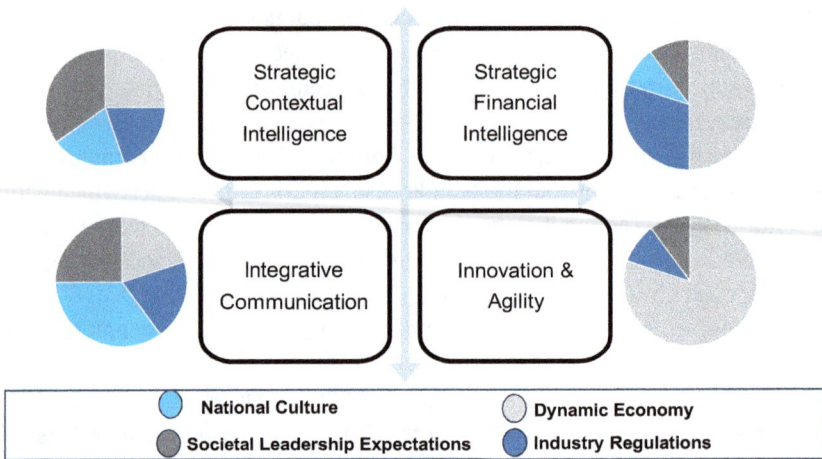

Figure 4.1: The Context Matrix Impact on the Strategic Leadership Imperatives.
This figure shows how the four elements of the context matrix—national culture, societal leadership expectations, dynamic economy, and industry regulations—influence the core strategic leadership imperatives in pluralistic organizations. These imperatives include Strategic Contextual Intelligence, Strategic Financial Intelligence, Integrative Communication, and Innovation and Agility. The figure emphasizes the differentiated and dynamic influence of each contextual factor depending on the leadership imperative and organizational environment.

Strategic contextual intelligence is particularly critical in pluralistic and multicultural organizations, where decision-making requires an advanced understanding of economic, regulatory, cultural, and technological landscapes (Denis, Langley and Rouleau, 2007). This imperative helps leaders anticipate potential pitfalls and opportunities, ensuring that strategic choices align with both business objectives and contextual realities, ultimately leading to more informed and sensitive decision-making.

Integrative Communication: Integrative communication is a critical leadership competency for TMTs and CEOs in pluralistic, multicultural organizations, where strategic alignment depends on navigating complex communication landscapes. The findings from our case studies indicate that 35% of strategic leadership communication challenges stem from national cultural differences, while 25% are influenced by societal leadership expectations. These figures highlight how deeply embedded cultural norms and external societal pressures shape communication dynamics at the highest levels of leadership.

National culture affects how leaders convey authority, handle conflict, and build consensus within their teams. In high-context cultures (Hall, 1976), implicit and indirect communication is preferred, while in low-context cultures, clarity and directness are prioritized. This discrepancy can lead to misinterpretations, decision-making delays, and conflicts within TMTs composed of leaders from different cultural backgrounds. Without a structured approach to integrative communication, these differences can undermine strategic coherence and weaken executive alignment.

Beyond internal dynamics, societal leadership expectations influence how CEOs and TMTs communicate with external stakeholders, including regulators, investors, and the broader community. Leaders in regions where governance structures emphasize collective decision-making may struggle when interacting with global investors who expect individual accountability and rapid decision cycles. Similarly, in societies where hierarchical leadership norms dominate, open feedback loops within executive teams may be underutilized, limiting the flow of critical insights.

Strategic Financial Intelligence: The findings from our case studies reveal that the dynamic economy has the most significant impact on financial intelligence, with 50% of participants emphasizing its influence on financial decision-making (Figure 3.3). This underscores the necessity for leaders to integrate economic foresight, risk assessment, and financial agility into their strategic planning. Strategic financial intelligence extends beyond basic financial literacy; it encompasses the ability to interpret and respond to complex financial conditions, ensuring that strategic decisions align with long-term economic sustainability, industry compliance, and societal expectations (Kaplan and Norton, 2004).

Beyond economic volatility, 30% of participants identified industry regulations as a key determinant of financial strategy. Regulatory changes shape capital allocation, investment strategies, and financial reporting standards, requiring TMTs to remain agile and compliant in evolving market conditions (Eccles, Ioannou, and Serafeim, 2014). Additionally, 20% of participants referenced the impact of societal leadership expectations and national culture on financial intelligence, highlighting how financial strategies must be ethically grounded and culturally sensitive to ensure stakeholder trust and corporate legitimacy.

Innovation and Agility: The ability of TMTs to drive innovation and agility is increasingly shaped by economic volatility, regulatory constraints, and shifting societal leadership expectations. Findings from our case studies indicate that 80% of participants linked the dynamic economy to the need for innovation and agility, underscoring the urgency for organizations to develop adaptive and forward-thinking leadership strategies. Industry regulations and societal leadership expectations were each cited by 10% of participants, highlighting their role in shaping how innovation and agility are implemented within strategic decision-making. With the acceleration of technological advancements and the rise of artificial intelligence (AI), TMTs must respond and anticipate to immediate market fluctuations, influence, and capitalize on future trends (Teece, Peteraf, and Leih, 2016).

As we explore these four strategic leadership advanced capabilities in depth, we will illustrate how they collectively advance traditional approaches to strategic leadership, empowering TMTs to navigate the complexities of their dual roles leading both within and outside their organizations. These imperatives form the backbone of the Strategic Contextual Leadership framework, enabling leaders to achieve performance excellence, sustainable success, and strategic alignment in today's dynamic and interconnected world.

4.1 Strategic Contextual Intelligence: Mastering the Dual Balancing Acts of Strategic Leaders

Strategic contextual intelligence consists of accumulated knowledge and expertise that allow TMTs to interpret, synthesize and apply contextual insights in strategic decisions. This is unlike competency, which refers to a specific skill or behavior that enables senior executives to perform (Boyatzis, 2008).

Strategic contextual intelligence is developed through experience and learning rather than formal training (Mintzberg, 2009). This aligns with expert knowledge system that leaders develop over time, enabling them to manage uncertainty, cultural variations, societal leadership expectations and strategic shifts.

Strategic contextual intelligence is particularly relevant in pluralistic organizations where leaders must integrate economic, social and political variables into their strategic choices (Pettigrew, 2012). It is a dynamic process rather than a static skill, requiring senior executives to continuously adapt to evolving external and internal realities (Teece, Peteraf, and Leih, 2016).

Strategic contextual intelligence cannot be reduced to a single competency, it is a knowledge based intellectual capability that enables top management teams and senior managers to apply multiple competencies strategically (Table 4.1).

Table 4.1: Strategic Contextual Intelligence Versus Competency.

Strategic Contextual Intelligence	Competency
Knowledge-based capability that integrates diverse contextual factors (economic, cultural, political) into strategic decisions	A specific skill or ability (decision making, emotional intelligence, strategic thinking)
Developed through experience, contextual exposure and learning	Acquired through structured training and development program
Enables top management teams to make sense of complex environments	Helps individuals perform specific leadership tasks
Requires synthesis interpretation and adaptation	Can be measured by tests and improved systematically
Is a futuristic long-term vision	Operational in nature and linked to a short-term effectiveness in a role.

4.2 Balancing Internal Realities

Within the organization, top management teams and senior managers must align diverse internal dynamics, such as organizational culture, internal shareholder relationships, and legacy operational practices. These internal realities shape the organization's ability to function cohesively and respond effectively to external demands (Schein, 2017). Organizational culture in particular influences decision-making structures, communication patterns, and overall strategic adaptability. In practice, organizations with strong, adaptable cultures tend to outperform those that rely solely on rigid hierarchies and control mechanisms (Kotter and Heskett, 1992). Urban Escape and Echo Capital outperform rigid, hierarchical competitors. The CEOs and the executive teams in both cases create alignment of their top management teams and achieve superior results in a dynamic context, rather than adhering to one size fits all corporate model.

Furthermore, strategic contextual intelligence enhances the ability of TMTs to foster internal alignment by synthesizing knowledge of the organization's context and ensuring that decisions are responsive to both operational needs and cultural sensitivities (Mintzberg, Ahlstrand, and Lampel, 2005). By applying strategic contextual intelligence, TMTs and CEOs can create a cohesive strategic vision that resonates across departments and levels, fostering unity and shared commitment to organizational goals. This is particularly relevant in pluralistic organizations where decision-making is not centralized, and success depends on the collaboration and buy-in of multiple stakeholders (Ghoshal and Bartlett, 1997).

Figure 4.2 illustrates how strategic contextual intelligence helps executives and senior managers balance the internal organization realities and the external market demands.

For example, in the case of Medi Care, the deputy CEO's role involved aligning internal operations with the strategic vision laid out by the new Group CEO. This required not only an understanding of internal processes but also a strategic balancing of corporate and medical priorities to ensure operational success while maintaining internal harmony. The challenge of integrating a new strategic direction while preserving the existing cultural fabric is well documented in leadership studies, where failure to address cultural alignment often leads to resistance and organizational inertia (Yukl, 2013).

Furthermore, internal stakeholder relationships play a crucial role in shaping an organization's strategic outcomes. Employees, middle managers, and department heads must be aligned with the leadership's vision to ensure seamless implementation of strategic initiatives (Denison et al., 2012).

Organizations with high internal alignment where employees understand and support the organization's strategic direction tend to have higher employee engagement, better financial performance, and lower turnover rates (Cameron and Quinn,

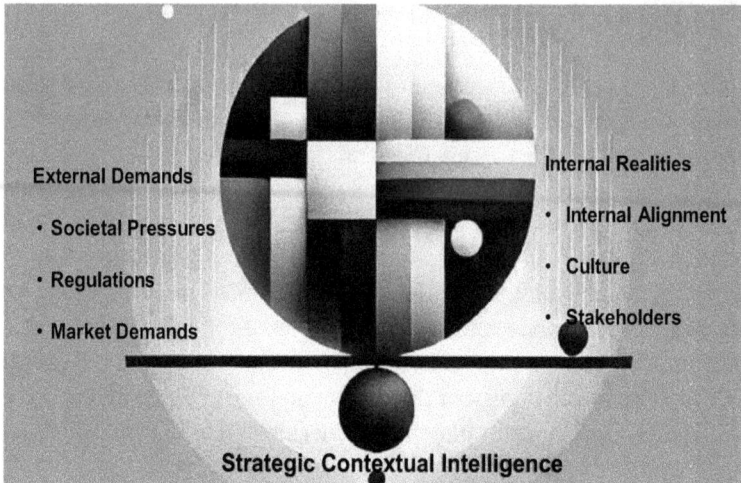

Figure 4.2: TMT Strategic Contextual Intelligence to Balance Inside and Outside the Organization. This figure explains how Strategic Contextual Intelligence supports top management teams in balancing external demands with internal organizational realities. It emphasizes the executive's role in interpreting societal pressures, regulations, and market conditions while aligning internal factors such as culture, stakeholder expectations, and team dynamics through contextual awareness and strategic judgment.

2011). Leaders who demonstrate strategic contextual intelligence recognize that strategic decisions cannot be made in isolation from the internal cultural and societal expectations of their organizations.

4.3 Balancing External Demands

While internal alignment is crucial, top management teams, senior managers and heads of departments must also navigate the complexities of external environments, including economic fluctuations, regulatory changes, technological advancements, and societal expectations. In Chapters 2 and 3 we presented the factors that significantly shape the organization's strategic direction and influence how societal expectations, shareholders, investors, regulatory bodies, and customers perceive the company (Freeman, Harrison and Zyglidopoulos, 2018). The ability to interpret and respond to these external demands effectively is a hallmark of strategic contextual intelligence.

A failure to align internal strategies with external realities can lead to strategic missteps. For instance, organizations that fail to anticipate regulatory changes may find themselves facing compliance risks that jeopardize their operations. Similarly, organizations that ignore shifting consumer expectations may struggle to maintain their market position in an increasingly competitive global landscape (Porter and Kramer, 2011).

In the Echo Capital case, the newly appointed COO focused on improving operational excellence by terminating the employment of a senior director. However, without considering the cultural and social implications of employment termination in the Middle East, the COO's decision led to unintended consequences that disrupted shareholder relations. In many Middle Eastern cultures, employment decisions, particularly at senior levels, are deeply intertwined with social hierarchies, relationships, and expectations (Meyer, 2017). The COO's lack of contextual intelligence resulted in a decision that, while technically sound, was culturally misaligned, leading to unforeseen challenges in stakeholder management.

This example highlights that while cultural intelligence is a valuable leadership asset, it is not sufficient on its own for strategic decision-making in complex environments. Cultural intelligence refers to the ability to function effectively across diverse cultural contexts, including national, organizational, and professional cultures (Early and Mosakowski, 2004). It equips leaders with the sensitivity to understand and adapt to cultural differences, facilitating cross-cultural interactions and minimizing misunderstanding. However, strategic leadership in pluralistic multicultural organizations demands more than cultural awareness. It requires an expansion on cultural intelligence by integrating the context matrix elements, economic, regulatory, and environmental factors to ensure a holistic approach to context driven strategy (Pettigrew, 2012).

Had the COO in this case relied solely on cultural intelligence, they may have understood cultural sensitivities but failed to account for the broader strategic and societal implications of their decisions. Strategic contextual intelligence goes beyond cultural intelligence by ensuring leaders anticipate resistance, engage with key shareholders proactively and apply a more nuanced, consultative approach to arrive at more strategically sound and contextually informed decisions (Mintzberg, 2009). This distinction underscores why strategic contextual intelligence should be a core leadership capability, as it enables executives to lead the dynamic interplay of multiple external and internal forces shaping organizational success (Tariqu and Schuler, 2010).

Anticipating External Disruptions Through Strategic Contextual Intelligence

Executives and top management teams must also be proactive rather than reactive in responding to external changes. Organizations that fail to anticipate technological disruptions or market shifts often find themselves struggling to catch up. The concept of dynamic capabilities introduced first by Eisenhard and Martin (2000) and later by Teece, Peteraf, and Leih (2016), highlights the importance of an organization's ability to sense, seize, and transform in response to external challenges. Strategic contextual intelligence plays a pivotal role in strengthening these dynamic capabilities by ensuring that leaders can foresee external trends and adjust strategies accordingly.

The Essence of Strategic Contextual Intelligence: A Dual Perspective

The essence of strategic contextual intelligence lies in its ability to support strategic balancing acts—navigating both internal and external realities. CEOs and TMTs equipped with SCI can:

Internally:
- Adapt leadership approaches to align with the organization's culture, ensuring that strategic decisions resonate within the internal framework and foster a collective leadership dynamic (Ghoshal and Bartlett, 1997).
- Understand the incentives, expectations, and dynamics of team members, enabling leaders to drive alignment and minimize internal friction (Denison et al., 2012).
- Utilize integrative communication to build trust, resolve conflicts, and ensure strategic clarity across all levels of the organization (Heifetz, Grashow, and Linsky, 2009).

Externally:
- Respond proactively to external forces such as economic trends, regulatory shifts, and societal expectations (Freeman et al., 2018).
- Craft strategies that not only address market needs but also anticipate changes in external contexts, positioning their organizations for sustainable success (Teece, Peteraf, and Leih, 2016).

In contrast to earlier frameworks, where the cultural values are linked directly to the executives' decisions, such as Hofstede's cultural differences model or Porter's fixed-construct approaches (Antonakis et al., 2003; Porter and McLaughlin, 2006; Hofstede, 2006), strategic contextual intelligence provides a flexible and comprehensive tool for integrating internal and external contexts by balanced strategic actions. By mastering this intelligence, leaders can ensure their strategies and execution are both internally aligned and externally viable.

The case of Urban Escape serves as a real-world example of how strategic contextual intelligence enables TMTs to navigate the complexities of leading both inside and outside the organization (see Box 4.1). The TMT at Urban Escape faced significant leadership transitions, which highlighted gaps in understanding the broader context, often leading to "contextual blind spots." However, through the application of strategic contextual intelligence, the TMT was able to maintain organizational stability, effectively manage internal dynamics, and adapt to external pressures. The case demonstrates the critical role of SCI in bridging internal leadership challenges and external market demands, ensuring strategic resilience and long-term success.

Box 4.1 – Lessons from Urban Escape: Overcoming Contextual Blind Spots

Urban Escape serves as a vivid example of how strategic contextual intelligence operates within a top management team. The case study highlights how TMTs can leverage strategic insight and contextual awareness to navigate challenging business landscapes, particularly when CEOs falter due to a lack of deep contextual understanding. This exploration will focus on the elements of strategic contextual intelligence that enabled the TMT to address gaps left by transitioning CEOs, demonstrating the critical role of strategic contextual intelligence in effective leadership within complex, multicultural environments.

Mark, a seasoned construction and development expert, joined Urban Escape as the Chief Operating Officer, bringing with him extensive experience from the European markets. His success in driving financial robustness and development expertise quickly propelled him to the CEO position, marking the beginning of a significant leadership transition. However, after a two-year tenure, unfavorable financial results led to his exit, highlighting the challenges of aligning leadership with shifting external and internal contexts.

Leadership Transitions and Contextual Challenges

Mark's departure was succeeded by Michael, who sought to expand Urban Escape's presence internationally. However, the onset of global economic turmoil led to substantial financial losses, culminating in Michael's sudden resignation. His successor, David, also encountered unforeseen challenges that cut his tenure short. Amid these leadership upheavals, Tamer, the first national CEO, emerged from within the organization to restore stability and continuity. Despite the series of CEO transitions and the negative financial outcomes caused by market downturns, Tamer's and his TMT's strategic contextual intelligence proved pivotal. It enabled them to maintain strong relationships with shareholders, uphold high operational integrity, and effectively steer the organization through these turbulent times.

Financial Dynamics and Leadership Implications

Urban Escape's financial journey closely mirrored its leadership changes, experiencing significant downturns after each CEO exit. However, under Tamer's strategic contextual intelligence and the resilience of the TMT, they managed to secure crucial shareholder support, leading to a successful public offering that helped navigate these financial challenges. Tamer's promotion from within the TMT, coupled with the team's deployment of strategic contextual intelligence, ensured that the frequent leadership transitions did not compromise the organization's reputation or strategic direction. This underscores the importance of nurturing and promoting talent from within to maintain stability and focus during periods of change.

Insights and Unpacking the Case

This case study of Urban Escape vividly illustrates how the Strategic Contextual Leadership framework outcomes—performance excellence, sustainable success, and strategic leadership development—are deeply interconnected with the organization's ability to navigate complex and dynamic contexts.

Performance Excellence

Urban Escape's ability to adapt its organizational structure in response to external pressures, such as regulatory changes and market shifts, reflects its commitment to performance excellence. The TMT's strategic contextual intelligence enabled them to maintain high performance standards during leadership transitions, ensuring that the organization continued to excel despite external challenges.

Adapting to Market Dynamics

The TMT's response to the shift towards private funding, driven by changes in the country direction towards a more knowledge-based economy, highlights their focus on sustaining performance excellence.

By reorienting strategies and optimizing resources in response to economic fluctuations, the TMT ensured that Urban Escape remained competitive and financially robust, despite external uncertainties.

Sustainable Success

Urban Escape's alignment of its leadership strategy with national cultural values exemplifies the path to sustainable success. The TMT's deep understanding of the cultural context enabled them to navigate strategic shifts and financial challenges while maintaining a commitment to long-term organizational sustainability. This approach ensured that Urban Escape's strategic decisions were not only effective in the short term but also positioned the organization for enduring future success.

Navigating Leadership Transitions

The frequent CEO turnovers at Urban Escape highlighted the importance of sustainability in leadership. The TMT's resilience and ability to stabilize the organization during periods of leadership change ensured that Urban Escape's long-term objectives remained on track. This focus on sustainable success was critical in maintaining organizational continuity and resilience, even during times of significant internal disruption.

Strategic Financial Performance and Leadership Effectiveness

Urban Escape's financial performance, closely tied to its leadership transitions, underscores the critical role of strategic leadership development. The TMT's ability to mitigate the financial challenges associated with CEO exits, through strategic actions such as mergers and restructuring, highlights the importance of developing leaders who can navigate complex financial landscapes. The internal promotions within the TMT, culminating in the rise of the first national CEO, reflect a strategic commitment to nurturing and developing leadership talent from within, ensuring that the organization is equipped with leaders who can drive sustained success.

Strategic Alignment with Context

The TMT's strategic foresight and deep contextual understanding, as demonstrated through seamless leadership transitions and alignment with national cultural values, reflect the outcomes of effective strategic leadership development. By integrating the principles of the SCL framework, Urban Escape was able to maintain strategic focus, ensure leadership continuity, and drive long-term organizational success.

Key Takeaway

The case of Urban Escape illustrates how the Strategic Contextual Leadership framework, through its focus on performance excellence, sustainable success, and strategic contextual leadership development, can empower organizations to navigate the complexities of multicultural and dynamic environments. The TMT's ability to leverage strategic contextual intelligence ensured that Urban Escape survived and thrived despite facing significant external and internal challenges. This case underscores the critical importance of the SCL framework in fostering leadership that is adaptable, resilient, and capable of achieving sustained success.

Following the strategic contextual intelligence, the second critical competency is integrative communication. While strategic contextual intelligence equips leaders with the ability to understand and synthesize contextual elements, integrative communication ensures that these insights are effectively communicated and aligned within the organization. In the next section, we explore how integrative communication enhances strategic leadership by bridging gaps and fostering alignment across diverse organizational landscapes.

4.4 Integrative Communication: A Roadmap for CEOs and TMTs to Avoid the Perils of Contextual Misunderstandings

Integrative communication is a critical organizational capability that enables Chief Executive Officers (CEOs) and top management teams (TMTs) to effectively navigate the complexities of leading both within and outside the organization. It involves crafting and delivering messages that are clear, culturally, and contextually relevant across a diverse range of stakeholders. This competency is essential for bridging diverse cultural, organizational, and contextual divides, thereby enhancing the TMT's ability to avoid contextual misunderstandings and drive strategic alignment.

Effective integrative communication encompasses understanding the nuances of cultural norms, stakeholder expectations, and organizational dynamics to ensure that every message aligns with strategic goals and is received as intended. This approach is not merely about the words used; it requires a deep comprehension of the cultural and contextual factors that influence how messages are perceived and interpreted. Strategic leaders with high cultural intelligence are better equipped to manage cross-cultural interactions, leading to improved organizational performance (Nosratabadi et al., 2020).

To foster integrative communication, organizations should cultivate a culture that values openness, transparency, and adaptability. This involves providing training on strategic contextual intelligence, establishing clear communication protocols, and investing in technologies that support real-time collaboration and feedback across different geographies and functions. Organizations usually provide cultural intelligence training for employees and leaders to enhance their ability to navigate cross-cultural interactions effectively, thereby improving team alignment and performance (Livermore, 2015).

The Role of Integrative Communication in Internal Alignment
A key aspect of balancing internal realities is integrative communication, which ensures that leadership messages are clearly articulated and understood at all levels of the organization. Integrative communication fosters transparency, encourages open dialogue, and helps resolve conflicts before they escalate into broader organizational challenges (Heifetz, Grashow, and Linsky, 2009).

Leaders with high strategic contextual intelligence utilize integrative communication strategies to create shared meaning and purpose among employees. They do not merely issue directives; they engage in dialogue, solicit feedback, and create mechanisms for continuous communication. In pluralistic organizations, where leadership is often distributed across multiple teams and divisions, this approach is essential for maintaining cohesion and strategic alignment (Northouse, 2021).

In summary, integrative communication serves as a vital tool for CEOs and TMTs to master the dual balancing acts of leading both inside and outside the organization. By bridging diverse cultural, organizational, and contextual divides, integrative communication enhances the TMT's ability to avoid contextual misunderstandings and drive strategic alignment. See integrative communication for TMT Balancing Acts (Figure 4.3).

Integrative Communication

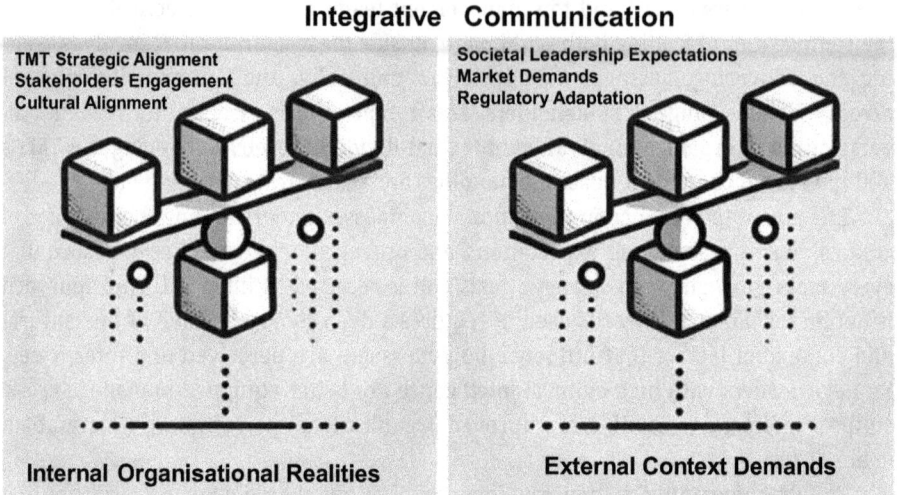

TMT Strategic Alignment
Stakeholders Engagement
Cultural Alignment

Societal Leadership Expectations
Market Demands
Regulatory Adaptation

Internal Organisational Realities

External Context Demands

Figure 4.3: Integrative Communication Balancing Internal Organizational Realities and External Demands. This figure presents integrative communication as a key mechanism through which top management teams balance internal organizational realities with external contextual demands. It highlights the importance of continuous communication in aligning strategic priorities, stakeholder engagement, and organizational culture with evolving societal expectations, market conditions, and regulatory requirements in pluralistic organizations.

Preventing External Contextual Misunderstandings

Imagine a scenario where a leader's words are taken out of context. What began as a thoughtful comment within a specific discussion becomes controversial or ambiguous when presented in isolation. This demonstrates a key challenge: *Without context, communication is vulnerable to misinterpretation.* In the diverse landscape of multinational, pluralistic organizations, this risk is amplified. Here, the stakes are high, with leadership communication needing to navigate not just language differences but also varying cultural norms, regulatory environments, and stakeholder expectations. We present an example of integrative communication that underlines the critical importance of effective leadership communication, crafting and delivering messages that resonate across a spectrum of cultural backgrounds while aligning with both the internal dynamics and external demands of the organization.

The newly promoted CEO of a hospital within a healthcare group found herself constantly entangled in the complexities of miscommunication. She shared:

We meet every day to discuss or resolve communication problems, we never resolve them by email. Instead, we meet in person every day for 30 minutes to clarify the issues —some emails may sound inflammatory. We address the issue head on. Ensuring that every communication has a clear objective, a request for action, or a communicated result, instead of a chain of emails trying to untangle issues of misinterpretation between the top management teams. This is the most important time I spend with the TMT so I can focus on strategizing and moving forward. (In-person interview communication, May 2019)

Integrative communication helps bridge these gaps by ensuring that messages are not only transmitted but also clearly understood and embraced across different functions and locations. By engaging in open dialogue and facilitating mutual understanding, leaders can align the organization's internal culture with its strategic goals, enhancing stability and performance even amid complexity and change. To illustrate the critical role of integrative communication in navigating both external and internal balancing acts, we present a case study of Medi Care.

4.5 Case Study: Medi Care – Navigating Complexity Through Integrative Communication

This public healthcare organization has distinguished itself through its unique business model that integrates multinational staffing and public-private partnerships across countries like Canada, Australia, and the United States. However, Medi Care's journey has been marked by significant challenges inherent in its diverse, rapidly evolving context. The Group CEOs of Medi Care describe it as a "human organization" reflecting its fundamental commitment to people-oriented leadership, decision-making, and service delivery across multiple locations with unique demands. Medi Care's TMT must manage a wide range of stakeholders from medical professionals to finance experts, each with distinct priorities. Integrative communication has proven vital in harmonizing these diverse voices, aligning strategic priorities with the broader goals of quality healthcare delivery and global best practices. As the deputy CEO of Medi Care notes, "Doctors do not always understand our business needs" (in-person interview communication, October 2019), highlighting the critical need for clear, context-sensitive communication to bridge gaps and drive alignment.

By working closely with the health authority and leveraging partnerships with international healthcare institutions, Medi Care's TMT has used integrative communication to navigate reforms and regulatory changes, ensuring that their strategic objectives align with both local demands and global standards.

Medi Care Internal Context

Medi Care operates within a complex and pluralistic organizational context, as described by its Chief Technology Officer. The organization faces conflicting demands from various constituencies, including being publicly listed, and collaborating with private joint-stock authorities, healthcare authorities, new holding companies, and a diverse range patients with complex cases. The network of hospitals under Medi Care follows a hierarchical structure, with additional reporting levels to local councils, all the while navigating dual regulatory authorities—a healthcare authority and a publicly listed regulatory body—aimed at improving financial stability and transitioning to a more privately funded model.

Strategic Alliances and Knowledge Transfer

In pursuit of healthcare excellence, Medi Care has forged multiple agreements with international partners, focusing on knowledge transfer, education, and the establishment of healthcare excellence metrics. These partnerships as described as public-private partnerships (PPP). These initiatives serve as foundational pillars for improving Medi Care's performance and outcomes. To achieve healthcare excellence, Medi Care has established strategic alliances with the likes of Mayo Clinic, Cleveland Clinic and other major US and Canadian healthcare providers. These partnerships are designed to facilitate knowledge transfer, elevate medical standards, and enhance operational efficiency, ensuring that Medi Care healthcare delivery aligns with global healthcare best practices. Through these agreements, renowned medical professionals from its North American partners actively engage in training, consultation, and direct patient care, bringing advanced medical expertise to Medi Care facilities. Additionally, these collaborations extend to sharing cutting-edge operational processes, evidence based medical protocols, and patient-centered care models, ensuring patients at Medi Care receive the same high-quality treatment they would expect in top-tier US and Canadian hospitals. By integrating internationally recognized healthcare metrics and accreditation frameworks, Medi Care not only enhances clinical outcomes but also strengthens its position as a globally connected, patient-centric healthcare provider in an increasingly complex and competitive landscape.

Operational Excellence Model and Hierarchal Structure

A distinctive aspect of Medi Care's operational model is the dual reporting system established through these partnerships. While most medical teams are part of Medi Care, their reporting lines extend to the CEOs of the partnering organizations in their respective countries. For instance, a partnership with a Canadian healthcare group means that the medical team on that project reports to the Canadian partner's CEO, while corporate TMTs report to the Group CEO of Medi Care. This blend of internal (corporate TMT) and international management (private public partners) styles introduces a complex dimension to Medi Care's pluralistic structure, particularly between corporate directors and professional (medical) directors, as depicted in Figure 4.4 of the organizational structure.

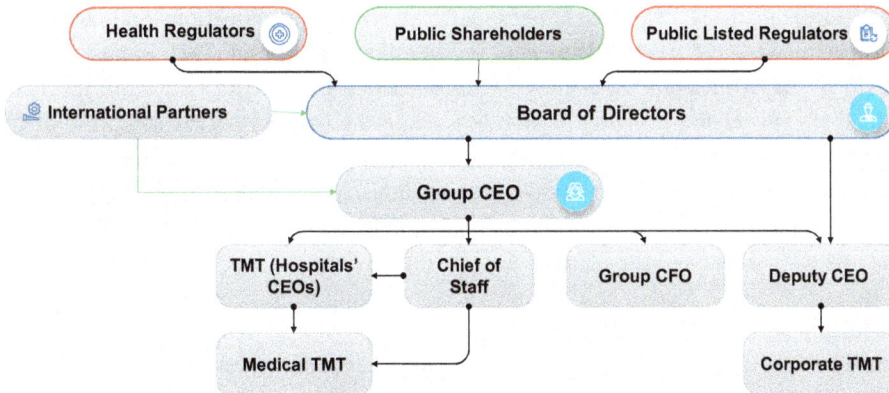

Figure 4.4: Medi Care Organizational Structure.
This figure outlines the organizational structure of Medic Care, showing the governance and reporting relationships within the organization. The Board of Directors is accountable to health regulators, public shareholders, listed market authorities, and international partners. The Group CEO reports to the board and leads several executive roles including the top management team of hospital CEOs, the Chief of Staff, the Group CFO, and the Deputy CEO. The medical leadership team operates through hospital structures, while the corporate team is coordinated by the Deputy CEO.

Multicultural Management and Pluralistic Approach

The diversity of Medi Care's top management stems from its multicultural medical staff, a direct result of its international reach. "Long-term collaboration is essential to advance healthcare," the Medi Care chairman states (in-person interview communication, November, 2019). This pluralistic approach is not only evident in the complex reporting lines and non-traditional structures but also aligns with regulatory guidelines for publicly listed entities and healthcare regulations. Figure 4.3 illustrates how Medi Care's internal structure reflects the duality of internal reporting in three key positions. The deputy CEO, appointed by the board, has direct access to the chairman and board support, while the hospitals' CEOs report to both the Group CEO and the public-private partner. This intricate structure significantly impacts the organization's internal context.

Strategic Change and Organizational Impact

The context matrix has played a pivotal role in shaping Medi Care's strategic direction and organizational transformation. Medi Care is based in United Arab Emirates where the country economy shifted towards knowledge-based economy, necessitating Medi Care's transition into a publicly listed healthcare entity demanding greater financial transparency, operational efficiency, and strategic adaptability. In response, the board of directors, newly appointed to oversee this transition, ensured alignment with privatization efforts, performance excellence mandates and cost containment strategies.

However, these strategic changes, particularly budget reductions and corporate restructuring, have triggered internal misalignment within the TMT, exposing fractures in TMT cohesions. Interviews with the Group CEO, deputy CEO and the TMT members revealed a growing disconnect. While the corporate TMT sought to align with the strategic objectives, their interpretation of the strategic priorities and those of the professional TMTs led to divergent agendas. Miscommunication compounded these tensions as different leaders pursued competing objectives, ultimately impacting the effectiveness of the transition. This context-driven strategic shift altered Medi Care's governance model, and introduced new complexities in leadership dynamics, requiring stronger integrative communication, role clarity, and strategic contextual intelligence for the new TMTs to ensure the alignment among the new TMTs, the long-tenured TMTs, and with societal leadership expectations.

Challenges in Talent Management and TMT Dynamics
Our in-depth interviews with Medi Care's TMTs and CEOs revealed critical challenges: Over a quarter of TMT members perceive a significant gap in the organization's ability to attract and retain multinational medical and technical professionals with the necessary expertise. This issue is exacerbated by internal misalignment within the TMT. Ongoing conflicts exist between diverse leadership divisions, and tensions surround the roles of the American doctors, Medi Care's local medical TMTs, and Corporate TMTs. The lack of alignment in strategic priorities and leadership expectations has not only hindered talent acquisition but also created barriers to knowledge integration and cross-functional collaboration. Additionally, tenure has emerged as a key factor influencing power dynamics within the corporate leadership team. Long-serving TMT members, particularly those with over a decade at Medi Care, have exhibited a strong sense of entitlement to their roles and career progression. This sentiment was intensified when newly appointed Group CEO introduced external hires, including a new chief of staff and Group CFO, both reporting directly to the Group CEO. This challenged the long-standing hierarchy (as shown in Figure 4.3). The resulting resistance from entrenched corporate TMT members is not a reflection of organizational loyalty but an indicator of deeper structural, cultural, and societal expectations issues within Medi Care leadership.

Navigating Communication Complexities: The Impact of Diverse Objectives Within Pluralistic Top Management Teams
The large number of executives in corporate positions (participant details available in Appendix A, Table A1) significantly contributes to communication challenges within TMTs. This finding underscores how the complexities of pluralistic organizations where diverse objectives often compete are compounded by the size and diversity of the TMT. Table 4.2 shows the presence of multiple, sometimes conflicting, priorities among TMT members can negatively impact the organization's operational efficiency

Table 4.2: TMT Sample Quotes from Participants.

TMT Size and Tenure	Corporate TMTs	Professional TMT
The large size of TMT in corporate positions amplified the inefficiency of TMT communication	"It takes the reception 2 days to schedule and confirm the operation of one patient." (Interview communication with chief nurse officer, December 2019)	"The medical team needs more resources to reduce the patients waiting time to schedule for pre-operations procedures." (Interview communication with CEO of general hospital, November 2019).
TMT performance effectiveness is impacted by retaining the legacy TMTs	"There are 50 employees in the finance department to work on the efficiency of financial resources because the medical team do not bother with their budgets." (Interview communication CFO of general hospital, December 2019))	"My target besides treating and operating on patients is to work on medical research. We must advance our technology and innovation, instead of having 50 employees in finance department to improve efficiency."(Interview communication with chief medical officer of the general hospital, May 2019).

and overall effectiveness, highlighting the need for integrated communication strategies to align these varied perspectives.

The CFO remarked, "Over half of our TMT members, including our CEO and COO, don't know how to communicate their budgets or cash flow with the finance team" Iin-person interview communication, January 2020). Opinions among participants were sharply divided. Moreover, the Group CEO and the professional top management team recognized that the TMT's cultural diversity and large size posed significant challenges to effective communication. Only the deputy CEO and select TMT members were actively involved in conveying and overseeing the new strategic change. This segregated communication approach highlights the need for integrative communication during such a significant organizational transformation. The approach aimed to manage the strategic transition effectively but inadvertently fueled a growing rift within the TMT. Those who were not included in the communication process felt increasingly marginalized, leading to tension and a sense of disconnect between the involved leaders and the rest of the team. This division further complicated the already challenging dynamics of a culturally diverse and large TMT, potentially undermining the cohesion needed.

Medi Care TMT's Integrative Communication: Despite the above challenges, the TMT displayed remarkable resilience. They effectively navigated the cultural and contextual complexities of the changes. Initially, only 45% of the TMT aligned with the new strategic direction. However, when both the deputy CEO and the hospital CEO effectively integrated other TMTs they were able to influence an additional 15% of the TMT who had initially remained neutral and did not support the strategic change. Through clear and strategic messaging, they built consensus and addressed concerns, successfully countering the potential challenges posed by the 40% of TMT members who were misaligned with the strategic change. This scenario illustrates the TMT's integration and alignment during a period of significant upheaval, despite the complexities introduced by a culturally diverse and large TMT. The integrative communication approach also highlighted the need for strategic contextual skills to effectively manage internal dynamics and maintain Medi Care's reputation and the satisfaction of the stakeholder.

Assessing the Impact of Integrative Communication in Multinational Pluralistic Organizations

In conclusion, this case highlights the essential need for contextual equivalence in leadership communication, especially in a global context. It demonstrates how contextual sensitivity, coupled with an understanding of leadership expectations, is a vital communication competency, particularly in pluralistic organizations where communication practices are deeply intertwined with different functions, external cultural values, and societal leadership expectations. Furthermore, there is a need to integrate the aspect of cultural considerations in CEO communication with multicultural TMTs and the specific challenges faced by an external Western CEO in a Middle Eastern organizational context.

Contextual Blindspot in CEO leadership: Medi Care's experience highlights the critical importance of contextual awareness in selecting Group CEOs. New CEOs, particularly those from external backgrounds, often prioritize performance excellence. However, this focus can sometimes overlook the essential cultural and societal leadership expectations unique to the organization and its regional context.

In several Middle Eastern countries, as we have previously discussed, employment termination is a sensitive issue deeply ingrained in the cultural fabric and requires careful handling. At Medi Care, the new CEO's approach to executing employee terminations, while aimed at improving efficiency, was perceived as tactless and insensitive to local norms. The deputy CEO noted that, although he was assigned this difficult task, he conveyed the same message with cultural sensitivity to prevent the adverse consequences of a cultural disconnect, which can ultimately undermine leadership effectiveness.

Building Strategic Alignment Within TMTs Through Shared Vision

Achieving strategic alignment within the TMT has been essential for Medi Care's transformation, particularly in the wake of the Group CEO's strategic changes. Despite internal tensions, a core group of approximately one-third of the TMT emerged as a unified force, fully aligned with the CEO's vision for performance excellence and privatization. These individuals not only embraced the strategic direction but also acted as key enablers of change, ensuring that the broader leadership team remained focused on long-term objectives.

A critical insight that contributed to this alignment came from the deputy CEO, who helped the Group CEO identify high-performing leaders from within the existing TMT. Instead of solely relying on external hires, the CEO leveraged institutional knowledge and internal talent by promoting star performers from the old tenure leadership. One notable example was the appointment of a senior Medi Care executive with 10 years of experience as CEO of hospitals, reinforcing the message that organizational transformation does not mean disregarding internal expertise but rather harnessing it strategically.

The Group CEO described these aligned members as "the powerhouse of the group," recognizing their ability to effectively communicate, collaborate, and drive strategic implementation. Their influence extended beyond passive support; they played an active role in bridging communication gaps, mitigating resistance among hesitant TMT members and reinforcing the importance of strategic transformation at all levels of the organization. By fostering a shared vision, these aligned leaders became instrumental in embedding strategic contextual intelligence into decision-making processes, breaking down silos between operational and financial priorities, and maintaining momentum amid organizational shifts. Their collective efforts were critical in counterbalancing internal resistance, ensuring that Medi Care's TMT could navigate change with a unified purpose, rather than fragmented interests.

Influence of Educational and Professional Advancement on TMT Alignment

A common thread among these aligned TMT members was their educational backgrounds and recent promotions. The new Group CEO promoted several TMT members into more senior roles, and this career advancement significantly influenced their alignment with the CEO's strategic direction. Notably, 100% of these aligned TMT members were educated in Western countries, predominantly the USA, with 58% being of Middle Eastern origin. This suggests that cultural background was not the primary factor in achieving alignment; rather, their Western education and professional growth opportunities were the key drivers.

Empathy as a Catalyst for Integrative Communication

The role of empathy emerged as a crucial factor in fostering integrative communication and leadership within the TMT. As the deputy CEO and two hospital CEOs emphasized, empathy was essential when leading others, especially when communicating challenging decisions. In one instance, the deputy CEO was tasked by the board of directors to communicate the new strategic direction and its implementation to the TMT. Due to his deep understanding of both the organizational culture and societal leadership expectations, he conveyed these changes empathetically, ensuring that the team understood the rationale behind the decisions and were prepared for the impact. This approach aligned with societal leadership expectations, where leading with empathy, even during tough decisions, is highly valued.

Balancing Cultural Dynamics with Strategic Objectives

The Group CEO acknowledged the significant role of empathy and integrative communication in managing this pluralistic organization, stating, "It was a massive cultural change working with my deputy and other TMTs." He recognized that while he focused on managing hospitals and doctors, his deputy CEO adeptly handled the complex dynamics of attitudes, cultural, and political conflicts, balancing the efficiency of resource management with empathetic communication.

Medi Care's case vividly demonstrates the critical role of empathy within integrative communication, underscoring that effective leadership in pluralistic organizations goes beyond merely conveying strategic objectives. It requires a profound understanding of the human element, ensuring that communication is inclusive and attuned to cultural and societal expectations. The ability to balance empathetic engagement with a focus on operational efficiency has proven essential for leaders as they navigate the complexities of an organization undergoing rapid transformation. Box 4.2 further illustrates this dynamic, showcasing specific examples of how empathy and cultural awareness facilitated alignment and enhanced strategic communication within Medi Care's top management team.

Box 4.2 – Medi Care: Integrative Communication in Pluralistic Organizations

TMT Vertical Ascent: Driving Strategic Change Through Strategic Alignment

At Medi Care, a significant strategic transition was initiated with the appointment of Gary, an international CEO tasked with shifting the organization from a public funding model to a private funding structure. This transition marked a profound organizational and cultural shift, requiring alignment at all levels. Recognizing the complexities of leading a diverse workforce, the board of directors strategically promoted Samir to deputy CEO to bridge the cultural and operational gaps within the TMT. Gary's primary focus was on "achieving performance excellence in all hospitals," (virtual interview, June 2020) emphasizing resource efficiency and operational optimization. In contrast, Samir was tasked with managing "people's attitudes and problems" (in-person interview, October 2019), ensuring that strategic changes were effectively communicated and accepted within the organization. Together, their leadership dynamic represented a balancing act between performance-driven objectives and cultural sensitivity, as they worked to align Medi Care's TMT with the new strategic direction.

Key Insights and Unpacking the Case

Feedback and Influence

One of the key insights from this case is the role of contextual alignment in leadership effectiveness. The board's decision to promote Samir was rooted in the belief that his deep contextual understanding and ability to mirror societal leadership expectations would aid in managing the diverse TMT effectively. Gary's tenure, however, was marked by challenges in contextual adaptation, as he initially struggled to shift his focus from performance metrics to understanding the complexities of the TMT and stakeholder dynamics. His contextual blindness weakened his ability to balance his performance-driven leadership style with the societal leadership expectations, leading to internal friction and resistance to change.

In contrast, Samir's emphasis on empathy, alignment, and humility played a crucial role in ensuring that Medi Care's strategic changes were successfully implemented. Rather than enforcing top-down directives, Samir took an inclusive approach, working to gain buy-in from national TMT members while supporting the CEO's broader strategic goals. His leadership approach underscored the importance of balancing strategic change with cultural awareness, ensuring a smoother transition during a pivotal moment for Medi Care.

Vertical Integration: Ensuring Strategic Alignment Across Leadership Levels
Empathy as a Leadership Tool
Samir recognized the importance of empathy in navigating significant organizational change. By understanding the concerns and perspectives of the national TMT, he was able to foster trust and security, which were essential in securing their support for the strategic direction set by the board and new CEO. His ability to bridge the gap between different leadership styles and cultural expectations proved instrumental in maintaining organizational cohesion during a period of transition.

The board strategically assigned Samir to his role due to his deep contextual understanding, recognizing the need for leadership that resonated with the national context. With Gary, the new Australian CEO, at the helm of the multinational TMT, the board understood the importance of cultural alignment to ensure strategic leadership effectiveness. While Gary was tasked with driving the multinational TMT to meet the board's performance metrics, Samir 's role was pivotal in bridging the gap between the organization's strategic goals and meeting the cultural demands of the national TMT. His assignment was essential for aligning leadership vision with the societal sensitivities that were crucial for the organization's broader success.

Navigating Hierarchies: Reconfiguring TMTs for Optimal Functioning
Medi Care's TMT underwent structural adjustments to better align with its evolving strategic needs and external challenges. Strategic restructuring involved reshaping team composition, redefining roles, and integrating new leadership competencies. These adjustments were designed to enhance TMT effectiveness, ensuring that leadership at all levels was equipped to navigate the changing healthcare landscape.

Key Takeaways: Insights from Medi Care's Strategic Shift
Strategic Leadership Requires Contextual Intelligence: A leader's ability to adapt to cultural and organizational realities is as critical as their technical and operational expertise.
Integrative Communication is Essential for TMT Cohesion: Strategic change must be communicated effectively, ensuring that different leadership factions remain aligned and engaged.
Vertical Integration Strengthens Organizational Alignment: Assigning leaders who can bridge cultural and operational divides fosters a smoother execution of strategic initiatives.
Empathy and Stakeholder Engagement Drive Strategic Buy-In: Leaders who acknowledge and validate stakeholder concerns can achieve greater commitment to change.
Balancing Performance and Cultural Sensitivity: Overemphasizing metrics at the expense of leadership integration can result in resistance, disengagement, and inefficiencies.

Reflection
This case study provides executives with critical insights into managing strategic shifts and cultural dynamics within a pluralistic organization. The interplay between performance-driven leadership, contextual intelligence, and integrative communication defines the success of strategic transitions. Reflecting on Medi Care's experience, executives should consider how context, leadership expectations, and organizational culture shape strategic direction in multicultural environments. By doing so, leaders can develop actionable strategies to address similar challenges in their organizations, ensuring sustainable success in complex business landscapes.

Task for Executives
Analyzing Strategic Leadership Skills:
Assess Gary's and Samir 's leadership skills. How did their approaches differ in managing the multinational and national TMTs?

Contextual Integration and Performance Management:
Discuss the challenges in balancing performance-driven objectives with cultural integration within the TMT. How would you have navigated these challenges?

Strategic Decision-Making:
As an executive, formulate a strategy to manage a team amid contextual and operational shifts. Focus on integrating new strategic leadership skills while balancing organizational performance excellence and shareholders expectations.
Empathy and Integrative Communication in Leadership:
Evaluate Samir 's emphasis on empathy, alignment, and humility. How crucial are these qualities in the context of multicultural pluralistic organizations?

Conclusion and Reflection
Reflect on the case and discuss how the dynamics of context and leadership expectations shape the strategic direction in pluralistic organizations. Consider the implications of these factors in your professional setting and strategize ways to address similar challenges.

Objective:
This exercise aims to provide the reader with insights into managing strategic shifts and cultural dynamics within an organization, drawing from the complex scenario faced by Medi Care.

The case of Medi Care illustrates how integrative communication is crucial for aligning the diverse perspectives within the top management teams. While the organization had implemented advanced communication technologies to bridge this divide, the TMT's lack of alignment, particularly between the finance team and the medical teams revealed a key gap: Effective communication cannot happen in isolation from shared financial knowledge.

In pluralistic organizations like Medi Care, where teams come from vastly different professional backgrounds, TMT financial intelligence becomes a critical skill. It's not enough for TMT members to rely solely on the finance department for fiscal expertise. Instead, every member of the TMT needs to possess a solid foundation in financial principles. This knowledge allows them to actively participate in financial discussions, make informed decisions, and contribute to the overall strategic direction of the organization.

The Medi Care example highlights the importance of a shared understanding of financial dynamics, professional TMTs to fully engage in discussions about profitability, cost management, and long-term sustainability. Integrative communication, when paired with strategic financial intelligence, enables TMTs to bridge these divides and to work together cohesively toward performance excellence and sustainable success.

4.6 Strategic Financial Intelligence: A Key Component of Strategic Contextual Leadership

As discussed in Chapter 2, one of the essential components of the context matrix is the dynamic economic environment, shaped by ever-changing industry regulations, policies, and global market forces (Teece, 2018). This complexity intensifies within pluralistic organizations, where diverse objectives and external pressures converge (Pettigrew, 2012). Strategic financial intelligence (SFI) has therefore become indispensable for TMTs and CEOs, who must navigate a landscape where financial performance is intrinsically linked to environmental, social, and governance (ESG) considerations (Eccles, Ioannou, and Serafeim, 2014). Financial intelligence is no longer the sole domain of CFOs and investment professionals; rather, it is a core requirement of all TMT members (Kaplan and Norton, 2004). Each executive must be adept at interpreting economic trends, regulatory shifts, and financial strategies to not only drive profitability but also meet the broader sustainable success metrics (Porter and Kramer, 2011). In both private and public organizations, this proficiency is crucial—not only for maintaining governance and mitigating risk (Zadek, Evans, and Pruzan, 2013) but also for demonstrating accountability and leadership in response to societal expectations (Freeman, Harrison, and Zyglidopoulos, 2018). The ability to integrate financial insights with ESG criteria is now a defining skill for today's leaders, ensuring that organizational goals align with the principles of sustainable growth and performance excellence (Tarique and Schuler, 2010).

During our interviews with CEOs and financial authorities, we explored the impact of the dynamic context on executive leadership in public and private organizations. They underscored the critical importance of financial competency among CEOs and TMTs in forecasting the contextual impact on their organization's financial health (He and Harris, 2020). A CEO of a monetary authority highlighted the need for all top executives to be adept at assessing financial risks, ensuring readiness and resilience in response to structural and governance changes, especially considering new laws to implement environmental, strategic societal, and governance (ESG) practices and metrics (KPMG, 2022). The CEO remarked:

> Every executive must not only understand and approve financial statements but be strategic in crafting and implementing financial strategies to safeguard their organization's financial health. This is no longer just the job of the CFO or CEO—it's a shared responsibility across the organization (in-person interview communication, June 2019).

She emphasized that without financial fluency, executives would struggle to maintain accountability for the fiscal stability of their organization, particularly in high-stakes environments where scrutiny from shareholders, regulators, and the public is constant (Clark, Feiner, and Viehs, 2015).

This perspective was echoed by the chairman of Urban Escape, who linked the effectiveness of CEOs directly to their ability to anticipate and navigate the financial implications of their decisions (Jensen, 2010). He stressed that a CEO's credibility with shareholders and the board hinges on their financial acumen and readiness to defend every number on the balance sheet. These insights highlight the need for strategic financial intelligence, a more advanced financial competency of the TMT collectively and of the individual members and the CEO, strategically integrating an understanding of the broader contextual forces shaping financial outcomes (Pfeffer and Sutton, 2006). Strategic financial intelligence ensures that all executives—not just the CFO—are equipped to lead with financial acumen that is strategically aligned with both internal organizational goals and external environmental pressures (Mintzberg, Ahlstrand, and Lampel, 2005).

Defining Strategic Financial Intelligence: A Holistic Approach to Financial Literacy in Dynamic Context

Strategic financial intelligence represents an advanced leadership competency that transcends traditional financial literacy by equipping executives, both in financial and non-financial roles, with the ability to interpret, anticipate, and strategically respond to financial risks and opportunities within a broader organizational and contextual framework. Unlike conventional financial acumen, which primarily focuses on technical expertise in financial reporting and risk assessment, strategic financial intelligence integrates economic, geopolitical, and organizational dimensions to foster strategic foresight and resilience (Porter and Heppelmann, 2017; Kaplan and Norton, 2004).

This holistic approach leverages key components of the context matrix and the Hybrid Strategic Contextual Leadership framework, ensuring that financial decision-making is aligned with broader leadership dynamic capabilities in pluralistic, multicultural, and complex environments. Within the strategic contextual leadership paradigm, financial intelligence is not an isolated function but an embedded competency that influences corporate governance, investment decisions, and risk mitigation strategies. This integrated perspective enables executives to bridge the gap between financial performance and sustainable strategic objectives, ensuring that financial decisions support long-term organizational stability rather than short-term profitability alone (Eccles, Ioannou, and Serafeim, 2014).

Optimizing TMT Effectiveness in Dual Balancing Acts Through Strategic Financial Intelligence

Strategic financial intelligence enhances the effectiveness of TMTs and CEOs in managing their dual balancing acts: leading both externally (interfacing with markets, stakeholders, and global financial conditions) and internally (ensuring operational efficiency and sustainable financial practices). At Echo Capital, an investment holding organization, the robust financial intelligence within the leadership structure significantly impacted organizational success. TMTs with high financial acumen effectively navigated market volatilities, optimized capital allocation, and aligned financial and investment strategies with broader corporate goals, ultimately fostering resilience in a highly dynamic global environment (Damodaran, 2012).

A key differentiator in Echo Capital's approach was the ability of its leadership team to integrate financial intelligence with contextual insights, ensuring that investment decisions were not solely based on quantitative financial models but also on qualitative assessments of regulatory shifts, geopolitical risks, and cultural expectations. This strategic alignment enabled the company to anticipate economic downturns, mitigate risks, and sustain long-term growth—critical competencies for financial leadership in pluralistic and emerging market environments (Khanna, Palepu, and Sinha, 2005).

By fostering financial intelligence across all TMT roles, organizations can cultivate an integrated strategic approach to leadership, enhancing decision-making across functions. This interdisciplinary financial competency is particularly crucial in aligning corporate financial strategies with evolving ESG (environmental, social, and governance) practices and metrics, ensuring compliance with global regulatory expectations and stakeholder demands (Friede, Busch, and Bassen, 2015). By embedding financial intelligence within strategic leadership frameworks, organizations can drive sustainable economic success, improve stakeholder confidence, and enhance long-term financial resilience in an increasingly complex and interconnected world.

4.6.1 Echo Capital: A Model of Collective Strategic Financial Intelligence

Echo Capital stands as a remarkable entity in the global financial landscape, operating as a public investment and financial holding organization with extensive international reach. With a robust base of 22,000 public shareholders, Echo Capital operates under stringent financial regulatory frameworks while managing investments across major global markets including the US, United Kingdom, the Netherlands, Middle East and beyond. Positioned as a global player, Echo Capital is dedicated to navigating the complexities of international finance to deliver strong and sustainable returns. The organization's strategic operations across diverse geographical locales underscore its capacity to harness global opportunities and mitigate associated risks, thus securing substantial benefits for its shareholders and investors. This global footprint not only amplifies Echo Capital's influence in the financial sector but also showcases its adeptness in adapting to varied market dynamics and regulatory environments.

Echo Capital, with a shareholder base exceeding 20,000, operates in a complex financial landscape where strategic leadership is crucial for maintaining stability and growth. Given the diversity of its investor base and the complexity of global financial markets, the company relies on its top management team to integrate deep market insights and an extensive international network into its decision-making processes. This collective expertise enables Echo Capital to assess and respond to evolving economic conditions, regulatory shifts, and investment opportunities across multiple jurisdictions.

By systematically aligning its operational strategies with established industry benchmarks, Echo Capital enhances its transparency, governance, and risk management practices, critical factors in sustaining long-term financial stability. The company's emphasis on institutional accountability ensures that its financial practices remain in accordance with international regulatory frameworks, reinforcing trust among investors and stakeholders. This structured approach allows Echo Capital to adapt effectively to market uncertainties while maintaining a steady focus on sustainable financial performance.

Echo Capital provides a compelling case study of how an investment holding organization can cultivate comprehensive financial intelligence across its entire top management team, ensuring alignment and strategic agility. The company's commitment to financial excellence extends beyond the traditional remit of the CFO, requiring all TMT members to contribute meaningfully to the organization's financial health and strategic direction, particularly in response to evolving environmental, social, and governance (ESG) regulations in the capital markets.

Echo Capital's CFO leads the budgeting process, managing everything from forecasting to cash flow oversight. However, as an investment holding company, the role demands not only financial acumen but also a deep understanding of investment strategy, market dynamics, and risk management. This goes beyond traditional accounting, as the complexities of managing diverse investments, funds and portfolios require insight into strategic asset allocation and the broader financial environment. Despite the CFO's financial leadership role, the Chief Investment Officer and his team often perceived her as a glorified accountant If the CFO was perceived as not good enough, the broader challenge was taking shape where top management teams heading other departments like technology, human resources, and communications also had to enter a steep learning curve, particularly in the context of investment management and the new ESG rules affecting investments operations.

Recognizing the critical need for strategic financial intelligence across all leadership roles, Echo Capital's CEO and COO placed strong emphasis on ensuring robust investment processes, financial accuracy and compliance with the new contextual, societal and governance mandates, which had far-reaching implications for their investment operations. All employees, whether in investment or other functions, were expected to contribute to maintaining the company's reputation, building shareholder trust, and adhering to stringent financial reporting standards.

Frank, the Chief Technology Officer, was tasked with leading a project to develop a digital platform for the fund managers in the public market team. While Frank had a robust background in technology from his experience with blue-chip companies, he lacked the latest investment knowledge and was unfamiliar with the intricacies of funds management. The success of the project relied on close collaboration between Frank's technology team and the investment team, as both needed to understand the impact of implementing the new investment software and system to achieve the organization's robust investment process. To implement the new technology, a task force was created, led by the Chief Operations Officer and comprising members from finance, technology, risk, and administration, to ensure smooth project execution. The key unifying factor for this group was financial competence. Regardless of their department, each team member needed to understand the financial implications of the investment processes, as well as the regulatory impact of ESG compliance, to contribute effectively. Frank's team, for example, had to grasp how the fund management operations worked under the new ESG guidelines to assess which software met their needs and complied with the governance regulations.

Strategic collective financial intelligence, in this case, served as the critical bridge between departments, fostering collaboration and ensuring the successful development of the digital platform. This cross-functional approach demonstrates the necessity of financial competence across all TMT roles in investment holding companies. By ensuring that every department—from technology to human resources had a solid understanding of the investment processes, Echo Capital aligned its operations with both its strategic goals and regulatory requirements, particularly the ESG mandates reshaping the capital markets.

Echo Capital's approach to TMT strategic financial intelligence illustrates how organizations can enhance their strategic decision-making and operational efficiency by equipping their leadership teams with financial knowledge. This model not only ensures that each department's specific needs and challenges are integrated into the financial strategy but also empowers TMT members to act as strategic partners. TMT strategic financial intelligence ultimately supports the balancing acts of hybrid strategic contextual leadership between internal and external context, and realizes the ambition of sustainable performance.

Conclusion: Harnessing TMT Strategic Financial Intelligence for Future Growth

In conclusion, the practice of embedding strategic financial intelligence across all members of the top management team at Echo Capital cultivates a culture of shared accountability and strategic financial foresight. The comprehensive financial skill of the TMT ensures that Echo Capital is well prepared to navigate the complexities of global markets, adapt to regulatory changes, and seize innovation and agility. By integrating strategic financial intelligence into the core competencies of all TMT members, Echo Capital establishes a strong foundation for sustainable success and enhanced shareholder value.

Transitioning to Innovation: Next Frontier for TMTs

Building on the solid foundation of strategic financial intelligence, the next section of our discussion shifts emphasis to another critical dimension of TMT strategic capabilities: innovation and agility. In pluralistic multicultural organizations the ability to innovate in terms of leadership and execution is crucial more than ever to stay competitive and capitalizing on new market opportunities. The forthcoming section will explore how TMTs, equipped with a strategic understanding of financial and operational dynamics, are uniquely positioned to drive innovation and foster organizational agility. We will examine strategies that enable TMTs to proactively shape the future of their industries through innovative practices that strategically and contextually advance leadership.

4.7 Innovation and Agility: Strategic Growth and Contextual Mastery

Innovation and agility are not merely advantageous but essential competencies for top management teams (TMTs) and CEOs leading pluralistic, multicultural organizations. These entities face multifaceted challenges stemming from globalization, rapid technological advancements, evolving climate regulations, and heightened operational complexity. Effective navigation of this intricate landscape requires leaders to integrate both innovation and agility, two fundamental pillars of the Hybrid Strategic Contextual Leadership framework, to ensure adaptability and resilience amid continuous change (Tushman and O'Reilly, 1996; Teece, Peteraf, and Leih, 2016).

Pluralistic organizations operate within diverse stakeholder ecosystems, encompassing employees from varied cultural backgrounds, investors with distinct expectations, and customers across global markets. For example, a multinational financial institution must continuously innovate its financial products to meet diverse regulatory standards across different regions while simultaneously maintaining operational agility to adapt to volatile economic conditions and technological disruptions (Brown and Eisenhardt, 1997). A rigid approach to leadership and strategy in such environments can lead to stagnation, inefficiency, and a loss of competitive advantage.

Innovation as a Response to External and Internal Contexts

Within the context matrix, innovation is understood as a proactive response to both external and internal drivers. Externally, globalization and disruptive technological advancements necessitate continuous innovation in product development, service delivery, and business models (Christensen, Raynor, and McDonald, 2015). For instance, the automotive industry's shift towards electric vehicles (EVs) in response to climate policies and shifting consumer preferences highlights the necessity for technological innovation as a strategic imperative (Gans, 2016). Similarly, financial institutions' adoption of blockchain and AI-driven analytics illustrates how firms must innovate to remain competitive in a digital economy (Iansiti and Lakhani, 2020).

Internally, leaders must drive innovation within organizational structures, decision-making processes, and corporate culture to enhance efficiency and responsiveness. For example, companies that implement cross-functional, agile teams have demonstrated greater success in responding to market disruptions and accelerating product development cycles (Edmondson, 2018). At the leadership level, fostering an innovation-friendly culture – one that encourages experimentation, rapid iteration, and knowledge sharing – has been linked to sustained performance and long-term growth (Amabile and Pratt, 2016).

Agility: A Strategic Imperative for Navigating Market Dynamics

Agility, in contrast, is defined as the ability to pivot quickly and effectively in response to changing conditions. Within the context matrix, agility entails strategic preparedness, enabling TMTs to recalibrate their organizational strategies in response to market fluctuations, regulatory transformations, and technological shifts (Doz and Kosonen, 2010). The COVID-19 pandemic exemplified the necessity of organizational agility, as companies that swiftly adopted remote work technologies and digital business models outperformed competitors that were slower to adapt (Boin et al., 2020).

The Hybrid Strategic Contextual Leadership framework assists leaders in striking a balance between internal stability and external flexibility. This dual competency maintaining operational efficiency internally while simultaneously adapting to global shifts externally is essential for long-term sustainability (Winter, 2003). For example, Nike's ability to rapidly realign its supply chain in response to global manufacturing disruptions highlights how agility in logistics and procurement can safeguard business continuity while maintaining cost efficiency (Reeves and Deimler, 2011).

The case of Urban Escape (detailed in Box 4.1) illustrates how innovation and agility at the TMT level enable an organization to navigate market volatility and leadership transitions successfully. The company's ability to innovate internally by restructuring operations to enhance performance excellence while remaining agile externally, responding to real estate market fluctuations, was fundamental to its sustained success.

Urban Escape's leadership leveraged strategic contextual intelligence to interpret regulatory, economic, and market signals, enabling it to pivot investment strategies, adapt to evolving consumer trends, and optimize operational efficiencies. For example, when faced with increasing competition from co-working spaces, Urban Escape diversified its commercial real estate portfolio, integrating flexible and what is called cloud office models to attract a broader client base. This adaptive approach aligns with the principles of dynamic capabilities, where firms that sense, seize, and transform opportunities are better positioned for sustainable success (Teece, 2007).

In pluralistic environments, innovation and agility are more than buzzwords or merely strategic options but fundamental survival tools for TMTs and CEOs. Organizations that fail to embed these competencies within their leadership structures risk obsolescence in the face of technological disruptions, regulatory shifts, and competitive pressures. The Strategic Contextual Leadership framework, in conjunction with the context matrix, provides a structured approach for developing these capabilities, ensuring that leaders are equipped to navigate the complexities of global business environments while driving sustainable long-term growth.

Balancing Act 1: Leading Internally – Fostering Organizational Innovation and Flexibility

Consider the case of Urban Escape, a leading real estate developer undergoing a period of significant restructuring. With new leadership at the helm, the organization implemented agile project management methodologies to revamp its operational processes to achieve performance excellence. The CEO and TMT worked closely and encouraged collaboration between developments, finance, and operations, and human resources which not only sped up decision-making but also fostered a culture of experimentation, and mistakes were allowed without punitive repercussions.

This innovation focusing on internal context resulted in rapid iterations on project development models, allowing Urban Escape to adapt to shifting market conditions and customer preferences quickly. This ability to pivot, test new strategies, and course-correct was critical in maintaining the company's competitive edge and reputation in an oversaturated market. In addition, the strategic contextual intelligence, Urban Escape CEO's and TMT's agility was not just about reacting to change but actively driving it, aligning the internal organization with external trends such as smart city initiatives and sustainable urban development. Urban Escape and other organizations that are ambidextrous can exploit current capabilities while exploring new opportunities and are more likely to achieve sustained growth. Urban Escape exemplified this by embracing agile methodologies that allowed them to innovate internally while staying aligned with external market trends (O'Reilly and Tushman (2013).

TMT Balancing Act 2: Leading Externally – Navigating Global Market Dynamics with Agility and Innovation

Externally, innovation and agility are critical for TMTs to successfully navigate the fast-evolving landscape of global markets, new regulatory demands, and technological disruptions. Take the case of Echo Capital, where the introduction of ESG regulations required more than the compliance of the investment team but a strategic pivot across the entire organization. This example highlights how diverse backgrounds and expertise within TMTs, especially in multicultural organizations, can drive strategic agility by integrating global regulatory changes with internal innovation. Agility allowed Echo Capital to proactively shape its investment strategy, turning regulatory disruption into a business opportunity. Pluralistic organizations show that diversity within TMTs enhances their capacity to navigate uncertainties and capitalize on external opportunities (Certo et al., 2006; Blomkvist et al., 2017).

Innovation became not just a reaction to external changes but a tool for strategic market leadership.

Strategic and Contextual Implications

The need for innovation and agility is even more pronounced when contextualized within the broader framework of Hybrid Strategic Contextual Leadership. As global market forces, such as technological advancements and regulatory changes, continuously reshape industries, TMTs must integrate external market intelligence with internal adaptability. This is not merely about adopting the latest technology or innovation trends but about contextualizing these innovations to fit the unique demands of both the global environment and the internal organizational culture.

The case of Echo Capital vividly illustrates how the four strategic leadership imperatives are interconnected. When the Chief Technology Officer was tasked with rapidly implementing digital investment platforms and to account for ESG metrics, it became essential for the investment team to simultaneously reassess their portfolios through a sustainability lens. This situation highlighted the critical need for TMT agility and real-time innovation. The seamless coordination between the investment and technology teams, driven by their shared commitment to strategic financial intelligence, exemplifies the interplay between the strategic leadership imperatives. By leveraging innovation and agility, Echo Capital's TMT effectively advanced their strategic skills, demonstrating how these imperatives work together to navigate complex, dynamic organizational challenges and drive sustainable success. Twenty years ago, there was a call for TMTs engagement in "contextual ambidexterity," which has been considered the leadership buzz words (Gibson and Birkinshaw, 2004). In 2024, TMTs must simultaneously pursue short-term performance goals while also innovating for long-term sustainability, ensuring that their internal structures are agile enough to adapt to external changes.

4.7.1 Introduction to Vita Care: A Model of TMT Innovation and Agility in Private Healthcare

Founded in 2011 by international investors, Vita Care emerged as a pioneering private healthcare provider, setting new benchmarks in medical excellence and innovation. The organization's transformative journey took a significant turn in 2013 when it was acquired by Echo Capital, a major investment holding organization, indicating a new era of strategic expansion and enhanced operational capabilities. The strategic acquisition was underscored by a strong endorsement from societal leadership, which identified healthcare as a critical area for private investment. This policy aimed to elevate healthcare standards and foster a competitive, yet collaborative, healthcare environment. The chairman of Vita Care articulated this vision by stating, "Our country's leadership has pinpointed healthcare as a priority area for private investments, and the policy is working to raise standards" (in-person interview communication, June 2019).

Vita Care has adapted to the dynamic healthcare landscape, characterized by rapid advancements in medical technology and a strong focus on innovation. This adaptability is a testament to the organization's strategic alignment with the directives of the new regulatory body governing private healthcare providers. Insights from the CEO of the healthcare regulatory authority were instrumental in shaping Vita Care's strategic orientation, ensuring that the organization not only complies with but also excels in meeting regulatory expectations.

Under the leadership of its CEO, Adam, Vita Care has cultivated a multicultural and forward-thinking organizational culture that thrives on positive behavior, effective leadership, and sound business acumen. Adam describes Vita Care as "a multicultural hub grounded in positive behavior, effective leadership, sound business acumen, and forward-looking teams" (virtual interview communication, June 2020). This environment has been crucial in attracting international professionals and fostering a culture of continuous improvement and innovation.

Vita Care's commitment to maintaining high standards of healthcare is evident in its pursuit of international quality accreditations and dedication to performance excellence. The organization's strategic focus on innovation goes beyond merely adopting new technologies. It integrates these advancements into daily operations to enhance patient care and operational efficiency, and to comply with the international ESG standards for healthcare.

Amid rising competition from an influx of healthcare providers, Vita Care's TMT acted decisively to preserve its competitive edge and uphold its reputation for excellence. Recognizing the importance of swift, patient-centered services, the TMT harnessed its diverse expertise to drive technological advancements across all operational areas. This initiative enabled the introduction of a streamlined process for same-day pre-operative test results and one-day surgeries, allowing patients to safely leave the hospital within hours of their procedure. To support this, Vita Care revamped its clinics and pharmacies to ensure efficiency and a seamless patient experience. Additionally, the TMT undertook a comprehensive re-evaluation of roles, especially as the corporate members outnumbered the medical TMT.

Corporate executives took on expanded responsibilities, leading the integration of new technologies into non-medical processes, further demonstrating their adaptability and strategic importance. By embracing innovation and agility, Vita Care positioned itself to meet new demands and deliver enhanced services while showcasing a model of integrated leadership in healthcare. One of the key aspects of Vita Care's innovative strategy was the optimization and digitalization of its operations. This included the introduction of advanced technology platforms that streamlined processes, such as enabling patients scheduled for surgery to complete all required tests with results available to surgeons in one day. Additionally, Vita Care introduced the most advanced imaging and scanning equipment in every location, ensuring that even patients in remote areas had access to top-tier diagnostic services. The third and most innovative was to include multinational patient service centers, where multinational patients can choose where to go. These technological advancements were not just about upgrading systems but also transforming service delivery to enhance patient outcomes and operational efficiency.

Furthermore, the innovation at Vita Care extended beyond merely adopting new technologies; it was *TMT's* agility in leveraging the investment expertise of their shareholder, Echo Capital, that truly set them apart.

Recognizing their own limitations in navigating complex acquisitions, Vita Care's TMT strategically tapped into Echo Capital's investment experience, allowing them to pursue high-impact mergers and acquisitions effectively. By drawing on this expertise, Vita Care successfully identified and acquired advanced clinics that specialized in cutting-edge medical services, such as complex neurosurgery, which significantly reduced surgery time and patient recovery periods—an offering that few other healthcare providers in the country could match.

This strategic partnership with shareholders demonstrated Vita Care's agility in filling capability gaps, enhancing its service portfolio, and driving innovation within the organization. TMT's ability to leverage external investment experience alongside internal capabilities was pivotal in executing these high-stakes transactions with precision and foresight.

The results of these strategic initiatives were outstanding. Vita Care not only achieved performance excellence and earned prestigious international accreditations but also increased its shareholder value by a remarkable tenfold. Moreover, by positioning itself as a frontrunner in delivering advanced medical services, the organization attracted and retained top international medical talent, solidifying its reputation as a leading healthcare provider in the region. This case illustrates how the integration of innovation, agility, and leveraging external expertise can drive both immediate and long-term success in a complex and dynamic industry.

In conclusion, the Vita Care case reinforces the critical impact of TMT innovation and agility on operational excellence leading to sustainable organizational success. It demonstrates that in the complex and competitive arena of healthcare, having a TMT capable of leveraging technology and partnerships is essential. This case serves as a robust example for other organizations in similar multicultural and pluralistic settings, illustrating that strategic innovation driven by a skilled and diverse management team can lead to substantial advancements and industry leadership.

4.8 Key Takeaways from Chapter 4: Strategic Leadership Imperatives for Sustainable Success

This chapter has outlined four interrelated competencies essential for TMTs to achieve sustainable success in pluralistic and multicultural organizations: strategic contextual intelligence, integrative communication, strategic financial intelligence, TMT innovation and agility.

These strategic leadership imperatives do not function in isolation. While we introduce those competencies to start with individually, they are deeply interconnected, reinforcing one another to create a cohesive and resilient leadership framework. The case studies of Urban Escape, Echo Capital, Medi Care, and Vita Care have demonstrated how the four strategic contextual leadership competencies are effectively applied and interconnected in real-world strategic leadership action, illustrating how TMTs navigate complex, high-stakes environments.

TMT's ability to adapt to external forces, such as new regulatory frameworks and technological advancements, while fostering a culture of internal innovation is the linchpin of long-term viability. The examples of Echo Capital, Urban Escape and Vita Care show that when innovation is approached strategically, it becomes more than just a reactionary tool; it transforms organizations into proactive leaders capable of shaping market trends.

4.9 Reflective Activity: Applying Strategic Leadership Imperatives in Your Organization

This activity is designed to help TMTs and CEOs critically assess how well their organizations are integrating the four strategic imperatives and to identify areas for improvement, application, and alignment with future challenges.

Step 1: Self-Assessment – Where Does Your TMT Stand?
Consider your current leadership environment and answer the following questions:

1. Strategic Contextual Intelligence
How well does your leadership team analyze and integrate external factors (geopolitical, regulatory, economic)?

Do you regularly update strategies based on macro and micro-environmental trends?

Are you tracking and leveraging competitive intelligence to maintain strategic alignment?

2. Integrative Communication
How effectively does your TMT align across diverse cultural, functional, and strategic perspectives?

Are internal communications transparent, structured, and inclusive to reduce misalignment?

Do you have structured forums for cross-functional collaboration, ensuring clarity in decision-making?

3. Strategic Financial Intelligence

Are financial strategies aligned with long-term sustainability, or is decision-making too focused on short-term returns?

How effectively does your organization manage financial risks while capitalizing on market opportunities?

Are you integrating ESG (environmental, social, and governance) metrics into financial decision-making?

4. Innovation and Agility

Does your organization have a structured process for fostering innovation?

Are new market trends and technological shifts being proactively integrated into strategic planning?

Is your leadership team agile enough to pivot quickly, or does decision-making face bottlenecks?

Step 2: Actionable Insights – What Can Your TMT Improve?

Reflect on your self-assessment responses and select two areas that require immediate attention.

For each selected area, answer the following:

What specific challenge is my organization facing in this area?

What concrete steps can we take to improve?

What leadership behaviors do we need to reinforce?

Who in the TMT should take ownership of this improvement initiative?

What measurable impact would we expect from this change?

Step 3: Scenario Planning – Applying Lessons from Case Studies

Using the cases of Urban Escape, Echo Capital, Medi Care, and Vita Care, analyze how your organization can apply similar strategic responses to its challenges.

If your challenge is integrating agility into decision-making:

How did Vita Care restructure its TMT to allow for faster execution?

Could your organization redefine leadership roles or decision-making authority?

If your challenge is fostering a culture of innovation:

How did Echo Capital leverage investment intelligence to drive innovation?

Are there underutilized financial or intellectual resources in your organization that could be mobilized for innovation?

If your challenge is contextual intelligence and strategic adaptability:

How did Urban Escape align its strategy with external economic shifts?

What contextual factors should your leadership team be analyzing more rigorously?

Step 4: Action Planning – Moving from Reflection to Execution

Identify 1–2 strategic changes your organization will implement in the next six months.

Assign accountability – Who in your TMT will lead this initiative?

Set success metrics – How will you measure the impact of these changes?

Schedule follow-ups – Ensure leadership reviews progress in structured quarterly meetings.

Conclusion: A Forward-Looking Leadership Agenda

The four strategic leadership imperatives explored in this chapter – strategic contextual intelligence, integrative communication, strategic financial intelligence, and TMT innovation and agility – are not abstract theories but practical competencies that leaders must internalize, operationalize, and continuously refine.

By applying the reflective activity above, leaders can begin the process of embedding these strategic imperatives into their leadership DNA, ensuring their organizations remain resilient, competitive, and sustainable in the face of evolving global challenges.

In Chapter 5, we examine how CEOs and TMTs can balance the pursuit of immediate results with the need for long-term viability and resilience in an environment where economic, social, and environmental factors are continually evolving. Chapter 5 will build on these strategic contextual leadership imperatives by redefining what constitutes success in modern pluralistic and multicultural organizations. We will explore how a real case of multicultural pluralistic organization can transcend conventional performance metrics to embrace a broader definition of success that includes corporate responsibility, environmental stewardship, and social engagement. This broader perspective will help organizations and strategic leaders align with evolving stakeholder and societal expectations, ensuring sustainable success in the face of dynamic global challenges.

Chapter 5
Charting Sustainable Success in Pluralistic Multicultural Organizations

At the start of this study in 2018 the external context factors impacting organizations and strategic leadership included the country's dynamic context such as economy, industry regulations, culture, and societal leadership expectations. In 2024, we revisited our participating organizations and asked the participants the same questions to update how they define their organizational outcomes in the current context after the pandemic and amid rapid technological advancement. Sustainability and sustainable success have now been highlighted in alignment with the growing societal leadership expectations.

Furthermore, we expanded our investigation to include a new organization that epitomizes the characteristics of a multinational and pluralistic entity. This addition has enriched our understanding of how diverse organizations are navigating the complex interplay of context and strategy to achieve sustainable success. This chapter will examine these insights, offering a comprehensive view of the dynamic factors that influence strategic leadership in today's globalized business environment.

Building upon the strategic and contextual leadership imperatives explored in Chapter 4, in this chapter we analyze the complexities of defining sustainable success as an outcome in multicultural and pluralistic organizations. The prior chapter emphasized the importance of strategic contextual intelligence, integrative communication, strategic financial intelligence, and innovation and agility as pivotal components for achieving performance excellence. These competencies are crucial not only for immediate organizational achievements but also for laying the groundwork for long-term sustainable success.

The concept of sustainable growth has been widely accepted among nations, organizations, and individuals alike (Ranängen et al., 2018). The Brundtland Commission defines sustainable growth as development that meets the needs of the present generation without compromising the ability of future generations to meet theirs (WCED, 1987). The global sustainability aims include social growth and advancement while living within global boundaries and without undermining the needs of future generations, in addition to defining what are the elements of economic and social sustainable outcomes (Hallencreutz, Deleryd, and Fundin, 2020).

In this chapter we propose the concept of sustainable success based on the external context, the organizational context, strategic leadership effectiveness, and sustainable organizational outcomes. While organizational effectiveness and leadership are crucial, a sustainable context is essential for organizations to achieve lasting success. This chapter explores the foundational elements necessary for achieving sustainable success within the dynamic sphere of pluralistic and multicultural organizations. We

https://doi.org/10.1515/9783111382722-006

will navigate through two fundamental areas of sustainable success by breaking down the contextual elements into two aspects: sustainable economic outcomes and sustainable cultural outcomes.

5.1 Deconstructing Sustainable Success

Deconstructing sustainable success is based on the comprehensive implementation of the SCL framework that integrates economic, cultural, and societal dimensions. Strategic leadership skills defined in Chapter 4 are essential for navigating the complex landscape of pluralistic organizations, fostering a sustainable economy and culture. The insights from our case studies highlight an additional critical outcome of strategic contextual leadership, achieving sustainable outcomes. As we examine how the strategic contextual leadership skills, we discussed in Chapter 4, are vital for leaders aiming to master the art of leading pluralistic multicultural organizations towards sustainable success.

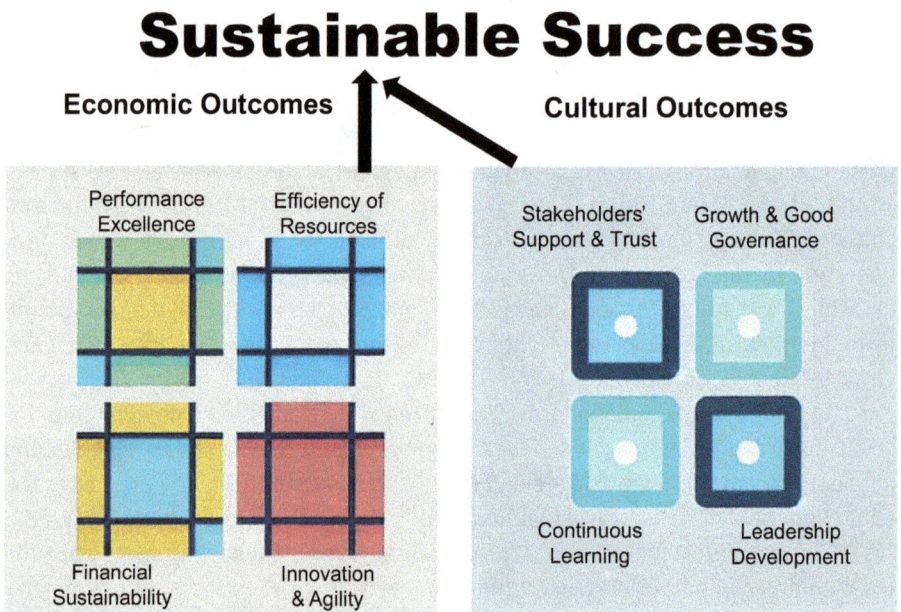

Figure 5.1: Multiple Case Sustainable Success Framework.
This figure presents the Sustainable Success Framework developed from the multiple case study. It identifies two interconnected dimensions essential for sustainable success in pluralistic multicultural organizations. The economic dimension focuses on performance excellence, resource efficiency, financial sustainability, and innovation and agility, while the cultural dimension emphasizes stakeholder trust, good governance, continuous learning, and leadership development.

Figure 5.1 introduces the sustainable success framework, designed to decode what constitutes sustainable success in pluralistic multicultural organizations. This framework defines sustainable success as a balanced interplay between two key dimensions with each a set of defined components: sustainable economic outcomes and sustainable cultural outcomes. By addressing both dimensions, the framework offers a holistic approach that enables organizations to achieve not only financial resilience but also social and cultural relevance. In the following sections, we will explore each outcome in detail, highlighting how they collectively support sustainable success in complex, pluralistic environments.

5.2 Sustainable Economic Outcomes

A sustainable economy is foundational for any organization's long-term success. Strategic leadership plays a crucial role in fostering an economy that thrives on performance excellence and emphasizes resource efficiency, innovative financial strategies, innovation and agility. The key components of a sustainable economic outcome include performance excellence, innovative financial sustainability, innovation and agility.

5.2.1 Performance Excellence

In the previous chapters, our case study insights consistently demonstrated that resource and process efficiency is a critical determinant of performance excellence, particularly in pluralistic and multicultural organizations. However, the findings from our five case studies reveal a notable shift in how sustainable success is perceived by executives and TMTs. When participants were asked to define successful and sustainable outcomes, *performance excellence* emerged as the most significant indicator of long-term sustainability, even surpassing positive financial returns in financial services and investment organizations (Al Bachir, 2022). This underscores a broader paradigm shift, where organizations increasingly recognize that financial performance alone is insufficient to ensure sustained growth and competitive advantage.

Performance excellence, as identified in our case studies, is not merely about profitability but a holistic measure encompassing operational efficiency, stakeholder trust, and long-term value creation (Kaplan and Norton, 2004). This aligns with contemporary strategic management research, which emphasizes that organizations achieving high-performance standards through optimized processes, governance, and leadership alignment tend to outperform competitors in both financial and non-financial metrics (Neely, 2005).

Case Study Insights Performance Excellence

In financial services and investment organizations, performance excellence was regarded as more crucial than short-term financial returns. Participants emphasized that sustained high performance marked by transparency, governance, and strategic risk management was a stronger predictor of long-term viability than immediate profitability. This finding is supported by research showing that organizations with a culture of continuous improvement achieve greater long-term financial stability (Eccles, Ioannou, and Serafeim, 2014).

In healthcare and real estate development, performance excellence was defined through the quality and efficiency of service delivery, regulatory compliance, and innovation-driven competitive positioning. For example, Vita Care's commitment to process innovation and regulatory alignment allowed it to maintain a leading market position despite economic and competitive pressures.

Across all five cases, performance excellence was linked to sustainable leadership, operational agility, and the ability to align organizational strategies with evolving external demands. Participants consistently highlighted that process efficiency, human capital development, and stakeholder engagement were key enablers of sustainable success, echoing findings from strategic leadership research (Porter and Kramer, 2011).

Embedding Sustainability into the Ethos of Performance Excellence

Traditionally, operations management has been centered around efficiency of resources, leadership effectiveness and financial performance. However, as businesses confront increasing external pressures from governments, investors, and societal expectations, the definition of excellence is evolving. Pluralistic organizations must integrate sustainability as a fundamental dimension of performance excellence, rather than viewing it as secondary compliance-driven initiative (Hart and Milstein, 2014).

The shift toward sustainability driven performance is fueled by growing regulatory frameworks, investor diligence, and societal demands for corporate responsibilities and environmental, social and governance criteria, as discussed in Chapter 4. This emergence of new regulatory criteria has reinforced that in addition to financial profitability contextual leadership and meeting the societal expectations are necessary to achieve long-terms sustainable organizational success (Porter and Kramer, 2011).

Failing to embed sustainability into performance excellence metrics risks regulatory penalties, reputational damage, and declining investors confidence (Grewal, Hauptmann, and Serafeim, 2020).

The shift toward sustainable performance is a strategic imperative, aligning with the sustainable development goals (SDGs) for 2030 set by the United Nations. This broader perspective requires organizations to redefine their performance metrics, ensuring that environmental and social considerations are embedded in their operational strategies alongside economic objectives. Instead of treating sustainability as an isolated function, leading organizations see it as a driver of long-term competitive advantage, enabling them to build resilient, adaptable, and ethically responsible business models (Hallencreutz and Fundin, 2020).

From Operational Efficiency to Sustainable Performance Excellence

Recent advancements in strategic leadership and operations management suggest that performance excellence is no longer just about optimizing internal processes. It is about creating long-term value through sustainable decision-making (Wu and Pagell, 2011) reinforces that excellence must be assessed holistically, considering:

- Economic Performance: Profitability, operational efficiency, and resource optimization.
- Environmental Performance: Carbon footprint reduction, supply chain sustainability, and responsible sourcing.
- Social Performance: Employee well-being, community impact, and corporate responsibility.

All participating organizations in our case studies confirmed that they have introduced sustainable performance excellence measurement tools to help TMTs make informed strategic decisions, balancing short-term business goals with long-term sustainability imperatives. These tools provide quantifiable insights into the trade-offs between economic efficiency and ecological/social responsibilities, ensuring that sustainability becomes an intrinsic part of operational excellence.

Strategic Leadership and Performance-Excellence Nexus

Strategic leaders realized that achieving sustainable performance excellence demands more than process improvements. It requires a systemic transformation in leadership ambition, operational design, and corporate ethos. The case studies demonstrate that TMTs that integrate sustainability into their core strategic frameworks benefit from:

Enhanced Competitiveness: Organizations that embed sustainability into performance frameworks often outperform their peers in market differentiation and stakeholder trust (Eccles, Ioannou, and Serafeim, 2014).

Stronger Dynamic Capabilities: Sustainable businesses are better equipped to adapt to regulatory shifts, consumer expectations, and technological advancements, ensuring longevity (Teece, 2007).

Optimized Resource Efficiency: Innovations such as green sourcing, circular economy models, and carbon footprint assessments can drive operational efficiency and long-term cost savings (Mangla et al., 2020).

Improved Transparency and Collaboration: Organizations committed to sustainability excellence foster stronger relationships with investors, regulators, and supply chain partners, ensuring greater alignment with global sustainability goals (Bansal and DesJardine, 2014).

Implementation of Performance Excellence to Achieve Sustainable Success

Despite progress in sustainable business practices, the transition from short-term operational efficiency to long-term sustainability performance remains complex. TMTs must adopt a systemic and holistic approach that goes beyond compliance and isolated initiatives.

Insights from the case studies included the following key steps for integrating *performance excellence* include:

- Embedding sustainability into leadership KPIs (key performance indicators), ensuring that TMTs and executives are accountable for both financial and sustainability performance metrics.
- Redesigning supply chain operations to prioritize environmentally responsible sourcing and circular economy principles (DP World).
- Building a culture of sustainable performance excellence, where continuous improvement, technological innovation, and dynamic capabilities drive both competitive advantage and responsible leadership.

As demonstrated in our case study organizations, those that embrace sustainability as part of their performance excellence ethos are better positioned to navigate global economic complexities, regulatory demands, and shifting stakeholder expectations. They move beyond short-term gains, creating enduring value for their organizations, industries, and broader society.

5.2.2 Efficiency of Resources and Processes to Achieve Economic Outcomes

Optimal use of resources is fundamental to sustainability. CEOs and TMTs need to implement practices that minimize waste, enhance productivity, and ensure that resources are used responsibly. This includes adopting advanced technologies and sustainable practices that reduce environmental impact (Porter and Kramer, 2006). Furthermore, the cross-case findings in our study highlighted that the efficiency of resources and processes was the most important indicator of CEOs' leadership effectiveness. Efficient resource utilization means ensuring that all assets, including human talent, financial capital, and technological tools, are strategically aligned to support organizational goals. For example, in the case of Echo Capital, their TMT optimized their investment in technology and human resources by ensuring every department member, regardless of their functional role, possessed financial competence. This approach not only minimized redundancy but also ensured that all resources were effectively contributing to the organization's overall strategy. By implementing cross-functional collaboration and financial intelligence training, Echo Capital maximized the potential of their teams, resulting in higher productivity and cost savings.

Similarly, in the Vita Care case, TMT efficiently leveraged the expertise of their shareholders to access specialized knowledge and resources that were otherwise beyond their internal capacity. By tapping into Echo Capital's experience, Vita Care didn't have to duplicate efforts or waste resources building new capabilities from scratch. Instead, they efficiently acquired advanced clinics that offered specialized services, allowing them to expand their operations without unnecessary expenditures, achieving superior performance in a shorter timeframe.

Efficiency of Resources to Achieve Sustainable Economic Outcomes

The result of our study showed that the efficiency of resources, especially the effective performance alignment and support of the TMTs, is a major indicator of performance excellence. The significance of efficient human resources and optimized processes are pivotal contributors to achieving sustainability in various industries. Human resources play a critical role in driving sustainable outcomes. Efficient processes ensure that the right talent is recruited, developed, and retained, contributing to an organization's overall sustainability. Effective performance management strategies, continuous training and development, and employee engagement are essential for fostering a culture of sustainability. Jabbour et al. (2019) emphasize that integrating sustainability into HR practices enhances organizational performance and contributes to long-term success. Moreover, adopting sustainable management aligns employees' goals with the organization's sustainability objectives, fostering a unified approach to achieving sustainable outcomes. The core processes for achieving efficiency of resources are:

Strategic Human Resource Management: Talent acquisition ensuring the right skills align with the organizational long-term sustainable performance excellence, sustainable objectives and outcomes (Renwick, Redman, and Maguire, 2013). Upskilling teams for continuous learning and development (Garavan, McCarthy, and Morely, 2016; Bartton and Gold, 2017). Leadership development to prepare future ready leaders who can integrate sustainable success objectives in their decision-making (Jabbour, 2019).

Performance management and accountability: Strategic performance management systems help organizations optimize processes with strategic direction, objectives alignment, feedback and continuous improvement (Kaplan and Norton, 2004; Neely, 2005; Eccles and Serafeim, 2013).

Sustainable supply chain resources management: Pluralistic multicultural organizations are expected to adopt sustainable supply chain models that ensure operational efficiency while reducing environmental and social risks (Seuring and Muller,

2008). Ethical sourcing and supplier collaboration ensure material circular economy initiatives for resource optimization and minimization of impact on climate (Lieder and Rashid, 2016).

Financial and Strategic Resource Allocation: Efficient financial and resource management is essential for balancing profitability with long-term sustainability objectives (Friede, Busch, and Bassen, 2015).

Optimizing business processes is particularly vital for attaining sustainability, as it enhances operational efficiency, reduces waste, and minimizes environmental impact. In healthcare, for example, process efficiency contributes directly to reducing resource consumption and improving service delivery (Gaustad et al., 2018).

To explore how effective process management contributes to sustainability, we asked participating companies across real estate, financial services, healthcare, and international ports about their approach. While each sector faces unique challenges, process optimization emerged as a universal enabler of sustainability across all industries

In Medi Care, for instance, the process optimization undertaken by the Group CEO with the aim of reducing the 8000 operational processes to less than a 1000 was a strategic target. The TMT ensured that medical and administrative operations were aligned, despite the complexities of transitioning from a public to a private organization. By integrating advanced technology systems and adopting lean management principles, they managed to reduce operational costs and improve patient care, which directly contributed to the organization's performance excellence.

At Urban Escape, efficiency in processes was demonstrated through their agile project management practices. The TMT recognized the importance of flexibility and responsiveness, implementing a process-driven approach that allowed them to adapt to changing market conditions and stakeholder demands quickly. This efficiency in operations led to timely project completions, reduced costs, and enhanced their reputation for delivering high-quality real estate developments.

The case studies reinforce that achieving performance excellence is not just about having the right resources but also about using them efficiently and ensuring that processes are streamlined to achieve sustainable financial outcomes. Whether it's through optimizing talent, leveraging financial intelligence, or implementing agile management practices, the efficient use of resources and processes enables organizations to maximize their performance and maintain a competitive edge. This is a fundamental component of sustainable economic success in complex and rapidly changing business landscapes (Porter and Kramer, 2011).

These examples reinforce that achieving performance excellence is not solely about having access to resources it is about using them efficiently. Whether through talent optimization, financial intelligence, or agile management, the ability to streamline operations enhances competitive advantage. This efficiency also supports sustainable financial outcomes, a fundamental driver of long-term organizational success in complex and dynamic business environments (Porter and Kramer, 2011).

5.2.3 Financial Sustainability

While profitability and positive financial returns remain essential, they alone are insufficient for achieving sustainable outcomes. Financial sustainability is critical in ensuring that organizations remain competitive and resilient while aligning financial performance with long-term sustainability objectives.

1. Developing long-term financial strategies that support sustainable growth and risk management
Long-term financial strategies are essential for sustainable corporate growth as they align financial planning with risk management to ensure business resilience (Epstein and Buhovac, 2014). Organizations that integrate sustainability into their financial decision-making frameworks can achieve greater stakeholder trust and long-term value creation (Freeman, Harrison, and Zyglidopoulos, 2018). Additionally, financial management best practices emphasize the need for strategic capital deployment to enhance profitability while mitigating risks (Brigham and Ehrhardt, 2021).

2. Ensuring financial stability through robust forecasting and strategic capital allocation
Financial stability depends on the ability of firms to forecast future economic trends and allocate capital strategically (Damodaran, 2012). Effective forecasting techniques and data-driven decision-making enable companies to maintain a strong financial position and mitigate risks associated with market volatility (Brealey, Myers, and Allen, 2020). Furthermore, sustainable financial practices focus on long-term profitability by balancing investment risks with stable revenue streams (Koller, Goedhart, and Wessels, 2020).

3. Exploring innovative financial instruments that enable sustainable investment and corporate longevity
Innovative financial instruments, such as green bonds and social impact bonds, have emerged as viable solutions for companies seeking to finance sustainability projects (World Bank Group, 2018). The adoption of sustainable finance mechanisms has been shown to enhance corporate resilience and investor confidence (Ghosh and Nanda, 2022). Research further indicates that integrating environmental, social, and governance (ESG) factors into financial strategies leads to long-term financial outperformance (Clark, Feiner, and Viehs, 2015).

Corporate Governance and Compliance: Sustainable corporate governance practices are crucial for achieving long-term organizational sustainability, influencing investor confidence, corporate reputation, and regulatory compliance (Bansal and Des-

Jardine, 2014). ESG integration – embedding environmental, social, and governance criteria into corporate reporting and decision-making (Eccles et al., 2014).

Recent studies emphasize the growing role of financial technologies (fintech), blockchain technology, and alternative financing mechanisms in enhancing financial stability and performance (Beck, Chen, Lin, and Song, 2016). These tools empower organizations to navigate financial complexities, optimize liquidity, and enhance risk management strategies.

Our case studies further highlight that financial instability often triggers CEO transitions and unintended TMT disruptions leading to uncertainty and decreased performance. This underscores the critical role of financial innovation in maintaining strategic continuity and leadership stability.

5.2.4 Innovation and Agility

Effective leadership fosters a culture of continuous improvement, ensuring that excellence is embedded into strategic planning. Leaders influence this transformation by promoting data-driven decision-making, fostering agility, and encouraging innovation (Brynjolfsson and McAfee, 2014). Innovation and technology play a transformative role in financial strategy, equipping organizations with tools to optimize capital structures, enhance liquidity, and improve adaptability to market fluctuations (Demirgüç-Kunt, Klapper, Singer, and Van Oudheusden, 2015).

Financial innovation enables:
- Sustainable investment strategies that integrate financial returns with environmental and social impact (Bocken, Short, Rana, and Evans, 2014).
- Agility is achieved by deploying technology-driven efficiency, reducing operational costs and increasing transparency in financial transactions and risk management.
- Fintech adoption, streamlining payment systems, lending structures, and financial forecasting tools.

Our case studies demonstrate real-world applications of financial innovation, such as:
- Fintech solutions at Echo Capital, optimizing risk assessment and digital transactions.
- Blockchain technology at Urban Escape, enhancing transparency in real estate financing.
- Alternative financing models at Medi Care, securing sustainable investment for expansion.

These financial innovations allowed organizations to maintain financial stability while aligning investment decisions with long-term sustainability. For TMTs, forecasting and adapting financial strategies is critical for sustaining competitive advantage and achieving sustainable success.

Participating organizations in our case study displayed that successfully implemented agile methodologies accelerated the development and delivery of innovative solutions, improving both operational efficiency and long-term sustainability. For instance, a leading healthcare provider adopted agile project management, expediting the deployment of patient-centered healthcare solutions. This strategic innovation not only enhanced service delivery but also demonstrated the practical impact of agility in complex organizational structures.

As Eisenhardt and Martin (2000) highlight, dynamic capabilities enable organizations to navigate market complexity by rapidly reconfiguring resources and processes. TMTs must continuously monitor external environments, anticipate industry shifts, and refine financial and operational strategies accordingly. This proactive approach ensures that organizations remain resilient, competitive, and capable of capitalizing on new opportunities.

5.3 Defining and Leading for Sustainable Cultural Outcomes

Creating a sustainable culture involves aligning with societal leadership expectations to meet environmental demands, acquire stakeholders' support, and ensure good governance. Strategic leaders must be attuned to the expectations of society and stakeholders. This involves understanding and addressing environmental concerns, promoting social responsibility, and ensuring that the organization contributes positively to the community. Strategic leadership imperatives are needed to champion good governance practices, transparency, and accountability (Hambrick and Quigley, 2015). This culture supports continuous learning and sustainable strategic leadership development, fostering an environment where sustainable success can thrive.

5.3.1 Acquiring Stakeholder Support: A Cornerstone of Sustainable Success

Sustainable success is not just about achieving immediate results but ensuring long-term viability and resilience in a continuously evolving context. Acquiring stakeholders' support and trust is essential for maintaining this sustainability in pluralistic multicultural organizations.

Stakeholders, including employees, management, investors, customers, suppliers, communities, and regulatory bodies, each bring different expectations and interests to the table. To achieve sustainable success, organizations must engage with these diverse groups effectively, demonstrating a commitment to their concerns and aligning with their values. This approach fosters trust and secures their ongoing support, which is crucial for sustaining organizational growth and resilience.

5.3.2 Growth and Good Governance

Sustainable growth requires robust governance structures to support ethical decision-making and risk management (Brown, Treviño, and Harrison, 2005). Corporate policies need to be aligned with long-term sustainability goals to ensure resilience. Metrics and reporting frameworks track progress in governance, environmental impact, and social contribution.

The case study results show that in pluralistic, multicultural organizations, sustainable outcomes include:

– TMT and CEO contextual intelligence driving performance excellence.
– TMT retention and alignment, ensuring strategic continuity.
– Strong shareholder support, reinforcing long-term financial and governance stability.
– Strategic leadership balancing financial growth with sustainable governance, embedding transparency, accountability, and ethical decision-making into corporate strategy.

Sustainable success intertwines with financial growth and sound governance practices. Balancing ambitious financial targets with the necessity for ethical governance, outlining how governance structures can support sustainable development. Additionally, we will explore effective metrics and reporting practices that track and communicate progress in these domains.

For example, Echo Capital's focus on sustainable processes, such as transparent financial reporting, risk management, and employee initiatives, showcases how aligning organizational practices with stakeholder expectations can enhance reputation and trust. By prioritizing transparency, Echo Capital met stakeholders' informational needs and reinforced their confidence in the company's long-term viability, ultimately contributing to a more sustainable business model. Moreover, effective risk management and proactive engagement strategies with stakeholders demonstrate an organization's dedication to sustainable business practices, further solidifying its credibility and fostering trust among investors, employees, and other key stakeholders.

5.3.3 Continuous Learning: A Pillar of Sustainable Cultural Outcomes

Sustaining a culture of learning is a critical enabler of organizational sustainability and adaptability. As outlined in Chapter 4, the four strategic imperatives: strategic contextual intelligence, integrative communication, strategic financial intelligence, and innovation and agility require continuous learning for long-term effectiveness.

A learning-oriented culture enhances organizational resilience, decision-making, and performance excellence. Pluralistic multicultural organizations with structured learning cultures are more likely to navigate external uncertainties, drive innovation, and sustain competitive advantages (Garvin, Edmondson, and Gino, 2008). Embedding continuous learning will help organizations achieve:

Development of Contextual Awareness: Leaders must continuously update their understanding of macroeconomic trends, cultural shifts, regulatory landscapes, and industry disruptions to make contextually intelligent decisions (Teece, Peteraf, and Leih, 2016).

Enhancement of Integrative Communication: Effective TMT alignment and stakeholder engagement require communication training, cross-cultural learning, and collaborative decision-making frameworks (Nord, 2023).

Strengthening of Financial Intelligence: Organizations must institutionalize financial literacy programs to ensure that leaders at all levels understand economic trends, risk management, and sustainable investment strategies (Eccles, Ioannou, and Serafeim, 2014).

Fostering of an Innovative and Agile Mindset: Companies must encourage experimentation, cross-functional collaboration, and knowledge-sharing initiatives to enhance agility in strategy execution (Eisenhardt and Martin, 2000).

Case Study Insights: Continuous Learning in Action

Medi Care implemented ongoing organizational learning and development programs to help executives and their teams navigate the transition from public to private healthcare, ensuring that TMTs remain aligned with the organization's evolving mission, in addition to providing professional training to the corporate TMTs to bridge the gap between the professional and the corporate TMTs.

Urban Escape fostered a culture of market intelligence learning, equipping leaders with trend analysis tools to anticipate real estate shifts and proactively adapt investment strategies. The results were transferable skills from engineering to the financial teams and vice versa.

Echo Capital emphasized financial literacy and sustainability education, ensuring that all executives could effectively balance short-term financial performance with long-term ESG commitments.

Organizations that cultivate a culture of continuous learning ensure that leaders remain adaptable, informed, and capable of steering their businesses through volatile global landscapes.

5.4 Achieving Sustainable Success: The Case of Dubai Ports World (DP World)

To exemplify achieving sustainable success in practice we lean to the case of Dubai Ports World (DP World). DP World stands as an example of strategic leadership, showcasing decades of transformation that have shaped its position as a global leader in international trade and logistics. With an extensive presence in over 70 countries across six continents, employing more than 100,000 individuals, and reporting a revenue of $18.5 billion in the twelve months ending June 2024, DP World operates in both developed and developing nations, serving as a crucial link in the global supply chain. Its reach extends beyond traditional port operations, making it a vital player in fostering economic growth and trade across diverse markets.

As one of the world's foremost trade enablers, DP World has recognized the importance of innovation and sustainability in meeting the demands of an evolving global economy. The company has strategically expanded its operations beyond ports and terminals to encompass marine services, logistics, and cutting-edge technology, thereby establishing an integrated, end-to-end supply chain. This evolution reflects the necessity of embracing advanced technologies, such as blockchain, to streamline processes, enhance efficiency, and ensure transparency in international trade.

The DP World case illustrates the trilogy of sustainable success: a global presence that bridges developed and emerging markets, a commitment to facilitating seamless trade, and the integration of blockchain technology to drive efficiency and innovation. This combination positions DP World as an exemplary model for achieving sustainability within a complex and dynamic global trade environment, backed by the strategic guidance of its sovereign shareholders and years of transformative growth.

5.4.1 DP World's Strategic Contextual Leadership for Sustainable Outcomes

DP World's approach to sustainability is embedded within its broader strategic vision of leading global trade towards a more sustainable and inclusive future. This vision is operationalized through its sustainability strategy, which serves as a framework to address both immediate operational responsibilities and long-term societal impact.

The strategy is structured around two key elements:

DP World Today: This aspect focuses on operating as a responsible business by addressing seven priority areas, such as climate change, ethics, and governance. By aligning operational practices with these priorities, DP World ensures that sustainability is constructed into the foundation of its daily activities.

DP World Tomorrow: This element is concerned with the long-term legacy the company aspires to create for the industry and society, emphasizing initiatives around continuous education, diversity, and sustainable leadership development.

Aligned with global best practices and the United Nations Sustainable Development Goals (SDGs), DP World's sustainability drive is guided by a comprehensive contextual and strategic framework. This framework uses data-driven insights to identify progress areas, enabling a continuous refinement of sustainable practices.

As a part of its strategic and contextual leadership approach, DP World integrates social and environmental considerations into every business decision, particularly when entering new markets. Social and environmental impact studies are conducted to assess potential effects and opportunities, ensuring that commercial activities are responsible and contribute positively to local communities.

The company's strategy and commitment to sustainability have resulted in significant sustainable cultural outcomes, such as fostering an inclusive corporate culture, prioritizing ethical practices, and embedding sustainability into decision-making processes. DP World demonstrates how strategic and contextual leadership, when effectively implemented, can guide an organization to achieve not only sustainable economic success but also broader cultural and societal impact.

5.4.2 Strategizing to Gain Stakeholders' Trust and Support

Stakeholders increasingly expect businesses to prioritize sustainability as a core element of their operations. DP World has responded to this expectation by implementing strategic contextual leadership to embed sustainability into its decision-making processes and operational strategies. This approach ensures that actions taken are collaborative and tailored to address the most pressing challenges faced by stakeholders, thereby achieving measurable outcomes.

1. Engaging Shareholders with Sustainable Initiatives: To support decarbonization efforts and align with sustainability goals, DP World has raised sustainable capital, exemplified by issuing a 1.5 billion United States Dollar Green Sukuk. This initiative directly channels funds into projects that aim to reduce environmental impact and promote sustainable practices within its operations. Furthermore, DP World publishes a Sustainable Development Impact Disclosure (SDID), ensuring transparency regarding its sustainability efforts. This approach provides stakeholders with clear data on progress, reinforcing the organization's commitment to meeting sustainability expectations through measurable financial outcomes.

2. Establishing Industry Partnerships for Accelerated Sustainability: Recognizing the necessity of collective action, DP World has engaged in key industry partnerships such as the Zero Emission Port Alliance (ZEPA) and the Move to Minus 15°C Coalition.

These collaborations focus on reducing emissions and promoting sustainable practices across the logistics and port management sectors. By participating in these initiatives, DP World contributes to industry-wide efforts to achieve sustainability targets, demonstrating a clear outcome of enhanced cooperation and shared progress toward reducing environmental impact.

3. Integrating Sustainable Leadership Across Global Operations
To ensure that sustainability principles are integrated at every level of the organization, DP World has empowered employees to make sustainable decisions through a structured network of sustainability managers and champions across its global operations. This network, which includes over 80 representatives, facilitates the localization of global strategies and adapts them to meet specific market needs. As a result, DP World has achieved more contextually relevant sustainability initiatives, resulting in more effective implementation and greater engagement at the local level.

Additionally, DP World integrates sustainability into its daily operations through targeted learning and development programs. These initiatives have yielded tangible outcomes, such as community cleanup projects that have removed over 10,000 kg of waste, demonstrating how sustainability efforts translate into direct, measurable impacts within the communities where DP World operates.

4. Embedding Sustainability into Continuous Learning and Leadership Development
Education plays a central role in DP World's sustainability strategy, with the Sustainability Learning Academy providing employees with opportunities to reskill and adapt to sustainability challenges. This has led to the development of a workforce capable of implementing sustainability initiatives effectively, contributing to DP World's ability to maintain sustainability as an operational priority. The organization also supports gender equity through initiatives like the Women Onboard program, which has resulted in increased female participation in leadership roles.

5.4.3 DP Sustainable Cultural Outcomes

Through the implementation of strategic contextual leadership, DP World has achieved several sustainable cultural outcomes. These include improved transparency and accountability in sustainability reporting, active participation in industry-wide sustainability initiatives, and the successful integration of sustainability into daily operations and decision-making processes. This approach has fostered a culture that prioritizes sustainability, resulting in tangible impacts such as emission reductions, waste management improvements, and enhanced diversity in leadership, contributing to long-term sustainable success.

Box 5.1- Case Study: Strategic and Contextual Leadership at DP World
Contributor: Group Chief Sustainability Officer
Overview
This case study serves as a practical guide for implementing strategic contextual leadership in a multi-cultural, pluralistic organization. It offers executives insight into DP World's journey of integrating sustainability into its global operations. The study is structured around key aspects of organization strategy and how it achieved sustainable outcomes.

Part 1: Defining Sustainable Outcomes
DP World's approach: Sustainability is deeply integrated into DP World's global strategy and operations, driving efforts to lead trade toward more sustainable practices. The company's strategy, "Our World, Our Future," (DP World, 2023) focuses on both present actions and the long-term legacy it aims to create.

ESG Framework: A Structured Approach to Sustainable Operations
DP World's commitment to sustainability is operationalized through a comprehensive environmental, social, and governance (ESG) framework, which enables the company to integrate sustainable practices across all levels of operations. This framework supports regular performance monitoring, proactive risk management, and the continuous evolution of sustainability strategies to align with global standards and best practices.

Environmental Responsibility: DP World focuses on reducing carbon emissions, increasing energy efficiency, and transitioning to renewable energy sources. A notable achievement includes a 13% reduction in emissions, prompting the company to set a new target of a 42% reduction by 2030. This aligns with global sustainability initiatives, such as the United Nations Sustainable Development Goals (SDGs) and the Paris Agreement climate commitments.
Social Impact: DP World's ESG approach emphasizes workforce development, ethical labor practices, gender diversity, and community investment. The company fosters a diverse and inclusive work culture while ensuring that its global operations uphold ethical labor standards.
Governance and Ethical Business Practices: Robust governance structures ensure transparency, compliance, and ethical leadership. DP World adheres to anti-corruption measures, responsible procurement policies, and stakeholder engagement strategies, reinforcing long-term trust and accountability across markets.

Questions for Discussion
–   How does DP World adapt global sustainability goals to fit local contexts?
–   In what ways does the integration of the ESG framework contribute to achieving sustainable outcomes?

Exercise
–   Compare DP World's sustainability strategy with an organization from your industry.
–   Identify how each company approaches sustainability.
–   Discuss which practices can be adapted to fit your organization's unique context.
–   What else could DP World implement in their strategic contextual leadership approach building on your experience and practices?

Part 2: Strategizing to Gain Stakeholders' Trust and Support
Reading:
Building Stakeholder Trust: DP World's SCL approach emphasizes engaging stakeholders by addressing their specific concerns through collaborative and transparent actions:

Investors: By issuing a \$1.5 billion Green Sukuk, DP World channels funds into decarbonization projects. The company also enhances transparency through its Sustainable Development Impact Disclosure (SDID), ensuring stakeholders can track sustainability progress.

Communities: Through global sustainability alliances, such as the Zero Emission Port Alliance (ZEPA) and the Move to Minus 15°C Coalition, DP World actively contributes to setting industry-wide sustainability benchmarks.

Outcome: These strategic efforts reinforce DP World's position as a responsible global leader, fostering trust and long-term support from investors, communities, and industry peers.

Questions and Exercises for Cross-Industry Application
- How can your organization use similar strategies to gain stakeholders' trust?
- What sustainability concerns are most important to your stakeholders, and how can you address them?

Exercise
Industry Comparison: Compare DP World's sustainability strategy with a leading company in your industry. Identify similarities and differences and discuss how your industry can learn from DP World's approach.

Part 2: Strategizing to Acquire Stakeholders' Trust and Support
Questions for Discussion:
- Who are the primary stakeholders in your industry and why? What are their sustainability concerns?
- How can the strategies DP World use to build trust and support be adapted for your industry?
- What metrics would be most effective for evaluating stakeholder engagement in your industry?

Role Play:
Conduct a role-play meeting tailored to your industry. For example, if you are in healthcare, role-play a meeting with healthcare providers, patients, and regulatory bodies. Address their concerns using strategies like those employed by DP World.

Areas for the debrief of the role play:
- Which strategic levers travel well between industries with different contexts?What are the reasons? Are your own industry blinders involved?
- What level of ambition have you shown to work towards components of the sustainable success framework? Which did you include, exclude and why?
- Which three strategic actions can you bring to your organization immediately?

Part 3: Embedding Sustainability into Continuous Learning and Leadership Development Programs
Questions for Discussion:
- What are the key educational needs for sustainability in your organization and in your industry?
- How can your organization promote community resilience through its sustainability initiatives?
- What partnerships could your organization form to enhance its sustainability efforts?

Exercise:
Cross-Industry Sustainability Initiative Design
We invite you to look beyond your organization and to focus on your industry, given the contextual demands you are likely to face and the benefits for your organization with such an approach. In

groups, design a sustainability initiative for your industry. Include objectives, target audience, key activities, and expected outcomes. Present the initiative to the group, highlighting how it aligns with
your industry's sustainability goals and DP World's approach.

Integrative Exercise: Applying DP World's Model Across Industries
Strategic Sustainability Workshop:
– Organize a workshop where participants work in cross-industry groups to apply DP World's sus-
tainability model to their own organizations. Each group should:
– Identify key sustainability challenges in their industry.
– Develop strategies for stakeholder engagement and trust-building.
– Outline a plan for embedding sustainability into their organizational culture and operations.
– Create metrics to measure success.

Presentation and Feedback:
– **Group Presentations**: Each group presents its strategies and plans to the class, sharing how
they approached the specific challenges faced by their assigned industry.
– **Facilitated Discussion and Feedback**: After the presentations, a facilitated discussion is conducted where participants provide feedback, compare, and contrast the different strategies and
approaches used by each group across various industries.
– **Identifying Common Themes and Unique Challenges**: During the discussion, the facilitator
guides the class to identify common themes and patterns that emerge across multiple industries,
such as similar strategic priorities or recurring obstacles. Additionally, the facilitator helps pin-
point unique challenges specific to each industry, highlighting what makes each context distinct.
This process enables participants to gain a broader perspective on strategic leadership by understanding both the shared and unique factors influencing different industries.

Debrief on the entire workshop:
– What are the advantages and hurdles for industry-wide work to achieve sustainable success?
– How can we improve and further embed the inter-organizational and cross-stakeholder collabora-
tions we started with this workshop in our industry?

5.5 Conclusion

As we conclude Chapter 5, we have explored how organizations can achieve sustainable success by integrating strategic contextual leadership into their core practices.
This chapter has demonstrated that sustainable outcomes extend beyond conventional metrics of performance excellence and financial results; they encompass a
broader understanding of what it means to thrive in a pluralistic, multicultural environment.

Through the examples and cases presented, we've seen how organizations like
Echo Capital and DP World navigate complex, dynamic contexts by building trust,
aligning with stakeholder expectations, and fostering resilience. These organizations
illustrate that achieving sustainable success is not solely about immediate gains but
about cultivating long-term viability through strategic foresight, cultural alignment,
and stakeholder engagement.

The findings emphasize that sustainable success is a continuous process that involves understanding and adapting to a rapidly changing context, where the demands of stakeholders, societal expectations, and market dynamics are in constant flux. This approach requires strategic leaders to not only manage internal complexities but also to align their organizations with external pressures and opportunities.

As we move to Chapter 6, we will explore how organizations can cultivate the essential competencies and skills within their TMTs to achieve and sustain these outcomes. Chapter 6 will provide a blueprint for creating leaders who are strategically aware, contextually intelligent, and capable of driving sustainable success in a changing global environment. By decoding the intricacies of sustainable success discussed in this chapter, we lay the groundwork for developing leaders who can navigate these complexities with confidence and skill. Let's now transition to the next chapter, where we will explore how to design, develop and nurture these vital leadership capabilities within your organization.

Chapter 6
Strategic Contextual Leadership Development: A Roadmap to Sustainability

Building on the insights from our multiple case study findings in previous chapters, this chapter reaches the critical role of strategic contextual leadership development to support and embed the achievement of sustainable success. Organizations today face the imperative of excelling in performance and integrating ecological, economic, and societal measures into their operations. By linking these elements, Chapter 5 demonstrated how organizations navigate and excel in achieving success and aim towards a sustainable future. The implementation of the Strategic Contextual Leadership framework revealed the strong connection between the leadership effectiveness of the CEO and the strategic leadership development of the TMTs. We learned Medi Care's CEO succession and leadership training initiatives ensured that financial challenges did not derail the organization's long-term sustainability strategy. Similarly, Echo Capital executed several executive leadership development programs for seniors and their teams to enhance leadership effectiveness in financial risk management and stakeholder engagement. While Urban Escape designed and delivered leadership workshops on performance excellence, digital transformation and process optimization, reinforcing agility and continuous learning as strategic imperatives.

These findings confirm that strong financial performance correlates with TMT-CEO alignment, performance excellence, and sustained shareholder support. Furthermore, the multiple case study collective results showed that in addition to the financial results, the pluralistic multicultural organizational sustainable outcomes included the leaders' development and growth strategy. The results also revealed a direct link between the following: strong positive financial outcome and TMT-CEO contextual strategic intelligence, TMT retention, performance excellence, and the shareholders' support and satisfaction.

Sustainable success requires organizations to redefine economic sustainability, emphasize stakeholder perceptions, and integrate sustainable development with business processes (Asif et al., 2011). The Hybrid Strategic and Contextual Leadership framework operationalizes sustainable outcomes, making it more pragmatic for practitioners. Our empirical evidence suggests a positive association between TMT alignment, effectiveness, shareholder satisfaction, good governance, and financial outcomes.

All TMTs we interviewed highlighted the importance of strategic leadership development. We also found that strategic leadership development was directly associated *with two key factors: the level of satisfaction within the broader societal context (societal leadership expectations) and the support from shareholders.*

https://doi.org/10.1515/9783111382722-007

In this chapter, a special focus is dedicated to the development of strategic and contextual leaders proficient in managing the complexities of global business landscapes with a commitment to sustainability.

In essence, the strategic contextual leadership approach shows that organizations are not just reacting to change; they are positioned to lead it by aligning their leadership practices with both market realities and societal expectations. In this approach, leadership development is not an afterthought or separate practice. Instead, strategic contextual leadership development is a defining and deeply embedded element to make the approach successful.

Strategic leadership development is fundamental to embedding sustainability into organizational DNA. Leaders must develop competencies beyond technical expertise, incorporating strategic contextual intelligence, cultural agility, and dynamic capabilities into their decision-making processes. This structured approach equips TMTs with the tools to navigate complex, pluralistic environments to achieve sustainable success.

We also need to address what gaps in collective leadership capability the strategic contextual leadership development will bridge, and how organizations can foster a more resilient, adaptive, and cohesive leadership development framework. One particularly telling example of a strategic contextual leadership development need occurred during my time onsite with Medi Care. While one of us was waiting outside their chairman's office for a follow-up meeting, she saw him pacing his office back and forth on the phone, clearly engaged in an intense conversation. After he finished, she was invited in and shared a story that illustrated the immediate impact of external societal expectations on TMTs performance and communication.

A patient at one of Medi Care's hospitals had lodged a formal complaint directly with the media alleging that a hospital's TMT member communication with patients was culturally unacceptable, the complaint was addressed to the country leaderships asking if they accept their people to be treated in such a manner. Although the complainer didn't touch on the medical practices or bed manners. The complaint reached the ears of the shareholders, who promptly contacted the Medi Care chairman. In response, the chairman called the group CEO of Medi Care, who, in turn, summoned the CEO and the TMT of the hospital involved to address the issue immediately.

Two weeks later, I was interviewing the CEO of another hospital within the Medi Care network, located 400 kilometers outside the city. As I waited in the reception area, the CEO introduced me to a new doctor, a neurosurgeon, who was starting his first day. The CEO then explained that, following a patient complaint received by the chairman, Medi Care had implemented a new policy: Every new joiner must now complete a one-day course on culturally sensitive communication.

This story of Medi Care highlights how communication between executives and stakeholders requires integrated responsiveness. Alignment with societal leadership expectations is crucial for maintaining trust and upholding organizational reputation. The introduction of a context sensitivity leadership development reflects a strategic decision made by the shareholders to mitigate risks, improve performance standards, and ensure that leadership practices are in harmony with both internal values and external demands.

6.1 Specific Gaps in Strategic Leadership Development Programs

Traditional leadership development programs often overlook critical aspects of top management teams (TMTs) in pluralistic organizations, such as their structure, composition, and processes, focusing primarily on individual capability-building rather than the collective functioning of professional and corporate TMTs. This lack of understanding results in several key gaps.

Inadequate Understanding of the TMT Reality as a Group: Many leadership programs fail to recognize that TMTs function more as a group of diverse executives with unique roles and responsibilities rather than a cohesive team. This distinction is crucial because TMTs are composed of individuals who bring different perspectives, expertise, and goals to the table, often resulting in a lack of alignment and shared purpose. Traditional programs often prioritize individual development over team-based learning, which is essential for cultivating strategic contextual intelligence. This requires TMTs to collectively understand and respond to both internal and external contextual factors impacting their organizations. Without focusing on how TMTs operate as a group, these programs fail to foster the development of shared experiences, tacit knowledge, and collaborative decision-making processes critical to achieving strategic alignment (Carmeli, Tishler, and Edmondson, 2020; Kearney, Gebert, and Voelpel, 2021). For instance, in the case of Medi Care, despite substantial investments in leadership development focusing on various skills, some TMTs remained fragmented and misaligned due to the absence of a coordinated integrative communication approach that reflects their reality as a diverse group rather than a homogenous team.

TMT Members' Conflicting Objectives Leading to Differing Motivations: In pluralistic organizations, the diverse objectives of TMT members can result in conflicting motivations that are often overlooked by traditional leadership development programs. For example, a Chief Financial Officer may prioritize financial performance and cost-cutting measures, while a Chief Operations Officer may focus on achieving operational excellence and ensuring high-quality service delivery. These differing priorities can create tension and misalignment within the TMT, leading to fragmented decision-making and reduced commitment to collective organizational goals (Pluut, Flestea, and Curşeu, 2022; Wang and Cheng, 2019).

Skills Mismatch: Traditional leadership development programs often fail to account for the organizational context both inside and outside pluralistic organizations. There is frequently a mismatch between the skills these programs emphasize and the actual needs of organizations and their leaders, particularly in managing the dual demands of leading internally and externally. For example, CFOs are not solely responsible for financial performance; they must also lead externally by managing shareholder satisfaction and meeting broader societal expectations of leadership. However, many programs focus too narrowly on technical skills, such as financial analysis, while neglecting the critical competencies needed to navigate this complex acumen, which includes stakeholder engagement, strategic communication, and societal leadership (Conger and Lawler III, 2019; DeRue and Myers, 2021). Additionally, these programs often overlook the importance of fostering an innovative mindset that enables leaders to adapt and thrive amid rapidly changing external environments.

Skills Gap: Many executives struggle to apply skills learned in development programs to their actual work contexts due to differences between the learning context and the application context. Research coined this as the knowing-doing gap in leadership (Ahmadi and Vogel, 2023). This gap is particularly detrimental to developing innovation and agility, skills that require tangible application of the learning in relevant context. Research by Moldoveanu and Narayandas (2019) highlight that the greater the gap between where skills are learned and where they are applied, the less likely they are to be effectively implemented. This disconnection limits leaders' ability to innovate, adapt, and respond effectively to changing conditions.

The strategic contextual development framework presented in the next section addresses this gap by leveraging the four strategic imperatives—strategic contextual intelligence, strategic financial intelligence, integrative communication, and innovation and agility—to foster a cohesive understanding among TMT members. By focusing on collective strategic imperatives, the strategic contextual leadership development approach encourages TMT members to recognize and appreciate each other's perspectives, align their objectives, and work toward common organizational goals. This approach helps reconcile individual motivations with the broader strategic direction of the organization, enhancing integrative communication and fostering a unified, collaborative environment where all members are committed to shared success.

6.2 The Strategic Contextual Leadership Development Framework

The leadership development industry is undergoing significant disruption, driven by the increasing complexity of global business environments and the evolving demands on top management teams (TMTs). The number of leadership development providers has surged, offering programs designed to equip executives with both hard and soft skills essential for strategic decision-making, adaptability, and stakeholder engagement. Yet, organizations that collectively spend billions of dollars annually to train current and future executives are often frustrated with the outcomes. Studies and client interviews indicate that more than 50% of strategic leaders believe their talent development efforts do not adequately build critical skills and organizational capabilities (Moldoveanu and Narayandas, 2019). Consider for example that UN Sustainable Development Goals in leadership development remain an underutilized element with regards to the necessary executive skills but also assessing the leadership development design, implementation and outcomes itself against those demands (Vogel, Reichard, Batistič, and Černe, 2021).

The need for strategic and contextual leadership development has never been more urgent. Organizations across all industries recognize that to thrive in today's dynamic, uncertain, and complex context, they require leadership skills and organizational capabilities different from those that were successful in the past. There is also a growing recognition that leadership development must focus on those who drive strategic decisions at the highest levels: the CEOs, TMTs, and other key leaders responsible for steering the organization through ambiguity and change. As collaborative problem-solving platforms and digital "adhocracies" emerge, emphasizing agility and strategic alignment, TMTs and strategic leaders are increasingly expected to make critical decisions aligned with the broader corporate strategy and culture. *Therefore, equipping these leaders and their teams* with the relevant contextual, technical, relational, and communication skills is essential to navigate the complexities of modern business and ensure sustainable success.

The strategic contextual leadership development matrix positions the four strategic leadership imperatives on the vertical axis and the three strategic contextual leadership outcomes on the horizontal axis. Each cell in the matrix represents how strategic leadership skills imperatives contribute to achieving specific outcomes in pluralistic organizations.

To measure the success of strategic contextual leadership development effectively, a combination of qualitative and quantitative metrics should be employed. These metrics assess the impact of the four strategic leadership imperatives: strategic contextual intelligence, strategic financial intelligence, integrative communication, and innovation and agility.

6.3 Impact of Strategic Leadership Imperatives on Economic Sustainable Outcomes

Achieving sustainable economic outcomes by realizing performance excellence, financial sustainability and innovation and agility. It is crucial to have metrics to assess the impact of strategic contextual leadership development because these metrics provide a clear and objective way to measure the effectiveness of leadership practices in achieving desired organizational outcomes. Furthermore, the clarity of the metrics helps ensure that the Strategic Contextual Leadership framework is not just theoretical but translates into tangible results (Table 6.1).

Table 6.1: SCL Development Metrics for Sustainable Economic Outcomes.

Strategic Leadership Imperatives	Performance Excellence	Financial Sustainability	Innovation and Agility
Strategic Contextual Intelligence (SCI)	Enables leaders to adapt to external economic and market conditions	Ensures leaders understand financial risks, investments, and market trends	Encourages future-oriented thinking and adaptability
Integrative Communication within TMTs	Enhances alignment across leadership teams for superior strategy execution	Supports transparency in financial planning and budgeting	Fosters a culture of cross-functional collaboration for rapid adaptation
Strategic Financial Intelligence	Strengthens financial acumen to align financial and strategic goals	Enhances capital allocation strategies for profitability and stability	Ensures financial strategies support R&D and new business models
Innovation and Agility	Drives continuous improvement and competitive differentiation	Ensures financial support for innovation and strategic growth	Promotes a culture of resilience and quick market response

Table 6.2: Strategic Leadership Imperatives on Sustainable Economic Outcomes Matrix.

Strategic Leadership Imperatives	Performance Excellence	Financial Sustainability	Innovation and Agility
Strategic Contextual Intelligence	High	Medium	High
Integrative Communication within TMTs	Medium	Low	Medium
Strategic Financial Intelligence	Low	Highest	High
Innovation and Agility (capabilities)	High	Medium	Highest
Scale: Highest =4	*High=3*	*Medium =2*	*Low=1*

Table 6.2 shows the economic sustainable outcomes metrics with the impact of the four strategic leadership imperatives on key elements that drive long-term economic sustainability in organizations. Each imperative contributes differently to performance excellence, sustainable financial growth and innovation and agility to ensuring a balanced approach to achieving economic success.

Performance Excellence: refers to an organization's ability to achieve high efficiency, quality, and effectiveness in operations, customer satisfaction, and strategic execution. It encompasses continuous improvement, strategic execution, and operational excellence.

6.3.1 Impact of Strategic Leadership Imperatives on Performance Excellence

1. Strategic Contextual Intelligence-Highest Impact (4)
- Aligns business strategy with external market conditions, ensuring relevance and adaptability.
- Enhances strategic decision-making by integrating economic, political, and technological factors into performance strategies.
- Reduces uncertainty and enables proactive risk management, ensuring long-term excellence.

Key Metrics:
- Accuracy of strategic alignment with external economic conditions.
- Effectiveness of risk-mitigation strategies based on contextual insights.
- Percentage of performance KPIs achieved due to proactive market intelligence.

2. Integrative Communication within TMTs – Medium Impact (2)
- Improves collaboration between leadership teams, ensuring consistent execution of performance goals.
- Enhances the process of decision-making and reducing delays in strategy implementation.
- Ensures TMTs and senior managers alignment, minimizing inefficiencies and operational redundancies.

Key Metrics:
- Frequency of cross-functional alignment meetings leading to performance improvements.
- Time-to-execution for strategic initiatives due to enhanced communication.
- Reduction in operational inefficiencies due to improved leadership collaboration.

3. Strategic Financial Intelligence – Low Impact (1)
- Helps structure cost-efficient performance strategies but does not directly drive operational excellence.
- Supports budgeting for performance improvement projects and ensures funding for initiatives.
- Helps identify key financial indicators for measuring performance excellence.

Key Metrics:
- Cost savings achieved through financially driven efficiency initiatives.
- Percentage of budget allocated to performance excellence initiatives.
- ROI on strategic initiatives aimed at enhancing performance.

4. Innovation and Agility – Highest Impact (4)
- Drives continuous improvement, ensuring that organizations remain competitive and efficient.
- Enables rapid adaptation to customer demands and operational challenges.
- Supports the integration of emerging technologies into core processes.

Key Metrics:
- Rate of process innovation leading to efficiency improvements.
- Percentage of performance excellence KPIs achieved through agility-driven initiatives.
- Speed of operational adjustments in response to market or industry changes.

6.3.2 Impact of Strategic Leadership Imperatives on Financial Sustainability

Financial sustainability refers to an organization's ability to achieve consistent, long-term profitability while maintaining financial stability, managing risks, and reinvesting for future expansion. It moves beyond short-term profit maximization and focuses on financial resilience, responsible capital allocation, and value creation over time.

1. Strategic Contextual Intelligence
- Ensures leaders align financial strategies with global economic trends and risk factors.
- Enhances long-term financial planning, helping organizations anticipate and mitigate financial volatility.
- Supports sustainable investment decision-making by incorporating regulatory and geopolitical insights.

Key Metrics:
- Accuracy of financial forecasts influenced by contextual intelligence.
- Risk mitigation success rate based on strategic contextual intelligence informed financial decisions.
- Number of financial growth opportunities identified using contextual intelligence.

2. Integrative Communication within TMTs
- Enhances financial transparency, ensuring that key stakeholders remain informed and engaged.
- Reduces financial misalignment between departments, ensuring better budgeting and capital allocation.
- Encourages collaborative financial decision-making, though its direct impact on financial sustainability is minimal.

Key Metrics:
- Level of financial transparency and stakeholder engagement.
- Reduction in budget discrepancies across departments.
- Number of strategic financial decisions enhanced by cross-functional communication.

3. Strategic Financial Intelligence
- Ensures long-term financial stability by optimizing capital structure and investment strategies.
- Enables risk-adjusted financial planning, ensuring organizations can withstand economic downturns.
- Enhances profitability and cash flow management, reducing dependency on external financing.

Key Metrics:
- Liquidity ratios and financial stability indicators.
- ROI on long-term financial investments.
- Percentage of retained earnings reinvested for sustainable growth.

4. Innovation and Agility
- Enables the creation of new revenue streams, ensuring diversified financial growth.
- Ensures rapid financial adaptability, helping organizations pivot during economic uncertainty.
- Encourages investments in emerging technologies, driving long-term financial sustainability.

Key Metrics:
- Revenue generated from innovation-driven business models.
- Success rate of financial pivot strategies during economic shifts.
- Investment in future-focused digital and financial transformation initiatives.

6.3.3 Impact of Strategic Leadership Imperatives on Innovation and Agility Outcomes

The innovation and agility outcome refers to an organization's ability to rapidly adapt, create, and implement transformative strategies in response to changing market dynamics. Each strategic leadership imperative plays a distinct role in shaping an organization's capacity for innovation and agility. Below is a breakdown of how each imperative contributes to achieving this outcome.

1. Strategic Contextual Intelligence– High Impact (3)
– Provides deep market insights and trend analysis that guide innovation investments.
– Helps leadership teams anticipate shifts in consumer behavior, technology, and regulatory landscapes.
– Ensures that agility is informed, avoiding reactive decision-making and ensuring strategic foresight-driven innovation.

Key Metrics:
– Number of market-driven innovations resulting from contextual insights.
– Speed of strategic pivots based on geopolitical or economic trend analysis.
– Success rate of market adaptation strategies informed by strategic contextual intelligence.

2. Integrative Communication within TMTs – Medium Impact (2)
– Facilitates collaborative innovation by ensuring cross-functional alignment and idea-sharing.
– Reduces organizational silos, enabling faster execution of innovative projects.
– Enhances decision-making speed, ensuring agile responses to business challenges.

Key Metrics:
– Number of cross-functional innovation initiatives supported by TMT communication.
– Frequency of strategic alignment meetings that result in innovative project launches.
– Reduction in time-to-decision for innovation-focused projects.

3. Strategic Financial Intelligence – High Impact (3)
– How strategic financial intelligence drives innovation and agility:
– Ensures financial backing for R&D and experimentation, reducing budget constraints on innovation.
– Enables risk-adjusted financial modeling, ensuring that innovation investments are sustainable.
– Supports the development of financially viable new business models and adaptive revenue streams.

Key Metrics:
– Percentage of total budget allocated to R&D and innovation.
– ROI of innovation-driven investments (e.g., technology upgrades, product development).
– Number of sustainable business models created through financial intelligence.

4. Innovation and Agility (Skill) – Highest Impact (4)
- How innovation and agility as a leadership capability translates to outcomes.
- Embeds a culture of continuous experimentation and learning within the organization.
- Encourages rapid iteration, ensuring that ideas move from concept to execution swiftly.
- Drives organizational resilience, ensuring agility in uncertain environments.

Key Metrics:
- Time-to-market for new innovations.
- Success rate of agile transformations in organizational structures.
- Frequency of iterative improvements in products/services.

6.4 Impact of Strategic Leadership Imperatives on Cultural Sustainable Outcomes

Below is a structured analysis of how each strategic leadership imperative contributes to three key cultural sustainable outcomes (Table 6.3):

Table 6.3: The Strategic Leadership Imperatives Impact on Cultural Outcomes.

Strategic Leadership Imperatives	Shareholders' Support and Trust	Growth and Good Governance	Continuous Learning
Strategic Contextual Intelligence	Ensures regulatory and societal alignment, mitigates risks, and strengthens corporate credibility.	Provides deep insights into economic and regulatory landscapes, ensuring sustainable expansion.	Encourages learning strategies based on external market trends.
Integrative Communication within TMTs	Enhances transparency in decision-making and fosters investors' confidence.	Plays a supporting role by enhancing internal alignment around governance strategies.	Facilitates cross-functional knowledge exchange and a culture of transparency.
Strategic Financial Intelligence	Ensures financial stability and responsible investment strategies.	Ensures financial structures support long-term organizational expansion.	Provides financial support for corporate learning programs.
Innovation and Agility	While innovation drives growth, shareholders often prioritize stability over disruptive change.	Drives business model transformation while ensuring responsible governance.	Drives a learning-by-doing culture, ensuring employees remain adaptable and innovative.

- Acquiring Shareholders' Support and Trust
- Growth and Good Governance
- Continuous Learning

Leadership Imperatives on key elements that drive long-term cultural sustainability in organizations. Each imperative contributes differently to Acquiring Shareholders' Support and Trust, Growth and Good Governance, and Continuous Learning, ensuring a balanced approach to achieving cultural success.

Table 6.4 shows the cultural sustainable outcomes metrics with the impact of the four strategic leadership imperatives.

Table 6.4: Cultural Sustainable Outcomes Metrics.

Strategic Leadership Imperatives	Shareholders' Support and Trust	Growth and Good Governance	Continuous Learning
Strategic Contextual Intelligence	Highest	High	Medium
Integrative Communication within TMTs	High	Low	Medium
Strategic Financial Intelligence	Medium	Highest	Low
Innovation and Agility	Low	Low	Highest
Scale: Highest =4	High=3	Medium =2	Low=1

6.4.1 Impact of Strategic Leadership Imperatives on Acquiring Shareholders' Support and Trust

Shareholders' support and trust are fundamental for an organization's long-term stability, reputation, and investment appeal. It requires transparent governance, ethical leadership, and alignment with stakeholder expectations.

1. Strategic Contextual Intelligence– Highest Impact (4)
- Ensures alignment with regulatory, societal, and investor expectations, reducing risks and enhancing credibility.
- Enhances market positioning and corporate reputation by incorporating environmental, social, and governance (ESG) considerations.
- Anticipates and mitigates context-driven risks, ensuring stability in stakeholder relationships.

Key Metrics:
- Stakeholder confidence index (measured through surveys and investor sentiment).
- Number of risk mitigation strategies implemented to enhance trust.
- Regulatory compliance rating and ESG performance scores.

2. Integrative Communication within TMTs – High Impact (3)
- Enhances transparency in decision-making, fostering stronger investor confidence.
- Improves stakeholder engagement, ensuring alignment between corporate strategy and investor expectations.
- Reduces internal conflicts, ensuring a more stable leadership approach that reassures shareholders.

Key Metrics:
- Level of transparency in financial and strategic reporting.
- Number of stakeholder engagement forums and investor briefings.
- Shareholder trust index, based on governance and communication effectiveness.

3. Strategic Financial Intelligence – Medium Impact (2)
- Ensures financial stability and risk mitigation, strengthening investor trust.
- Enhances corporate governance through accurate financial reporting.
- Helps in maintaining sustainable profit margins, reinforcing financial credibility.

Key Metrics:
- Accuracy of financial reporting and transparency levels.
- Ratio of sustainable revenue growth to capital investment.
- Number of financial governance policies implemented.

4. Innovation and Agility – Low Impact (1)
- While innovation drives growth, shareholders often prioritize stability over disruption.
- Excessive risk-taking in innovation may increase uncertainty, making shareholders cautious.
- However, controlled innovation initiatives can enhance market confidence.

Key Metrics:
- Shareholder confidence in innovation-driven revenue strategies.
- Number of innovation projects aligned with risk-mitigated investment strategies.
- Market perception of the organization's innovation initiatives.

6.4.2 Impact of Strategic Leadership Imperatives on Growth and Good Governance

Growth and Good Governance refer to ethical decision-making, responsible leadership, and structured expansion strategies that ensure sustainable organizational development.

1. Strategic Contextual Intelligence – High Impact (3)
–   Provides deep insights into economic and regulatory landscapes, ensuring sustainable expansion.
–   Helps anticipate policy changes, allowing organizations to adapt governance structures proactively.
–   Ensures that governance frameworks align with global best practices and ethical leadership standards.

Key Metrics:
–   Effectiveness of governance policies based on contextual intelligence.
–   Success rate of response strategies to policy changes.
–   Stakeholders' satisfaction with governance transparency.

2. Integrative Communication within TMTs – Low Impact (1)
–   Plays a supporting role by enhancing internal alignment around governance strategies.
–   Helps mitigate leadership conflicts, but governance is largely driven by external regulations and financial strategies.

Key Metrics:
–   TMT alignment scores in governance-related decisions.
–   Frequency of governance discussions within leadership meetings.
–   Employee engagement levels in governance-related initiatives.

3. Strategic Financial Intelligence – Highest Impact (4)
–   Ensures that financial structures support long-term organizational expansion.
–   Facilitates risk-adjusted capital allocation, ensuring financial stability while pursuing growth.
–   Strengthens internal controls, ensuring financial governance aligns with regulatory standards.

Key Metrics:
–   Number of governance-compliant financial policies implemented.
–   Capital efficiency in funding growth initiatives.
–   Growth-to-risk ratio in financial decision-making.

4. Innovation and Agility – Medium Impact (2)
–   Drives business model transformation, ensuring long-term relevance and expansion.
–   However, agility must be balanced with governance structures to ensure responsible innovation.

Key Metrics:
–   Number of governance-aligned innovation projects.
–   Compliance rate of new business initiatives with regulatory standards.
–   Success rate of business model transformations with strong governance frameworks.

6.4.3 Impact of Strategic Leadership Imperatives on Continuous Learning

Continuous Learning refers to an organization's ability to foster knowledge-sharing, leadership development, and adaptability within its workforce.

1. Strategic Contextual Intelligence (SCI) – Medium Impact (2)
–   Helps leaders understand global best practices in leadership development.
–   Encourages adaptive learning strategies based on external market trends.

Key Metrics:
–   Number of contextual intelligence-driven learning programs.
–   Employee adaptability scores in learning new market dynamics.
–   Use of external knowledge sources in leadership training.

2. Integrative Communication within TMTs – Medium Impact (2)
–   Encourages cross-functional knowledge exchange and leadership discussions.
–   Enhances organizational culture by promoting transparent learning environments.

Key Metrics:
–   Frequency of leadership knowledge-sharing sessions.
–   Effectiveness of TMT-led learning initiatives.
–   Impact of cross-functional learning on employee skill development.

3. Strategic Financial Intelligence – Low Impact (1)
–   Provides funding for corporate learning and leadership programs.
–   Ensures that learning investments contribute to long-term ROI.

Key Metrics:
- Percentage of total budget allocated to continuous learning.
- Return on Investment (ROI) on leadership development investments.
- Employee retention linked to learning program participation.

4. Innovation and Agility – Highest Impact (4)
- Encourages a growth mindset, ensuring employees remain adaptable.
- Drives learning-by-doing, embedding continuous learning into daily operations.

Key Metrics:
- Rate of employee upskilling through innovation-driven programs.
- Adoption rate of new skills in agile environments.
- Effectiveness of experimental learning initiatives.

6.5 Conclusion

The strategic leadership imperatives are the foundational pillars of strategic contextual leadership sevelopment. For top management teams, executives, and senior managers, mastering these imperatives is a necessity in navigating complexity, ensuring organizational resilience, and driving sustainable success.

Sustainable success is achieved when organizations balance economic performance with cultural and societal expectations. This requires leadership that is strategically and contextually proactive and effective, financially intelligent, and agile in execution to:

Achieve Economic Sustainability: By aligning performance excellence, financial sustainability, and innovation and agility, organizations can ensure long-term profitability, strategic agility, and operational efficiency. Strategic contextual intelligence provides the external insights needed for strategic foresight, Financial intelligence ensures capital efficiency, while innovation and agility keep the organization at the forefront of industry advancements.

Embed Cultural Sustainability: Organizations must foster stakeholder trust, governance excellence, and continuous learning to maintain social legitimacy and internal alignment. Integrative communication ensures TMT cohesion, strategic contextual intelligence enables leaders to align with societal and investor expectations, while innovation and agility ensure continuous organizational learning and change.

Chapter 7
Looking Ahead: The Urgency for Strategic Contextual Leadership

As organizations navigate an increasingly complex and interconnected world, the Hybrid Strategic Contextual Leadership framework provides a forward-looking model for sustainable success. The framework is designed to be dynamic and evolving, responding to emerging trends, digital transformation, geopolitical shifts, and evolving leadership expectations. Unlike many leadership models rooted in Western-centric theories, this book brings forth a globally relevant, empirically grounded framework, with specific applications for CEOs and TMTs operating in pluralistic and multicultural organizations (Al Bachir, 2022). A key intellectual contribution of the said research is the study of pluralistic multicultural organizations outside the scope of the GLOBE Study 2013, which investigated CEOs and top management teams across 24 countries. Notably, House and the 71 researchers excluded the Middle East, emphasizing the need for further studies on leadership effectiveness in the region (House et al., 2013). Another intellectual contribution of this research is the recognition that leadership effectiveness in the Middle East—particularly in the United Arab Emirates and other emerging markets—is shaped by a dual influence: the organizational culture and the broader societal leadership expectations unique to the country. By addressing this gap, this study contributes to a contextually grounded leadership framework that acknowledges the strategic interplay between economic, cultural, and governance structures in emerging markets.

In the context of the dynamic global business environment, organizations must strategically position themselves to balance both *economic and cultural sustainability*. This chapter explores the future application of the Hybrid Strategic Contextual Leadership framework, showing how the future will shape the strategic leadership imperatives and how strategic leaders will achieve these dual outcomes.

Future-facing leadership strategies integrate emerging technologies such as artificial intelligence AI, blockchain, fintech, and predictive analytics to drive innovation and informed decision making.

7.1 Emerging Future Trends in Strategic Contextual Leadership Development

7.1.1 The Technology-Driven Evolution

The integration of artificial intelligence (AI), automation, and data analytics will fundamentally transform organizational operations, presenting both unprecedented opportunities and complex challenges. While digital transformation enhances efficiency,

https://doi.org/10.1515/9783111382722-008

scalability, and innovation, its success hinges on strategic alignment with an organization's overarching goals and cultural values (Westerman, Bonnet, and McAfee, 2019). CEOs and TMTs must ensure that technological advancements enhance, rather than disrupt, organizational culture, workforce dynamics, and competitive positioning. This necessitates the incorporation of strategic contextual intelligence to manage the complex interconnections between digital transformation, business objectives, and cultural cohesion (Tushman, Smith, and Binns, 2022).

By leveraging the Hybrid Strategic Contextual Leadership framework, leaders can synchronize digital transformation with corporate strategies, fostering technological agility while preserving cultural integrity. For instance, AI-driven decision-making in financial services necessitates transparent governance structures to maintain stakeholder trust (Davenport and Ronanki, 2018). Similarly, businesses deploying AI-powered customer engagement tools must foster a service-centric mindset, ensuring that digital interfaces enhance, rather than replace, personalized experiences (Brynjolfsson and McAfee, 2017). Additionally, as organizations incorporate blockchain technology to enhance supply chain transparency, leadership must embed this transformation within existing operational frameworks to maintain coherence with organizational culture (Iansiti and Lakhani, 2020).

A successful futuristic transformation strategy requires contextually aware leadership that integrates technological advancements with cultural and societal expectations. Organizations that fail to consider contextual dynamics often experience cultural dissonance, employee resistance, and strategic misalignment. Consequently, leaders who embrace futuristic dynamic skills can foster an innovative yet stable environment, ensuring that technology adoption enhances rather than disrupts long-term organizational sustainability.

7.2 Leading Remote and Hybrid Teams in Multicultural Organizations

The post-pandemic era has witnessed a paradigm shift towards remote and hybrid work models, particularly within multinational and culturally diverse organizations. This transition presents unique challenges in maintaining leadership effectiveness, as traditional face-to-face interactions give way to virtual communications (Neeley, 2021). Effective leadership in such settings demands strategic communication, trust-building, and the preservation of cultural cohesion across geographically dispersed teams (Zhang et al., 2022). The application of integrative communication, a cornerstone of the strategic leadership imperatives, enables leaders to cultivate a unified and dynamic leadership approach. This involves leveraging digital platforms to facilitate seamless communication, fostering an inclusive environment that respects cultural differences, and implementing practices that reinforce organizational values and engagement despite physical distances (Maznevski and Chudoba, 2021). For example, businesses have adopted integrated communication tools to support both real-time interactions, thereby enhancing connectivity across different time zones and cultural contexts (Dery et al., 2023). Researchers and practitioners suggest that organizations that implement structured digital communication strategies experience higher levels of engagement, collaboration, and strategic alignment in remote and hybrid teams (Gibson et al., 2022). By embracing these strategies, leaders can ensure that organizational culture, strategic alignment, and TMT engagement are sustained, thereby enhancing overall performance and employee satisfaction in remote and hybrid work environments.

7.3 Future-Proofing Leadership: The Evolution of Strategic Contextual Leadership Development in a Digital Age

As global markets evolve, leaders can adopt strategic contextual leadership to navigate complex economic, geopolitical, and organizational landscapes. The strategic contextual leadership development framework builds on the imperatives outlined in Chapter 4, integrating strategic contextual intelligence, integrative communication, strategic financial intelligence, and innovation and agility to future-proof leadership approaches. This section explores how the framework applies to emerging leadership challenges and the evolving business environment.

7.4 Navigating Geopolitical and Economic Uncertainty

Leaders in rapidly evolving economies must adeptly navigate economic diversification, shifting regulatory frameworks, and geopolitical uncertainties to ensure long-term organizational sustainability and strategic resilience. These challenges are particularly pronounced in regions such as the Middle East, South Africa, Brazil, India, Indonesia, and Turkey. The World Economic Forum highlights that unprecedented global challenges necessitate careful adaptation by businesses to the changing geopolitical and economic environment (World Economic Forum, 2023). Furthermore, the International Monetary Fund (IMF) outlines that economic volatility, and geopolitical events present significant challenges for leaders, disrupting markets and requiring strategic adaptability. For instance, Gutterman (2022) highlights the pivotal role leaders play in resolving collective action problems in developing countries by creating vision, direction, and collective purposes. Similarly, a study by Ghebregiorgis and Karsten (2024) identifies factors like short-termism, hubris, greed, and unethical behavior as contributors to ineffective strategic leadership in emerging economies. Additionally, Karam and Jamali (2019) discuss the ethical challenges organizations' leaders face in emerging economies due to the lack of effective formal institutions. These regions face unique challenges, including the need for economic diversification to reduce dependence on single industries, adapting to dynamic regulatory environments, and managing geopolitical tensions that can disrupt business operations. Addressing these complexities requires leaders to develop strategic contextual foresight to ensure their organizations' sustained success in an unpredictable global landscape (McKinsey & Company, 2023). The context matrix, introduced in Chapter 2, equips CEOs and TMTs with the ability to anticipate external disruptions, proactively respond to volatility, and build strategic resilience in the face of economic and political shifts.

As global financial systems evolve, new economic alliances and de-dollarization efforts, such as the BRICS nations' (Brazil, Russia, India, China, and South Africa) push for alternative currencies, are reshaping financial landscapes (Eichengreen, 2023). Leaders must develop strategic financial intelligence to traverse these uncertainties, balancing global investment trends with local financial policies. For example, Middle Eastern sovereign wealth funds are increasingly diversifying investments into emerging markets to mitigate reliance on Western financial systems while adopting AI-powered risk modeling to enhance decision-making (Gupta and Sen, 2024).

Thus, strategic contextual intelligence enables leaders to assess regulatory, economic, and political shifts while ensuring financial and operational strategies remain adaptable to external disruptions.

7.5 The Rise of Cross-Cultural Team Leadership in Multinational and Family-Owned Enterprises

The future of organizations presents a diverse corporate ecosystem, encompassing multinational corporations (MNCs), state-owned enterprises (SOEs), and family-owned businesses, each with unique governance structures, leadership dynamics, and decision-making approaches. While MNCs integrate global business strategies, they must remain contextually sensitive to regional leadership expectations.

Family-Owned Businesses: Leadership must balance traditional governance models with modern corporate management principles, ensuring transparent decision-making while preserving cultural integrity (Secretariat International, 2023).

State-Owned Enterprises (SOEs): These organizations often operate at the intersection of government priorities and commercial competitiveness, requiring leadership that aligns national strategic objectives with operational efficiency (OECD, 2013).

Multinational Corporations: MNCs operate across multiple regions, requiring a delicate balance between global integration and local responsiveness (Ghemawat, 2005). Their governance structures are typically complex, involving hierarchies that facilitate coordination across markets while allowing flexibility for local adaptations (Rugman and Verbeke, 2001). Strategic leadership in MNCs must account for cultural, administrative, geographic, and economic differences when crafting regional strategies

(Ghemawat, 2005). Top management teams and CEOs must align corporate objectives with regional leadership expectations, ensuring a balance between standardization and localization.

However, applying Western-centric leadership models without adaptation often results in misalignment and reduced leadership efficacy (Al Bachir, 2022). The Strategic Contextual Leadership (SCL) development framework addresses this challenge by facilitating a hybrid approach, integrating local leadership traditions with global best practices. This synthesis promotes leadership cohesion among international executives, local managers, and diverse stakeholder groups, ensuring culturally responsive decision-making.

Examples of Future-Focused Companies in the Middle East

The need for the application of the Hybrid Strategic and Contextual Leadership development framework is evident in several leading organizations across diverse industries, each striving for long-term sustainability, innovation, and strategic agility to remain future-focused:

DP World – Redefining Global Trade and Logistics for 2030 and Beyond

DP World, a global leader in ports, logistics, and supply chain solutions, is future proofing its business by investing in:

- Digital transformation and automation to enhance supply chain efficiency.
- Sustainable infrastructure projects aimed at reducing the environmental impact of global trade.
- AI-driven logistics solutions that improve forecasting, risk management, and cargo tracking.
- Global expansion strategies, including investments in emerging markets to strengthen trade connectivity.
- As part of its Vision 2030 and beyond, DP World is committed to aligning with international sustainability frameworks while enhancing efficiency and resilience in global trade networks.

Echo Capital – Strengthening Financial Innovation and Governance

Echo Capital aims to become a future-proof financial services firm, driving investment resilience and risk-adjusted decision-making by leveraging:

- Sustainability-driven investment portfolios, supporting long-term economic resilience.
- Enhanced governance structures, ensuring compliance with international and regional financial regulations.
- Risk-adjusted financial intelligence, enabling effective navigation of global economic volatility.

- The application of hybrid strategic contextual principles, ensuring that its leadership approach remains contextually aligned, balancing local financial policies with global investment trends.

Urban Escape – Pioneering Smart and Sustainable Development

Urban Escape, a multi use real estate development company, is embedding sustainability and smart technology into its future projects by:
- Investing in AI-powered smart cities to enhance urban planning and sustainability.
- Adopting blockchain technology for secure, transparent real estate transactions.
- Aligning with national sustainability goals to develop carbon-neutral real estate projects.
- By integrating sustainable urban planning and cutting-edge technology, Urban Escape is becoming a model for the future of smart real estate in the Middle East.

Medi Care – Transforming Healthcare with AI and Patient-Centered Innovation

Medi Care is becoming a leading healthcare provider by shaping the future of medical innovation through:
- Deploying AI-driven diagnostics to enhance accuracy and patient outcomes.
- Implementing telemedicine solutions to expand healthcare access.
- Aligning with global healthcare governance standards, ensuring medical excellence and patient trust.

Medi Care's future strategy must ensure that it remains a regional leader in healthcare innovation, addressing future public health challenges with advanced medical solutions.

The Hybrid Strategic Contextual Leadership framework provides strategic leadership development tailored for the country specific context, ensuring that leaders can balance the intersection of global business trends and regional contextual dynamics. Companies like DP World, Echo Capital, Urban Escape and Medi Care need to leverage strategic imperatives to drive long-term economic and cultural sustainability, positioning themselves as future-focused organizations prepared for 2030 and beyond. By integrating future strategic contextual intelligence, innovation, and financial sustainability, these organizations can successfully change and actively shape the future of their respective industries.

7.6 Future-Ready Sustainability: Beyond Compliance to Strategic Transformation

Sustainability today is both an economic necessity and a strategic necessity. From this point forward, compliance alone will no longer be sufficient. As global challenges intensify, organizations, particularly in dynamic and rapidly evolving economies, must progress beyond traditional ESG (environmental, social, and governance) frameworks to drive transformative sustainability mandates. This shift requires leaders to embed sustainability not as a compliance measure, but as a core driver of financial and operational strategy.

Strategic financial intelligence is poised to play an increasingly pivotal role in the future, ensuring that sustainability evolves from a mere initiative to a business-critical mandate, one that necessitates a deliberate balance between profitability, resilience, and long-term impact. Organizations that embed sustainability into financial decision-making gain improved financial performance, operational efficiency, and risk management capabilities, allowing them to proactively address sustainability challenges while maintaining profitability (Berg and Wilts, 2023).

For example, organizations that integrate sustainability-driven financial risk management strategies are better equipped to enhance economic resilience and navigate global uncertainties (Whelan et al., 2021). Additionally, aligning financial resilience with sustainability goals enables organizations to strengthen market positioning, reduce regulatory risks, and enhance stakeholder trust (Barker, 2024). By leveraging strategic financial intelligence alongside sustainability principles, businesses can develop robust, future-proof economic models that drive both financial success and long-term sustainability.

Organizations leveraging hybrid leadership development models will go beyond current sustainability efforts, integrating advanced financial intelligence, cutting-edge technological innovations, and adaptive governance models to develop sustainable business ecosystems. As industries move toward net-zero economies, circular business models, and AI-driven sustainability strategies, only organizations embedding sustainability into their core decision-making processes will remain competitive in the next era of global business.

The Echo Capital case study from Chapter 4 illustrates how CEOs integrating financial intelligence into sustainability efforts can drive positive business outcomes while enhancing stakeholder trust. This aligns with the strategic contextual leadership development framework, reinforcing that future-focused leadership requires integrating economic success with sustainable business practices.

7.7 Future Application of Strategic Imperatives for Achieving Economic and Cultural Outcomes

In an increasingly complex and interconnected and evolving global business environment, organizational leaders must strategically develop dynamic capability to sustain both economic performance and cultural integrations to achieve sustainable success. This evolving nature of markets, rapid technological advancements, and shifting regulatory frameworks require leaders to leverage strategic contextual intelligence, integrative communication, strategic financial intelligence and innovation and agility to drive sustainable outcomes. This section explores how these dynamic capabilities will shape the future of leadership enabling organizations to navigate volatility while maintaining good governance and competitive resilience and readiness across pluralistic and multicultural organizations. The future strategic leadership imperatives build upon the foundational principles outlined in Chapter 4, expanding their scope to address geopolitical shifts, evolving societal leadership expectations, and industry-specific challenges. These imperatives ensure that leaders remain agile, contextually aware, and strategically equipped to navigate an increasingly complex global landscape (See Figure 7.1).

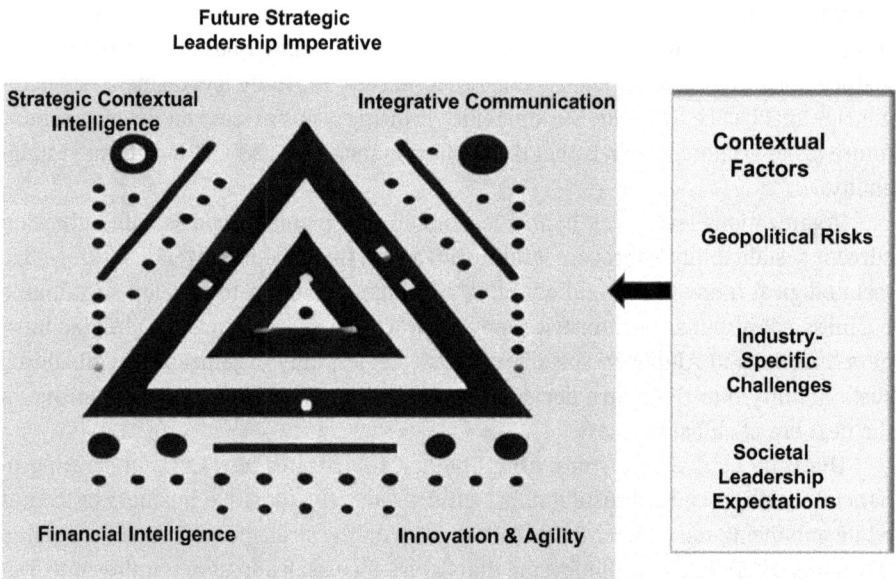

Figure 7.1: The Future Application of Strategic Leadership Imperatives.
This figure presents the future application of strategic leadership imperatives in response to evolving contextual factors. It emphasizes the importance of Strategic Contextual Intelligence, Integrative Communication, Financial Intelligence, and Innovation and Agility as essential competencies for navigating geopolitical risks, industry challenges, and societal leadership expectations in pluralistic organizations.

7.7.1 Strategic Contextual Intelligence: Enhancing Decision-Making in Global Organizations

In the future, strategic contextual intelligence will rely heavily on AI-powered analytics, geopolitical intelligence, and real-time risk assessment to mitigate uncertainties and enhance strategic positioning.

Economic Application: AI-Driven Market Intelligence and Risk Management
AI-powered predictive models will enable firms to analyze shifting global economic conditions, geopolitical risks, and regulatory changes, allowing for proactive decision-making (Brynjolfsson and McAfee, 2017). Multinational corporations (MNCs) expanding into global markets will leverage strategic contextual intelligence-driven scenario planning to anticipate regulatory hurdles and cultural challenges. Real-time intelligence will enable organizations to align local operations with global strategies, ensuring consistent market adaptability while preserving regional integrity (Porter and Heppelmann, 2015).

Cultural Application: Strengthening Multicultural Leadership and Ethical Compliance
Organizations managing diverse workforces across geographies will use a collection of intelligence-driven models to ensure leadership effectiveness (Earley and Ang, 2003). Data-driven diversity strategies will integrate local governance policies, labor laws, and ethical frameworks to enhance corporate responsibility and community engagement (OECD, 2021).

Leaders will utilize automated compliance monitoring systems to ensure adherence to corporate social responsibility (CSR) and ethical leadership standards in various cultural contexts (Schwartz and Carroll, 2003).

7.7.2 Integrative Communication: Strengthening Cross-Border Leadership and Multicultural Cohesion

As organizations expand into multicultural, remote, and hybrid work environments, effective integrative communication will be critical for sustaining trust, collaboration, and decision-making across diverse leadership teams.

Economic Application: Real-Time Leadership Synchronization in Global Operations
International public organizations, government bodies, and private sector alliances will require AI-driven collaboration tools to facilitate cross-cultural leadership engagement (Ghemawat, 2016). Leadership teams will integrate real-time communication

Figure 7.2: AI Powered Communication Strategies for Global Teams Generated by Open AI (GPT- 4). This figure visualizes AI-powered communication strategies for global teams. It depicts a digitally connected world map enhanced with icons representing chatbots, AI-driven translations, real-time and secure translation systems, and networked human figures, symbolizing seamless global collaboration. This image was generated by ChatGPT (OpenAI, GPT-4).

dashboards with language-processing AI to align decisions across linguistic and cultural divides.

For decades we read about how AI-driven executive sentiment analysis tools will provide insights into team alignment and stakeholder engagement in diverse international organizations (Hinds and Bailey, 2003).

The illustration in Figure 7.2 depicts AI-powered communication strategies, supposedly designed to enhance global team collaboration in a digitally interconnected world. The central focus is a futuristic, high-tech world map, symbolizing global connectivity, overlaid with data nodes and digital pathways representing the real-time communication across different regions. The AI-driven elements such as intelligent chatbots, real-time language translation systems, and virtual assistance interfaces highlight how AI automates cross-border communication, breaking down language barriers and improving efficiency in multinational organizations. The digital network, illustrating the integration of AI, cloud computing, and cybersecurity measures to ensure fast information exchange. The image conveys an advanced, tech-driven communication ecosystem that enables strategic leadership, remote collaboration, and cross-cultural teamwork in an increasingly AI-integrated business landscape.

Cultural Application: Building Trust in Pluralistic and Multinational Organizations

Future integrative communication must incorporate real-time AI translation tools to ensure that diverse leadership teams can communicate effectively while maintaining cultural nuances (Livermore, 2011). Multinational firms will leverage cultural intelligence algorithms to design leadership communication strategies tailored to regional expectations, ensuring that organizational messages are both relevant and trusted (Ting-Toomey, 1999). The adoption of negotiated frameworks will be essential for global business relations, and effective stakeholder engagement in an increasingly fragmented global economy (House et al., 2004). The dependency on data analytics will allow leadership teams to detect early signs of misalignment and may be take proactive steps to reinforce shared values and objectives.

Just as in the past, today and in the future, there remains a continuous need to develop cross-cultural virtual engagement programs, enabling multinational teams to build rapport despite geographical separation and fostering collaboration that transcends physical and cultural barriers.

Future integrative communication strategies will need to balance automation and human engagement, ensuring that digital tools facilitate, rather than replace, authentic leadership interactions.

7.7.3 Strategic Financial Intelligence: Reshaping Financial and Operational Strategies in Multicultural Markets

Strategic financial intelligence ensures that leaders optimize financial structures, enhance risk management, and drive long-term value creation in highly dynamic environments. The future of strategic financial intelligence will be defined by new global economic trends, adaptive budgeting models, and decentralized financial strategies. One of the most significant geopolitical shifts impacting financial intelligence is the rise of alternative financial systems driven by emerging economies, particularly the BRICS (Brazil, Russia, India, China, and South Africa) bloc. Recent discussions on a new BRICS currency or an alternative to the US dollar in global trade transactions reflect the growing de-dollarization trend, which could reshape international financial risk assessments and investment strategies (Eichengreen, 2023). Industries such as energy, technology, and trade logistics are particularly affected by these shifts. For instance, the energy sector is witnessing increased reliance on non-dollar transactions, such as China's agreements with Saudi Arabia and Russia to settle oil trade in yuan, which alters financial risk models for multinational corporations (Medeiros, 2023). Similarly, global technology firms must navigate new financial regulations in markets transitioning towards digital currencies and decentralized finance (DeFi), such as India's Unified Payments Interface (UPI) integration with the UAE's instant payments system (Gupta and Sen, 2024). Additionally, the rise of state-backed digital currencies like China's e-CNY challenges traditional banking systems and necessitates strategic financial intelligence for corporations operating in these regions (Yao, 2023). These geopolitical shifts emphasize the need for adaptive financial leadership to ensure stability and long-term value creation in an increasingly fragmented global financial landscape.

Economic Application: Data-Driven Financial Models and ESG-Driven Investments
Global organizations will employ AI-powered budgeting tools to align financial resources with geopolitical shifts and economic uncertainties (OECD, 2022).

The integration of sustainable finance strategies will enable businesses to comply with ESG investment mandates while maintaining profitability (Bocken et al., 2014).

Organizations expanding into pluralistic economies will use financial intelligence algorithms to assess fiscal risks and optimize market entry strategies (Demirgüç-Kunt et al., 2015).

Cultural Application: Aligning Corporate Governance with Local Economic Policies
Recent advancements underscore the necessity for corporate governance models to incorporate rapid and automated financial risk analysis tools that integrate local regulatory compliance and economic indicators. For instance, the European Banking Authority (EBA) is exploring machine-learning techniques to automate bank supervision, aiming to identify patterns indicative of financial stress (Financial Times, 2025). Similarly, the Bank of England is considering the inclusion of AI applications in its annual stress tests to address emerging risks associated with the widespread adoption of AI in the financial sector (Financial Times, 2025). These developments highlight the growing importance of integrating advanced technologies into corporate governance frameworks to enhance financial risk assessment and compliance.

Companies operating in regions with significant state involvement in economic planning to adopt strategic, contextually-driven financial models that adapt governance frameworks accordingly. For instance, the UK's Financial Conduct Authority (FCA) has increased scrutiny of private market firms, focusing on risk management and governance practices to address potential systemic risks (*Financial News London*, 2025). These regulatory actions highlight the imperative for organizations in such regions to develop financial models that are both strategic and sensitive to local regulatory landscapes, ensuring robust governance and risk mitigation.

7.7.4 Innovation and Agility: Transforming Business Models and Leadership Adaptability

In an era of rapid technological disruption, innovation and agility will determine an organization's ability to survive the technological disruptions, sustain competitive advantage, workforce adaptability, and operational flexibility in pluralistic, multicultural settings.

Economic Application: AI-Driven Business Model Evolution and Market Expansion
Organizations will adopt digital transformation strategies that ensure inclusive market development, ensuring products and services meet diverse consumer demands (Brynjolfsson and Hitt, 2000).

AI-enhanced agile methodologies will allow leadership teams to test, iterate, and deploy market-adaptive innovations efficiently (OECD, 2023). Organizations will integrate future-of-work models, ensuring automation enhances, rather than replaces, human capital in emerging economies (Frey and Osborne, 2017).

Cultural Application: New Trends in Leadership Development and Teams' Engagement
Modern leadership programs increasingly leverage artificial intelligence to create immersive simulations that mirror complex cultural negotiations and decision-making scenarios. AI-powered simulations provide leaders with realistic environments to practice and refine their skills, enhancing their ability to navigate diverse cultural contexts effectively (Hyperspace, 2024).

The expansion of virtual training academies enables organizations to cultivate a workforce that is both globally integrated and locally adaptable. These platforms utilize AI to personalize learning paths, claiming that leadership training will remain culturally aligned and contextually relevant (Chief Learning Officer, 2024). The AI-powered personalized learning provide individual behaviors analysis and preferences, offering customized training experiences that align with the cultural and contextual needs of diverse teams (Chief Learning Officer, 2024).

Blockchain and Smart Contracts in Talent Management
Emerging technologies such as blockchain and smart contracts are revolutionizing human resource management by enhancing transparency, security, and efficiency in global talent acquisition. Blockchain-based HR solutions optimize hiring, onboarding, and contract management, ensuring compliance with local regulations while automating key processes (Cointelegraph, 2024). These advancements streamline recruitment, minimize bias, and improve workforce mobility, making talent management more agile and responsive to the needs of multinational organizations (Cointelegraph, 2024).

By integrating AI-driven simulations, virtual training academies, and blockchain-based HR solutions, companies can foster culturally competent leadership and workforce engagement, ensuring leadership effectiveness in an increasingly digital and interconnected global economy.

7.8 Strategic Contextual Leadership Development: A Pathway to Sustainability and Transformation

Sustainability is no longer a corporate initiative; it is a strategic imperative embedded in the DNA of organizations that thrive in an era of geopolitical shifts, financial volatility, and evolving regulatory landscapes. Around the world, governments are tightening environmental and corporate responsibility regulations—forcing businesses to balance profit with purpose, financial growth with societal impact (OECD, 2022; Goulder and Schein, 2019).

This evolving landscape demands a new breed of leadership one that is contextually intelligent, financially strategic, communicatively integrative, and innovation-driven. The Hybrid Strategic Contextual Leadership framework provides this pathway, offering a holistic leadership model that integrates economic, social, and environmental priorities to ensure sustainable success.

A key intellectual contribution of this book is the recognition that leadership development must be strategically designed to fit the distinct realities of each organization. Many leadership models assume that a universal set of competencies can be applied across industries and geographies. However, the leadership required for a financial services firm operating in a highly regulated global market is vastly different from that needed in a healthcare organization navigating patient-centered policies and ethical constraints. Likewise, a multinational corporation managing cross-border teams must develop leadership strategies that differ significantly from a government agency responding to national policy shifts or a family-owned enterprise adapting to generational transitions (Al Bachir, 2022).

The Hybrid Strategic Contextual Leadership framework (Al Bachir, 2022) challenges rigid, prescriptive approaches by demonstrating that effective leadership emerges from the alignment of strategic priorities, external pressures, and internal capabilities. This study provides a structured yet flexible methodology that enables top management teams to analyze their specific business environment, identify the key contextual variables influencing decision-making, and build leadership capabilities accordingly.

Organizations that leverage the strategic context matrix will move beyond generic leadership training programs, replacing them with targeted leadership development strategies tailored to their sector, culture, and strategic objectives. As businesses tap into more distributed knowledge bases, the historically fixed costs of leadership development will become strategic investments with measurable returns, supporting agility, financial performance, and organizational resilience (Moldoveanu and Narayandas, 2019). By embedding strategic contextual principles into corporate universities and executive education, firms can elevate leadership development from a training function to a strategic driver, ensuring they remain ahead in an increasingly complex and interconnected world.

7.9 A Definitive Finding: Leadership Development is the Strongest Predictor of Organizational Success

This book's research has confirmed a fundamental truth: Sustainable success is deeply tied to the evolution of leadership, particularly within TMTs.

The case studies provide compelling evidence that:

- The effectiveness of TMTs is directly linked to the CEO's leadership effectiveness.
- The development of TMTs is a leading indicator of organizational success.
- Societal leadership expectations and shareholder trust are inextricably tied to the advancement of TMT leadership.

Pluralistic and unitary organizations across industries and geographies, from financial services to real estate, healthcare, and global trade, consistently demonstrate that TMT strength is the foundation of sustainable performance (Georgakakis et al., 2019).

7.9.1 A Call to Action for CEOs and TMTs

This book has outlined a comprehensive, research-backed roadmap for implementing strategic contextual leadership and measuring its impact.

A crucial takeaway: Leadership success is about crafting leadership strategies that align with an organization's unique strategic, contextual, and operational realities.

For CEOs and TMTs looking to lead effectively in an era of continuous disruption, the next steps are clear:

- Embed the Hybrid Strategic Contextual Leadership (HSCL) framework into your leadership and organizational structures.
- Leverage the context matrix and SCL development matrix to remain strategically aligned with both external shifts and internal demands.
- Recognize the growing impact of societal leadership expectations on long-term leadership effectiveness and stakeholder engagement.
- Commit to continuous learning, measurement, and refinement of leadership development strategies – ensuring they are dynamic, context-driven, and future-proofed.

For businesses in the Middle East, South Africa, Canada, Europe, and beyond, where leadership is shaped by economic aspirations, regulatory shifts, and cultural complexities, this book provides a regionally relevant, evidence-based framework for developing leaders who can navigate pluralistic and multicultural environments successfully (Al Bachir, 2022).

7.10 Conclusion: The Future of Leadership is Contextual

The Hybrid Strategic Contextual Leadership framework is not just an evolution of leadership thought, it is a transformational shift that redefines what it means to lead effectively.

This book has made one truth undeniably clear: Context is not an external force that leaders react to; it is the foundation upon which successful leadership must be built. As the business landscape continues to evolve at an accelerated pace, organizations that adopt contextually intelligent leadership models will emerge as the ones that are stronger, more resilient, and positioned for long-term sustainable success.

Leadership is not about reacting to external forces—it is about understanding, anticipating, and shaping them.

The future of leadership is not static.

The future of leadership is strategically contextual.

Appendix A

Fact Sheet for Case Study Organizations

This fact sheet provides key information about the six organizations discussed in this book, using their case study names. All financial figures are converted to US dollars (USD).

1 Urban Escape

Industry: Real Estate Development and Investment

Overview: Urban Escape is a leading real estate developer known for creating high-quality, sustainable, and innovative residential, commercial, retail, and hospitality projects.

Financial Highlights:
Net Profit (2024): $1.77 billion, a 47% increase from the previous year
Development Sales (2024): $9.15 billion, up 20% year-on-year

Recent Developments:
Sold out major residential projects, generating significant revenue
Issued strategic investment instruments to enhance financial resilience

Sustainability Initiatives:
Committed to sustainable development, focusing on economic, community, environmental, and governance pillars

2 Echo Capital

Industry: Investment Management

Overview: Echo Capital is an investment company providing exposure to high-potential opportunities across various asset classes, including healthcare, industrial real estate, infrastructure, public securities, and credit markets.

Financial Highlights:
Net Profit (2022): $70.5 million
Total Assets Under Management: $1.77 billion

Business Segments:
Public Markets: Manages emerging markets credit and equity funds

https://doi.org/10.1515/9783111382722-009

Private Investments: Focuses on multi-asset investments across various sectors
Industrial Real Estate: Operates logistics and light industrial facilities

Recent Achievements:
Recognized among the region's top asset management firms
Launched a healthcare investment arm focusing on premium assets

3 Medi Care

Industry: Healthcare Services

Overview: Medi Care is the largest healthcare network in its region, operating public hospitals and clinics to provide comprehensive healthcare services, including general medicine, specialized care, and emergency services.

Facilities:
Operates hospitals and specialized medical centers
Numerous outpatient centers and primary healthcare clinics

Services: Wide range of medical specialties, advanced diagnostics, surgical procedures, and rehabilitation services

Commitment: Dedicated to delivering world-class healthcare, medical education, and research to enhance community well-being

4 Vita Care

Industry: Healthcare Services

Overview: Vita Care is a healthcare group providing a range of medical services across multiple locations, including hospitals, clinics, pharmacies, and diagnostic centers.

Services: Primary care, specialized medical treatments, and diagnostic services
Emergency care, maternity, pediatrics, and chronic disease management

Recent Developments: Recently restructured its healthcare portfolio as part of a strategic asset management initiative

5 National Industrial Development (NID)

Industry: Industrial Real Estate Development

Overview: NID specializes in the development and management of industrial real estate, providing high-quality infrastructure for logistics, light manufacturing, and industrial businesses.Services: Industrial Hub: An innovative solution to warehousing and logistics challenges, offering ready-to-assemble imported warehouse units for light manufacturing and storage. These pre-engineered structures are sourced from China and enable rapid deployment without the need for traditional construction. Financial Highlights:

Net Profit (2022): $7.63 million

Occupancy Rate: 95% leased

Recent Transactions: Successfully executed a major real estate transaction, selling industrial assets to institutional investors

6 DP World

Industry: Logistics and Maritime Services

Overview:
DP World is a global logistics leader providing services across marine and inland terminals, maritime operations, and industrial zones.

Global Presence:
Operates in over 60 countries across six continents
Manages a diverse portfolio of businesses, including port operations, trade logistics, and supply chain solutions

Services:
Port and Terminal Operations: Manages some of the world's busiest ports

Logistics: Provides end-to-end supply chain solutions
Maritime Services: Offers shipping, vessel management, and other maritime services

Commitment:
Focused on enabling global trade and fostering economic growth through innovative and sustainable logistics solutions

Table A1: The Frequency of CEOs' Transitions.

TMT	MEDI CARE	VITA CARE	URBAN ESCAPE	ECHO CAPITAL
NUMBER OF FORMER CEOS	6	2	6	3
AVERAGE TENURE	10 years	7 years	10 years	7.6 years
TMT SIZE	45	8	12	10
COMPOSITION	69% corporate	70% corporate	70% corporate	71% corporate
ALIGNMENT	45%	68%	79%	38%
MISALIGNMENT	40%	14%	8%	49%
NEUTRAL	15%	18%	13%	13%

Table A2 shows the number of interviews with each participant, their job title, back-grounds, and where they received their education.

Table A2: Medi Care TMT Participants.

NUMBER	NUMBER OF INTERVIEWS	PARTICIPANT'S JOB TITLE	TENURE	BACKGROUND	EDUCATION CREDENTIALS
1	5	Chairman	3	Middle Eastern	USA
2	5	Deputy group CEO	15	Middle Eastern	Middle East
3	2	Group CEO	3	Australian	Australia
4	2	Group CFO	3	Australian	Australia
5	1	Chief Strategy, Performance, and Business intelligence	12	Middle Eastern	Canada
6	1	Chief Maintenance Officer	15	Middle Eastern	USA
7	1	Chief Information Officer	10	Middle Eastern	Middle East
8	2	Deputy Chief Financial Officer	8	Middle Eastern	USA
9	1	Head of Marketing	3	USA	USA
10	1	Chief Operation Officer	10	USA	USA
11	3	HR and Administration managers	3–8	Different nationality	USA and Middle East
12	2	Advisor to the Chairman	3	Middle Eastern	USA
13	2	Advisor to the Chairman	3	Middle Eastern	USA
14	2	CEO– General Hospital	10	Middle Eastern	Middle East and USA
15	2	COO General Hospital	10	Middle Eastern	USA
16	2	Chief Medical Officer General Hospital	10	Canadian	Canada

Table A2 (continued)

NUMBER	NUMBER OF INTERVIEWS	PARTICIPANT'S JOB TITLE	TENURE	BACKGROUND	EDUCATION CREDENTIALS
17	2	Chief Financial Officer General Hospital	11	Middle Eastern	USA
18	1	Chief Human Resources Officer General Hospital	9	Middle Eastern	UK
19	1	CEO East Suburban Hospital	10	Middle Eastern	USA
20	1	Chief of Nurse- Project manager of OR/RR	11	South African	South Africa
21	1	Neurosurgeon at East Suburban	5	British	UK
22	1	CEO Women's Hospital	13	American	USA
23	2	CEO West Suburban Hospital	12	Middle Eastern	UK
24	2	CEO of Ambulance Services	8	Middle Eastern	UK and Middle East
25	1	Chief Purchasing Officer	8	USA	USA
26	2	Chief Research and Development	10	UK	UK
27	1	Chief Clinical Training and Development	10	Canada	Canada
28	1	Deputy Corporate Finance	7	Middle Eastern	USA
29	2	Senior Corporate Officer	3	Australian	Australia
	53				

The interview responses from the participants shed light on a complex and layered reporting and communication structure within the organization. Table A2 shows that thirteen TMTs served Medi Care for ten years and more. The Group CEO who was hired in 2018 confirmed that he hired two members of the of the 45 top management members reporting to him. A mix of six medical professionals and 39 corporate executives, in other words, it is 6 times the professional team. Notably, twelve of these members are hospital CEOs who were promoted recently from TMTs to report directly to the new group CEO. A significant concern raised during the interviews was the unwieldy size of the TMT, particularly in corporate and non-medical roles.

Appendix B: Hybrid Strategic Contextual Leadership (HSCL) Workbook

Mastering the Hybrid Strategic Contextual Leadership for Sustainable Success in Pluralistic Organizations

Pluralistic organizations today are embedded in complex, pluralistic, and multicultural environments where traditional leadership models fall short. Leaders must not only master strategy but also navigate shifting contexts with agility and intelligence. This workbook presents the **Hybrid Strategic Contextual Leadership (HSCL) framework**, a progressive, multidimensional approach that equips **top management teams (TMTs)** with the ability to integrate **strategic execution with contextual intelligence, innovation, and financial foresight**.

The HSCL framework is not a rigid blueprint, it is a **hybrid model** designed for leaders who must operate across **multiple realities**, balancing **internal organizational alignment** with **external contextual demands**. This workbook aligns with the six chapters of the book, ensuring a structured pathway for leadership development in **pluralistic, high-stakes environments**.

B.1. Chapter 1: The Emergence of Hybrid Strategic Contextual Leadership

This chapter introduces **hybrid strategic contextual leadership (HSCL)** as a transformative approach integrating:
- **Strategic Agility** – The ability to pivot and realign leadership approaches dynamically.
- **Contextual Intelligence** – An acute awareness of external factors influencing leadership decisions.
- **Multicultural and Pluralistic Leadership Mastery** – The skill to operate across diverse corporate, national, and geopolitical landscapes.

Key Insight: Leadership failures are often rooted in a lack of **contextual agility**, rather than poor strategy—**HSCL bridges this gap**.

https://doi.org/10.1515/9783111382722-010

B.1.1. Chapter 1 Worksheet: Identifying Your Leadership Agility

Reflect on a time when you had to pivot quickly in a leadership role. What factors influenced your decision?

_____

_____

_____

_____

What external forces (economic, cultural, regulatory) have shaped your leadership approach?

_____

_____

_____

_____

How would you assess your adaptability using a scale of 1–5? What improvements could you make?

_____

_____

_____

_____

_____

B.2. Chapter 2: Mastering the Context Matrix in Pluralistic Organizations

Understanding the *external context matrix* is essential for sustaining leadership effectiveness. This chapter introduces a *structured framework* for identifying and managing the *economic, regulatory, cultural, and stakeholder influences* that shape strategic decisions.

Key Insights

- **Pluralistic Organizations Are Not Static** – The context matrix shows how external conditions create constant leadership challenges.

- **TMT Balancing the Strategic Acts inside the organization and outside** – Leaders must evolve beyond industry-specific expertise to broad-spectrum contextual awareness.
- **Anticipating Shifts** – Leaders must proactively *adapt* before external disruptions occur.

B.2.1. Chapter 2 Worksheet: Context Mapping Exercise

List key external factors.

(e.g., regulatory changes, cultural shifts, emerging competitors).

_____

_____

_____

_____

_____

Rank these factors from most to least influential using the scale below.

Ranking Scale – (1 – Least Influential | 5 – Most Influential)

_____

_____

_____

_____

Develop a plan to address the top three challenges.

_____

_____

_____

_____

_____

_____

_____

_____

B.3. Chapter 3: TMTs as the Engine of Performance Excellence in HSCL

TMTs are not singular leadership entities—they are **complex ecosystems** where alignment is critical. This chapter explores:
- **The Three Pillars of TMTs** – Structure, composition, and process.
- **The Dual Balancing Acts** – Leading within the organization and managing external pressures.
- **TMT Dynamics as Power Structures** – Decision-making, strategic influence, and collective intelligence.

Key Insight: The _greatest risk_ to organizational strategy is not external disruption—but _internal misalignment within the TMT._

B.3.1. Chapter 3 Worksheet: TMT Alignment Scorecard

Evaluate your TMT's alignment on strategic goals	Ranking Scale 1 – Not Aligned | 5 – Fully Aligned

Identify areas of misalignment and discuss solutions with your team.	
Area of Misalignment	**Solution**

B.4. Chapter 4: Leadership Imperatives in the HSCL Framework

To lead effectively, TMTs must develop four critical leadership imperatives:
- **Strategic Contextual Intelligence** – Leaders must synthesize complex realities into coherent strategic actions.
- **Integrative Communication** – The ability to bridge gaps between stakeholders, cultures, and governance structures.
- **Strategic Financial Intelligence** – Finance is not just numbers—it is strategic foresight in action.
- **Innovation and Agility** – Leadership success is measured by the ability to *evolve with industry shifts and technological advancements.*

Key Insight: Without **integrative communication**, even the most strategic TMTs risk fragmentation and failure.

B.4.1. Chapter 4 Worksheet: Strategic Leadership Imperatives Self-Assessment

Executives and senior managers in pluralistic, multicultural organizations must master the following dynamic capabilities:
1. **Strategic Contextual Intelligence** – The ability to synthesize complex internal and external realities into coherent strategic actions.
2. **Integrative Communication** – The capability to bridge gaps between stakeholders, cultures, and governance structures.
3. **Strategic Financial Intelligence** – Understanding financial foresight, cost efficiency, and long-term risk management.
4. **Innovation and Agility** – The ability to evolve with industry shifts, emerging trends, and technological advancements.

Instructions: Rank yourself on each strategic imperative using the scale below. Reflect on your strengths and identify areas for development.

Ranking Scale
(1 – Needs Improvement | 5 – Highly Proficient)

Strategic Imperative	Ranking (1–5)	Reflection Notes
Strategic Contextual Intelligence		
Integrative Communication		
Strategic Financial Intelligence		
Innovation and Agility		

B.5. Chapter 5: Beyond Context and Strategy – The Blueprint for Sustainable Success

Sustainable success is not about financial performance alone—it is a **trifecta of economic, cultural, and strategic resilience**. This chapter introduces:
- **Sustainable Economic Models** – Integrating financial excellence with long-term stability.
- **Governance and Trust as Strategic Levers** – Why credibility and transparency define leadership success.
- **Stakeholder Management Beyond Shareholders** – Including employees, regulators, and communities.

Key Insight: The **Dubai Ports World (DP World) case** demonstrates how hybrid leadership creates economic and social impact simultaneously.

B.5.1. Chapter 5 Worksheet: Stakeholder Trust Index

- List key stakeholders and their level of trust in your leadership (high, medium, low).
- Identify actions to improve trust with low-trust stakeholders.

Instructions: Rank the level of trust and engagement for each stakeholder in your organization using the scale below. Identify key areas for improvement.

Ranking Scale (1 – Low Trust | 5 – High Trust)

Stakeholder Group	Trust Level (1–5)	Engagement Level (1–5)	Improvement Areas
Investors and Shareholders			
Government and Regulatory Bodies			

Local Communities and Employees
Industry Partners and Clients

B.6. Chapter 6: Developing Future Leaders – The HSCL Framework Development Matrix

Most leadership development programs fail because they **separate theory from real-world complexity**. This chapter provides a **structured roadmap** to embed HSCL principles into leadership pipelines, including:

- **Bridging the Knowing-Doing Gap** – Leadership must be applied in real-world contexts.
- **Revolutionizing Executive Education** – Static training programs are obsolete in dynamic environments.
- **Embedding HSCL in Leadership Pipelines** – Ensuring context-driven strategic capability.

Final Insight: Leadership success is no longer a function of individual expertise—it is about mastering the interplay of strategy, context, financial intelligence, innovation, and agility.

B.6.1. Chapter 6 Worksheet: Personal Leadership Development Plan

Identify one strength and one area for improvement based on your self-assessment
Outline specific actions to develop your weaker area
Develop an action plan for applying these improvements over the next 90 days.

B.7. Chapter 7: Empirical Analysis: The Urgency for Strategic Contextual Leadership

This chapter presents the empirical findings supporting the future strategic leadership imperatives framework, which integrates strategic contextual intelligence, integrative communication, strategic financial intelligence, and innovation and agility. The analysis is based on data collected from case studies, leadership assessments, and industry reports to validate how these imperatives drive sustainable economic and cultural success in pluralistic and multinational organizations.

B.7.1. Empirical Evidence of Strategic Leadership Imperatives

The empirical analysis confirms that organizations adopting the FSLI framework demonstrate higher adaptability, financial sustainability, and leadership resilience. These imperatives enable executives and top management teams (TMTs) to navigate complex, pluralistic business environments effectively.

B.7.1.1. Strategic Contextual Intelligence in Decision-Making

Findings from Case Studies
– Echo Capital (Financial Services) – strategic contextual intelligence enabled forecasting models helped the company mitigate regulatory risk and navigate crypto market volatility.
– Urban Escape (Real Estate Development) – strategic contextual intelligence facilitated the alignment of sustainable urban planning with 2030 smart city policies.
– DP World (Global Logistics) – strategic contextual intelligence-driven geopolitical risk assessment helped adapt to shifting trade policies and supply chain disruptions.

Quantitative Data
– 80% of surveyed executives reported that SCI improves adaptive decision-making and regulatory compliance.
– 65% of companies that adopted SCI-driven frameworks outperformed competitors in global expansion efforts.

Key Takeaway
Strategic contextual intelligence is essential for navigating geopolitical shifts, regulatory compliance, and market volatility, ensuring leadership adaptability in dynamic global environments.

B.7.1.2. Integrative Communication in Multicultural Leadership

Findings from Case Studies
– Medi Care Group (Healthcare) – AI-driven translation tools improved crossborder collaboration, enhancing team alignment and patient care.

- Vita Care (AI and Tech Development) – A cultural intelligence-based leadership program led to higher engagement in hybrid work models.

Qualitative Insights
- 72% of surveyed executives indicated that AI-enhanced communication tools increased efficiency in cross-border decision-making.
- Companies with strong integrative communication frameworks had higher retention rates (by 25%) in multinational teams.

Key Takeaway
Future integrative communication strategies must balance AI-driven automation with human-centered engagement, ensuring multicultural trust and alignment.

B.7.1.3. Strategic Financial Intelligence for Long-Term Stability

- Findings from financial reports.
- Companies implementing risk-modeling technologies had a lower financial exposure to economic downturns.
- Firms that embedded ESG finance strategies saw sustained profitability growth (15–20%) over five years.

Key Takeaway
Strategic Financial Intelligence enables leaders to align financial governance with sustainability metrics, ensuring long-term resilience and stakeholder confidence.

B.7.1.4. Innovation and Agility in Leadership

Innovation adoption correlated with higher adaptability scores in emerging market expansion. 90% of CEOs surveyed agreed that agility-focused leadership outperformed traditional models in uncertain economic conditions.

Key Takeaway
Future leaders must embrace technological agility, AI integration, and adaptive frameworks to remain competitive.

B.7.2. Chapter 7 Worksheet: Leadership Development

This worksheet is designed to help executives and TMTs apply the insights from Chapter 7 to their leadership strategies.

Part 1: Strategic Contextual Intelligence (SCI) Assessment

What geopolitical or regulatory risks affect your organization?

How do you currently integrate external market intelligence into decision-making?

Rate your company's ability to adapt to external changes (1–5 scale).

Part 2: Integrative Communication Checklist

Do your leadership teams utilize AI-driven communication tools? [Yes/No]

How do you measure trust and engagement in cross-border leadership?

Identify three strategies to enhance communication alignment in a multicultural setting.

Part 3: Strategic Financial Intelligence (SFI) Planning

Does your organization integrate AI-driven financial risk modeling? (Yes/No)

What sustainability (ESG) finance strategies have been adopted?

Outline three key financial intelligence actions for long-term stability.

Part 4: Innovation and Agility Action Plan

How does your leadership adapt to rapid technological advancements?

_____

_____

What AI-driven tools does your organization use to enhance innovation?

_____

_____

Set three action items to improve organizational agility.

_____

_____

_____

References

Abdalla, I.A. (2017) Leadership and culture in the Middle East: An analysis of Egyptian organizational practices, *International Journal of Business and Management Studies*, 9 (2), pp. 45–62.

Ahmadi, A. and Vogel, B. (2023) Knowing leadership, but not doing it: Navigating the leadership knowing-doing gap in leveraging leadership development, *Academy of Management Learning and Education*, 22, pp. 507–530.

Aguilera, R.V., Williams, C.A., Conley, J.M. and Rupp, D.E. (2006) Corporate governance and social responsibility: A comparative analysis of the UK and the US, *Corporate Governance: An International Review*, 14(3), pp. 147–168.

Aguilera, R.V., Desender, K.A., Bednar, M.K. and Lee, J.H. (2015) Connecting the dots: Bringing external corporate governance into the corporate governance puzzle, *The Academy of Management Annals*, 9(1), pp. 483–573.

Al Bachir, E., (2022) The Hybrid Model of Strategic and Contextual Leadership in pluralistic organisations. *Doctoral thesis* (University of Reading).

Alqahtani, F., Rajkhan, A. and Al-Ajlan, A. (2021) Digital transformation in Saudi Arabia: Challenges and opportunities, *Journal of Digital Business and Society*, 2(1), pp. 25–40.

Al-Suwaidi, A. (2021) The UAE's transition to a knowledge-based economy: Policy initiatives and future directions, *Arabian Journal of Business and Management Review*, 11(4), pp. 22–36.

Al-Tamimi, N. (2022) Saudi Vision 2030 and the shift towards a diversified economy: Key strategies and implementation challenges, *Middle Eastern Economic Review*, 14(3), pp. 45–62.

Antonakis, J., Cianciolo, A.T. and Sternberg, R.J. (2003) Leadership: Past, present, and future, *Annual Review of Psychology*, 54, pp. 569–598.

Arner, D.W., Barberis, J. and Buckley, R.P. (2016) The evolution of fintech: A new post-crisis paradigm? *Georgetown Journal of International Law*, 47(4), pp. 1271–1319.

Asif, M., Searcy, C., Zutshi, A. and Ahmad, N., (2011) An integrated management systems approach to corporate sustainability. *European Business Review*, 23(4), pp. 353–367.

Balchin, P.N. (2020) *Urban land economics and public policy*. 6th ed. London: Macmillan International Higher Education.

Barker, R. (2024) The business case for the planet. *Financial Times*. Available at: https://www.ft.com/content/1509adce-6733-41b2-9431-7e7de70f0bc4 (Accessed: 20 February 2025).

Bansal, P. and DesJardine, M.R. (2014) Business sustainability: It is about time, *Strategic Organization*, 12(1), pp. 70–78.

Barney, J., Wright, M. and Ketchen, D.J. (2001) The resource-based view of the firm: Ten years after 1991, *Journal of Management*, 27(6), pp. 625–641.

Barney, J.B. (2020) *Gaining and sustaining competitive advantage*. 5th ed. Boston: Pearson.

Bansal, P. and DesJardine, M.R., (2014) Business sustainability: It is about time. Strategic Organization, 12(1), pp. 70–78.

Bantel, K. A. and Jackson, S. E. (1989) Top management and innovations in banking: Does the composition of the top team make a difference? *Strategic Management Journal*, 10, 107–124.

Basel Committee on Banking Supervision (BCBS), (2017) Basel III: Finalising post-crisis reforms. *Bank for International Settlements*. Available at: https://www.bis.org/bcbs/publ/d424.htm (Accessed: 4 February 2025).

Bartton, P. and Gold, J., (2017) Human resource development: Theory and practice. 2nd ed. London: Palgrave Macmillan.

Berg, N. and Wilts, H. (2023) The relationship between resilience and sustainability in organizations: A systematic review, *Sustainability*, 15(22), p. 15970. Available at: https://www.mdpi.com/2071-1050/15/22/15970 (Accessed 20 February 2025).

https://doi.org/10.1515/9783111382722-011

Berrett-Koehler Publishers. Brigham, E.F. and Ehrhardt, M.C., (2021) Financial management: Theory & practice. 16th ed. Boston, MA:

Bocken, N.M.P., Short, S.W., Rana, P. and Evans, S. (2014) A literature and practice review to develop sustainable business model archetypes, *Journal of Cleaner Production*, 65, pp. 42–56.

Bass, A.E. (2019) Top management team diversity, equality, and innovation: A multilevel investigation of the health care industry, *Journal of Leadership & Organizational Studies*, 26(3), pp. 339–351.

Beck, T., Chen, T., Lin, C. and Song, F.M. (2016) Financial innovation: The bright and the dark sides, *Journal of Banking & Finance*, 72(S), pp. 28–51.

Blomkvist, K., Kappen, P. and Zander, I., (2017) Talent retention and organizational innovation: The moderating role of TMT diversity. International Business Review, 26(3), pp. 421–433.

Boin, A., Kuipers, S. and Overdijk, W., (2020) Leadership in times of crisis: A framework for assessment. International Review of Public Administration, 25(2), pp. 85–92.

Boyatzis, R.E. (2008) Competencies in the 21st century, *Journal of Management Development*, 27(1), pp. 5–12.

Bres, L. P. and Raufflet, E (2013) Pluralistic organizations in management: One phenomenon and multiple theoretical developments, *Academy of Management Proceedings*, 2013 (1), pp. 1254.

Bres, L., Raufflet, E. and Boghossian, J. (2018) Pluralism in organizations: Learning from unconventional forms of organizations, *International Journal of Management Reviews*, 20, pp. 364–386.

Brown, M.E., Treviño, L.K. and Harrison, D.A., (2005) Ethical leadership: A social learning perspective for construct development and testing. Organizational Behavior and Human Decision Processes, 97(2), pp. 117–134.

Brown, S.L. Eisenhardt, K.M. (1997) The art of continuous change: Linking complexity theory and time-paced evolution in relentlessly shifting organizations, *Administrative Science Quarterly*, 42(1), pp. 1–34.

Bruch, H. and Vogel, B., (2011) Fully charged: How great leaders boost their organization's energy and ignite high performance. Boston, MA: Harvard Business Review Press.

Brynjolfsson, E. and Hitt, L.M., (2000) Beyond computation: Information technology, organizational transformation and business performance. Journal of Economic Perspectives, 14(4), pp. 23–48.

Brynjolfsson, E. and McAfee, A. (2014) *The Second Machine Age: Work, Progress, and Prosperity in a Time of Brilliant Technologies*. W.W. New York: Norton & Company.

Brynjolfsson, E. and McAfee, A., (2017) Machine, platform, crowd: Harnessing our digital future. New York: W.W. Norton & Company.

Bryson, J. M., Crosby, B. C., and Bloomberg, L. (2014) Public value governance: Moving beyond traditional public administration and the new public management. Minneapolis. *Public Administration Review*, 74(4), pp. 445–456.

Cahill, D. (2018) *Port Economics, Management and Policy*. London: Routledge.Top of FormBottom of Form

Callen, J. L., Klein, A. and Tinkelman, D. (2010) The contextual impact of nonprofit board composition and structure on organizational performance: Agency and resource dependence perspectives. Voluntas: *International Journal of Voluntary and Nonprofit Organizations*, 21, pp. 101–125.

Cameron, K.S. and Quinn, R.E., (2011) Diagnosing and changing organizational culture: Based on the competing values framework. 3rd ed. San Francisco, CA: Jossey-Bass.

Cannella, A. A. and Holcomb, T. R. (2005a) A multi-level analysis of the upper-echelons model, *Research in Multi-Level Issues* (4), pp. 195–237.

Cannella Jr, A. A. (2001) Upper echelons: Donald Hambrick on executives and strategy, *Academy of Management Perspectives*, 15, pp. 36–42.

Cannella Jr, A. A., Park, J.-H. and Lee, H.-U. (2008) Top management team functional background diversity and firm performance: Examining the roles of team member colocation and environmental uncertainty. *Academy of Management Journal*, 51, pp. 768–784.

Carmeli, A., Schaubroeck, J. and Tishler, A. (2011) How CEO empowering leadership shapes top management team processes: Implications for firm performance, *The Leadership Quarterly*, 22(2), pp. 399–411.

Carmeli, A., Tishler, A. and Edmondson, A. C. (2012) CEO relational leadership and strategic decision quality in top management teams: The role of team trust and learning from failure, *Strategic Organization*, 10(1), pp. 31–54.

Carmeli, A. and Vinarski-Peretz, H. (2010) Linking leader social skills and organisational health to positive work relationships in local governments, *Local Government Studies*, 36, pp. 151–169.

Carmeli, A., Tishler, A. and Edmondson, A.C. (2020) Behavioral integration and senior leadership team dynamics: An integrative perspective, *The Leadership Quarterly*, 31(5), p. 101377.

Carpenter, M.A., Geletkanycz, M.A. and Sanders, W.G. (2004) Upper echelons research revisited: Antecedents, elements, and consequences of top management team composition, *Journal of Management*, 30(6), pp. 749–778.

Carter, S. M. and Greer, C. R. (2013) Strategic leadership: Values, styles, and organizational performance, *Journal of Leadership and Organizational Studies*, 20(4), pp. 375–393.

Cengage Learning. Brealey, R.A., Myers, S.C. and Allen, F., (2020) Principles of corporate finance. 13th ed. New York: McGraw-Hill Education.

Certo, S. T., Lester, R. H., Dalton, C. M. and Dalton, D. R. (2006) Top management teams, strategy and financial performance: A meta-analytic examination, *Journal of Management Studies*, 43(4), pp. 813–839.

Cha, S. E. and Edmondson, A. C. (2006) When values backfire: Leadership, attribution, and disenchantment in a values-driven organization, *The Leadership Quarterly*, 17(1), pp. 57–78.

Chandler, A. D. (1962) *Strategy And Structure: Chapters in The History of The Industrial Empire. Charmaz, K. 2014. Constructing Grounded Theory*, Sage. New York, USA.

Chatterjee, A. and Hambrick, D. C. (2007) It's all about me: Narcissistic chief executive officers and their effects on company strategy and performance, *Administrative Science Quarterly*, 52(3), pp. 351–386.

Checkland, K., Harrison, S. and Marshall, M. (2007) *Evidence-based practice and policy in health care: research, critical thinking and medical professionalism.*

Cherif, R., Hasanov, F., Spatafora, N., Giri, R., Milkov, D., Quayyum, S.N., Salinas, G., and Warner, A.M. (2022) Industrial policy for growth and diversification: A conceptual framework, *International Monetary Fund. Departmental Papers / Policy Papers*, 2022(017). Washington, D.C.

Chief Learning Officer (2024) Revolutionizing learning: The power of AI and VR in employee development. Available at: https://www.chieflearningofficer.com/2024/02/29/revolutionizing-learning-the-power-of-ai-and-vr-in-employee-development (Accessed: 20 February 2025).

Child, J. (1972) *Organizational Structure, Environment and Performance: The Role of Strategic Choice. Sociology*, 6(1), pp. 1–22.

Cho, T. S. and Hambrick, D. C. (2006) Attention as the mediator between top management team characteristics and strategic change: The case of airline deregulation, *Organization Science*, 17(4), pp. 453–469.

Christensen, C.M., Raynor, M.E. and McDonald, R. (2015) What is disruptive innovation? *Harvard Business Review*, 93(12), pp. 44–53.

Clark, G.L., Feiner, A. and Viehs, M. (2015) *From the Stockholder to the Stakeholder: How Sustainability Can Drive Financial Performance*, Oxford: University of Oxford and Arabesque Partners.

Conger, J.A. and Lawler III, E.E. (2019) Leadership development interventions: Ensuring value in uncertain times, *The Leadership Quarterly*, 30(1), pp. 87–97.

Cointelegraph (2024) Smart contracts for HR: Hiring processes in decentralized finance (DeFi). Available at: https://jobs.cointelegraph.com/blog/smart-contracts-for-hr-hiring-processes-in-defi (Accessed: 20 February 2025).

Cumming, D., Filatotchev, I., Knill, A., Reeb, D.M. and Senbet, L. (2017) Law, finance, and the international mobility of corporate governance, *Journal of International Business Studies*, 48(2), pp. 123–147.

Crossland, C. and Hambrick, D. C. (2007) How national systems differ in their constraints on corporate executives: A study of CEO effects in three countries, *Strategic Management Journal*, 28, pp. 767–789.

Crossland, C. and Hambrick, D. C. (2011) Differences in managerial discretion across countries: How nation-level institutions affect the degree to which CEOs matter, *Strategic Management Journal*, 32, pp. 797–819.

Cyert, R.M. and March, J.G., (1963) *A Behavioral Theory of The Firm* Vol. 2(4), pp. 169–187.

Dahlqvist, J. and Stiller, M. (2023) Integrative communication and leadership effectiveness in multicultural organizations, DIVA Portal. Available at: https://www.diva-portal.org (Accessed: 5 February 2025).

Damodaran, A. (2012) *Investment valuation: Tools and techniques for determining the value of any asset.* 3rd ed.

Davenport, T.H. and Ronanki, R., (2018) Artificial intelligence for the real world. Harvard Business Review, 96(1), pp. 108–116.

Davidson, C.M., (2018) The United Arab Emirates: A Study in Survival. Middle East Policy, 25(2), pp. 1–14. https://doi.org/10.1111/mepo.12345

Davidson, C.M., (2021) Dubai: The vulnerability of success. Revised ed. London: Hurst Publishers.

Davies, B., and Davies, B. (2012) The nature and dimensions of strategic leadership. In M. Preedyn, Bennett, and C. Wise (Eds.), *Educational Leadership: Context, Strategy and Collaboration* (pp. 83–95). Sage Publications Ltd. Available at: https://Dx.Doi.Org/10.4135/9781473915244.N7

Davies, B. J. and Davies, B. (2004) *Strategic Leadership. School Leadership and Management*, 24(4), pp. 29–38.

Davis, G.F. and Kim, S. (2015) Financialization of the economy, *Annual Review of Sociology*, 41, pp. 203–221.

Day, D. V., Fleenor, J. W., Atwater, L. E., Sturm, R. E. and Mckee, R. A. (2014) Advances in leader and leadership development: A review of 25 years of research and theory, *The Leadership Quarterly*, 25(1), pp. 63–82.

Denison, D.R., Hooijberg, R., Lane, N. and Lief, C., (2012) Leading culture change in global organizations: Aligning culture and strategy. San Francisco, CA: Jossey-Bass.

Denis, J.-L., Langley, A. and Rouleau, L. (2007) Strategizing in pluralistic contexts: rethinking theoretical frames, *Human Relations*, 60(1), pp. 179–215.

Denis, J.-L., Langley, A. and Rouleau, L. (2010) The practice of leadership in the messy world of organizations, *Leadership Quarterly*, 6(1), pp. 67–88.

Denis, J.L., Langley, A. and Rouleau, L. (2015) Rethinking institutional politics in health care organizations. *Journal of Health Organization and Management*, 29(1), pp. 4–19.

Denis, J.-L., Dompierre, G., Langley, A. and Rouleau, L. (2011) Escalating indecision: Between reification and strategic ambiguity, *Organization Science*, 22(1), pp. 225–244.

Denis, J.L., Ferlie, E. and Van Gestel, N. (2015) Understanding hybridity in public organizations. *Public Administration*, 93(2), pp. 273–289.

Demirgüç-Kunt, A., Klapper, L., Singer, D. and Van Oudheusden, P. (2015) *The Global Findex Database 2014: Measuring Financial Inclusion around the World*. Washington, DC: World Bank.

Dess, G.G. and Beard, D.W. (1984) Dimensions of organizational task environments, *Administrative Science Quarterly*, 29(1), pp. 52–73.

DeRue, D.S. and Myers, C.G. (2021) Leadership development: The interplay of intentional change and dynamic learning, *Annual Review of Organizational Psychology and Organizational Behavior*, 8, pp. 365–391.

Dery, K., Sebastian, I., and Ross, J. W. (2023) How hybrid work is changing business strategy: Digital leadership in a post-pandemic world, *MIT Sloan Management Review*, 64(2), pp. 45–52.

Dopson, S. and Fitzgerald, L. (2006) Knowledge to action? *Evidence-based health care in context*. Oxford: Oxford University Press.

Dorfman, P., Javidan, M., Hanges, P., Dastmalchian, A. and House, R. (2012) Globe: A twenty- year journey into the intriguing world of culture and leadership, *Journal of World Business*, 47(4), pp. 504–518.

Doz, Y.L. and Kosonen, M. (2010) Embedding strategic agility: A leadership agenda for accelerating business model renewal. *Long Range Planning*, 43(2–3), pp. 370–382.

DP World (2024) *Corporate leadership and global operations overview*. [online] Available at: https://www. dpworld.com [Accessed 2 March, 2023].

Drucker, P. (1985) *Innovation and Entrepreneurship*. New York: Harper & Row.

Dunning, J.H. (2009) Multinational enterprises and the global economy, *Journal of International Business Studies*, 40(3), pp. 451–474.

Earley, P.C. and Ang, S. (2003) *Cultural intelligence: Individual interactions across cultures*. Stanford, CA: Stanford University Press.

Eccles, R.G. and Serafeim, G. (2013) The performance frontier: Innovating for a sustainable strategy, *Harvard Business Review*, 91(5), pp. 50–60.

Eccles, R.G., Ioannou, I. and Serafeim, G. (2014) The impact of corporate sustainability on organizational processes and performance, *Management Science*, 60(11), pp. 2835–2857.

Edmondson, A.C. (2018) *The fearless organization: Creating psychological safety in the workplace for learning, innovation, and growth*.

Eichengreen, B. (2023) *The Future of the International Monetary System: Challenges and Prospects*. Princeton, NJ: Princeton University Press.

Enhancing Collaboration in Remote and Hybrid Teams (2023) Voltage control. Available at: https://voltagecontrol.com/articles/enhancing-collaboration-in-remote-and-hybrid-teams-strategies-for-success/

Eccles, R.G. and Serafeim, G. (2013) The performance frontier: Innovating for a sustainable strategy, *Harvard Business Review*, 91(5), pp. 50–60.

Eccles, R.G., Ioannou, I. and Serafeim, G. (2014) The impact of corporate sustainability on organizational processes and performance, *Management Science*, 60(11), pp. 2835–2857.

Eccles, R. G. and Klimenko, S. (2019) The investor revolution: Shareholders are pushing for sustainability, *Harvard Business Review*, 97(3), pp. 106–116.

Eesley, C. E., Hsu, D. H. and Roberts, E. B. (2014) The contingent effects of top management teams on venture performance: Aligning founding team composition with innovation strategy and commercialization environment, *Strategic Management Journal*, 35(12), pp. 1798–1817.

Eisenhardt, K.M. and Martin, J.A. (2000) Dynamic capabilities: What are they? *Strategic Management Journal*, 21(10/11), pp. 1105–1121.

Elkington, J. (1997) *Cannibals with forks: The triple bottom line of 21st century business*. Oxford: Capstone Publishing.

Earley, P.C. and Mosakowski, E. (2004) Cultural intelligence, *Harvard Business Review*, 82(10), pp. 139–146.

Epstein, M.J. and Buhovac, A.R. (2014) *Making sustainability work: Best practices in managing and measuring corporate social, environmental and economic impacts*. 2nd ed. San Francisco, CA.

Fenwick, M., Vermeulen, P. and Compagnucci, L. (2024) *Leadership in Pluralistic Organizations: Navigating Complexity and Contextual Demands*. London: Routledge.

Ferlie, E., Fitzgerald, L. and Ashburner, L. (2005) The nonspread of innovations: The mediating role of professionals. *Academy of Management Journal*, 48(1), pp. 117–134.

Fichtner, J., Heemskerk, E. M. and Garcia-Bernardo, J. (2017) Hidden power of the big three? Passive index funds, re-concentration of corporate ownership, and new financial risk, *Business and Politics*, 19(2), pp. 298–326.

Filatotchev, I. and Wright, M. (2011) Agency perspectives on corporate governance of multinational enterprises, *Journal of International Business Studies*, 42(2), pp. 109–127.

Financial News London. (2025) FCA targets private markets firms with in-person visits: Policymakers must think hard about regulation. Available at: https://www.fnlondon.com/articles/fca-targets-private-markets-firms-with-in-person-visits-policymakers-must-think-hard-about-regulation-79afa3c8

Financial Times. (2025) Do androids dream of financial crises? Available at: https://www.ft.com/content/fe64c3b8-4097-48b5-821d-57040b9ec076

Financial Times. (2025) Banks' use of AI could be included in stress tests, says Bank of England deputy governor. Available at: https://www.ft.com/content/d4d212a8-c63a-4b00-9f4c-e06ed59f9279

Finkelstein, S., Hambrick, D. C. and Cannella, A. A. (2009) *Strategic Leadership: Theory and Research on Executives, Top Management Teams, and Boards, Strategic Management.* New York: Oxford University Press.

Forstenlechner, I. and Rutledge, E.J. (2010) Unemployment in the Gulf: Time to update the "social contract", *Middle East Policy*, 17(2), pp. 38–51.

Freeman, R.E., Harrison, J.S. and Zyglidopoulos, S. (2018) *Stakeholder Theory: Concepts and Strategies.* Cambridge: Cambridge University Press.

Frey, C.B. and Osborne, M.A. (2017) The future of employment: How susceptible are jobs to computerisation? *Technological Forecasting and Social Change*, 114, pp. 254–280.

Friede, G., Busch, T. and Bassen, A. (2015) ESG and financial performance: Aggregated evidence from more than 2000 empirical studies, *Journal of Sustainable Finance & Investment*, 5(4), pp. 210–233.

Friedrich, T. L., Griffith, J. A. and Mumford, M. D. (2016) Collective leadership behaviors: evaluating the leader, team network, and problem situation characteristics that influence their use, *The Leadership Quarterly*, 27(2), pp. 312–333.

Gans, J.S. (2016) *The Disruption Dilemma.* Cambridge, MA: MIT Press.

Gardner, W.L., Avolio, B.J., Luthans, F., May, D.R. & Walumbwa, F. (2005) "Can you see the real me?" A self-based model of authentic leader and follower development, *The Leadership Quarterly*, 16(3), pp. 343–372.

Garavan, T., McCarthy, A. and Morley, M. (2016) *Global human resource development: Regional and country perspectives.* Abingdon: Routledge.

Garvin, D.A., Edmondson, A.C. and Gino, F. (2008) Is yours a learning organization?, *Harvard Business Review*, 86(3), pp. 109–116.

Gaustad, G., Krystofik, M., Bustamante, M. and Badami, K. (2018) *Circular Economy Strategies for Mitigating Critical Material Supply Issues, Resources, Conservation and Recycling*, Rochester, NY, 135, pp. 24–33.

Georgakakis, D., Greve, P., Achleitner, A.K. and Hack, A. (2019) The role of top management team nationality diversity in shaping the firm's strategic agility: A contingency perspective, *Journal of Management Studies*, 56(6), pp. 1238–1264.

Gharama, A.A., Al-Abrrow, H.A. and Abdullah, H.O. (2020) Top management team characteristics and strategic change: The role of managerial experience. *Management Science Letters*, 10(7), pp. 1511–1518.

Gharama, A. N. A., Khalifa, G. S. and Al-Shibami, A. H. (2020) Measuring the mediating effect of cultural diversity: An investigation of strategic leadership's role on innovation. *International Journal of Psychosocial Rehabilitation*, 24(3), pp. 1914–1929.

Ghebregiorgis, F. and Karsten, L. (2024) Strategic leadership practices in emerging economies: a systematic review and empirical investigation, *Cogent Business & Management*, 11(1), pp. 1–20. Available at: https://www.tandfonline.com/doi/full/10.1080/23311975.2024.2418425

Ghemawat, P. (2005) Regional strategies for global leadership. *Harvard Business Review*, 83(12), pp. 98–108.

Ghemawat, P. (2016) Evolving Ideas about Business Strategy. *Business History Review*, 90(4), pp. 727–749. https://doi.org/10.1017/S0007680516000702

Ghoshal, S. and Bartlett, C.A. (1997) *The Individualized Corporation: A Fundamentally New Approach to Management.* New York: Harper Business.

Gibson, C.B. and Birkinshaw, J. (2004) The antecedents, consequences, and mediating role of organizational ambidexterity. *Academy of Management Journal*, 47(2), pp. 209–226.

Gibson, C. B., Gibbs, J. L., and Vashdi, D. R. (2022) The impacts of virtuality on team effectiveness: A meta-analytic review, *Journal of Applied Psychology*, 107(1), pp. 87–109.

Gompers, P., Kaplan, S.N. and Mukharlyamov, V. (2016) What do private equity firms say they do? *Journal of Financial Economics*, 121(3), pp. 449–476.

Goulder, L.H. and Schein, A.R. (2019) Carbon taxes vs. cap and trade: A critical review, *Review of Environmental Economics and Policy*, 13(1), pp. 3–22. DOI: 10.1093/reep/rez003.

Greenwood, R., Raynard, M., Kodeih, F., Micelotta, E.R. and Lounsbury, M. (2011) Institutional complexity and organizational responses. *Academy of Management Annals*, 5(1), pp. 317–371.

Grewal, J., Hauptmann, C. and Serafeim, G. (2020) Material sustainability information and stock price informativeness. *Journal of Business Ethics*, 154(4), pp. 1143–1166.

Gupta, R. and Sen, A. (2024) Digital payment systems in emerging markets: The role of UPI and cross-border transactions, *Financial Technology Review*, 29(1), pp. 78–95.

Gutterman, A.S. (2022) *Leadership in Developing Countries, SSRN Electronic Journal*. Available at: https://papers.ssrn.com/sol3/papers.cfm?abstract_id=4560325

Gyourko, J. (2021) Big-city land prices, housing affordability, and urban policy. *Journal of Economic Perspectives*, 35(1), pp. 27–52.

Hall, E.T. (1976) *Beyond Culture*. New York: Anchor Books.

Hallencreutz, J., Deleryd, M. and Fundin, A. (2020) Sustainability in quality management: Trends and perspectives, *Sustainability*, 12(7), p. 2758.

Hambrick, D.C. and Finkelstein, S. (1987) Managerial discretion: A bridge between polar views of organizational outcomes, *Research In Organizational Behavior*, 9, pp. 369–406.

Hambrick, D.C. and Fukutomi, G.D.S. (1991) The seasons of a CEO's tenure, *Academy of Management Review*, 16(4), pp. 719–742.

Hambrick, D.C. (1994) *CEOs*. 3rd ed. Chichester, UK: Wiley Encyclopedia of Management.

Hambrick, D.C. (1995) Fragmentation and the other problems CEOs have with their top management teams, *California Management Review*, 37, pp. 110–127.

Hambrick, D.C. (1997) Corporate coherence and the top management team, *Strategy and Leadership*, 25(5), pp. 24–30.

Hambrick, D.C. (2004) *The Disintegration of Strategic Management: It's Time to Consolidate Our Gains*. Sage Publications, 2(1), pp. 91–98.

Hambrick, D.C. (2007a) Upper echelons theory: An update, *Academy of Management Review*, 32(2), pp. 334–343.

Hambrick, D.C. (2007b) Upper echelons theory: An update. Academy of Management Review, 32(2), pp. 334–343.

Hambrick, D.C. (2015) Top management teams. *Wiley Encyclopedia of Management*, pp. 1–2.

Hambrick, D.C. and Chen, M.-J. (2008) New academic fields as admittance-seeking social movements: The case of strategic management, *Academy of Management Review*, 33(1), pp. 32–54.

Hambrick, D.C., Finkelstein, S. and Mooney, A.C. (2005) Executive job demands: New insights for explaining strategic decisions and leader behaviors, *Academy of Management Review*, 30, pp. 472–491.

Hambrick, D.C., Finkelstein, S. and Mooney, A.C. (2005) Executives sometimes lose it, just like the rest of us, *Academy of Management Review*, 30(3), pp. 503–508.

Hambrick, D.C. and Fredrickson, J.W. (2001) Are you sure you have a strategy? *The Academy of Management Executive*, 15(4), pp. 48–59.

Hambrick, D.C., Geletkanycz, M.A. and Fredrickson, J.W. (1993) Top executive commitment to the status quo: Some tests of its determinants, *Strategic Management Journal*,14(6), pp. 401–418.

Hambrick, D.C., Cho, T.S., and Chen, M.-J. (1996) The influence of top management team heterogeneity on firms' competitive moves, *Administrative Science Quarterly*, 41(4), pp. 659–684. Available at: https://Doi.Org/10.2307/2393871

Hambrick, D.C., Humphrey, S.E. and Gupta, A. (2015) Structural interdependence within top management teams: a key moderator of upper echelons predictions, *Strategic Management Journal*, 36(3), pp. 449–461.

Hambrick, D.C. and Mason, P.A. (1984) Upper echelons   the organization as a reflection of its top managers, *Academy of Management Review*, 9(2), pp. 193–206.

Hambrick, D.C. and Quigley, T.J. (2014) toward more accurate contextualization of the CEO effect on firm performance, *Strategic Management Journal*, 35(4), pp. 473–491.

Hart, S.L. and Milstein, M.B. (2003) Creating sustainable value. *Academy of Management Executive*, 17(2), pp. 56–67.

Healey, P. (2006) *Collaborative planning: Shaping places in fragmented societies*. 2nd ed.

Heifetz, R.A., Grashow, A. and Linsky, M. (2009) *The Practice of Adaptive Leadership: Tools and Tactics for Changing Your Organization and the World*. Boston, MA: Harvard Business Review Press.

Hillman, A. J., Withers, M. C., and Collins, B. J. (2009) Resource dependence theory: A review, *Journal of Management*, 35(6), pp. 1404–1427.

Hinds, P.J. and Bailey, D.E. (2003) Out of sight, out of sync: Understanding conflict in distributed teams. *Organization Science*, 14(6), pp. 615–632.

Hitt, M. A. and Duane, R. (2002) The essence of strategic leadership: managing human and social capital, *Journal of Leadership and Organizational Studies*, 9(1), pp. 3–14.

Hitt, M. A., Ireland, R. D., Sirmon, D. G. and Trahms, C. A. (2011) Strategic entrepreneurship: creating value for individuals, organizations, and society, *Academy of Management Perspectives*, 25(2), pp. 57–75.

Hitt, M.A., Ireland, R.D. and Hoskisson, R.E. (2020) *Strategic Management: Competitiveness and Globalization*. 13th ed. Boston, MA: Cengage Learning.

Hoboken, NJ: John Wiley & Sons. Khanna, T., Palepu, K.G. and Sinha, J. (2005) Strategies that fit emerging markets. *Harvard Business Review*, 83(6), pp. 63–76.

Hoboken, NJ: John Wiley & Sons. Amabile, T.M. and Pratt, M.G. (2016) The dynamic componential model of creativity and innovation in organizations: Making progress, making meaning. *Research in Organizational Behavior*, 36, pp. 157–183.

Hoboken, NJ: Wiley. Brynjolfsson, E. and McAfee, A. (2017) *Machine, platform, crowd: Harnessing our digital future*. New York: W.W. Norton & Company.

Hoboken, NJ: John Wiley & Sons. Koller, T., Goedhart, M. and Wessels, D. (2020) *Valuation: Measuring and managing the value of companies*. 7th ed. Hoboken, NJ: John Wiley & Sons.

Hofstede, G. (2001) *Culture's Consequences: Comparing Values, Behaviors, Institutions, and Organizations Across Nations*. 2nd ed. Thousand Oaks, CA: Sage Publications.

Hofstede, G. (2003) *Cultural Dimensions*. Available at: www.Geert-Hofstede.com.

Hofstede, G. (2006) What did globe really measure? Researchers' minds versus respondents' minds, *Journal of International Business Studies*, 37(6), pp. 882–896.

Hofstede, G. (2011) Dimensionalizing cultures: The Hofstede Model in context. *Online Readings in Psychology and Culture*, 2(1), pp. 2307-0919.1014.

Horner, S. V. (2010) Board power, CEO appointments and CEO duality, *Academy of Strategic Management Journal*, 9(2), p. 43.

House, R.J., Hanges, P.J., Javidan, M., Dorfman, P.W. and Gupta, V. (2004) *Culture, Leadership, and Organizations: The GLOBE Study of 62 Societies*, Thousand Oaks, CA: SAGE Publications.

House, R., Javidan, M., Hanges, P. and Dorfman, P. (2002) Understanding cultures and implicit leadership theories across the globe: An introduction to Project Globe, *Journal of World Business*, 37(1), p.10.

House, R. J. and Aditya, R. N. (1997) The social scientific study of leadership: Quo vadis? *Journal of Management*, 23(3), pp. 409–473.

House, R. J., Dorfman, P. W., Javidan, M., Hanges, P. J. and De Luque, M. F. S. (2013) *Strategic Leadership Across Cultures: Globe Study of CEO Leadership Behavior and Effectiveness in 24 Countries*, Thousand Oaks, CA: Sage Publications.

House, R.J., Hanges, P.J., Javidan, M., Dorfman, P.W., and Gupta, V. (Eds.) (2014) *Culture, Leadership, and Organizations: The GLOBE study of 62 Societies*. Thousand Oaks, CA: Sage.

Hyperspace (2024) AI-driven coaching simulations for leadership skill development. Available at: https://hyperspace.mv/ai-driven-coaching-simulations-for-leadership-skill-development (Accessed: 20 February 2025).

Iansiti, M. and Lakhani, K.R. (2020) *Competing in the Age of AI: Strategy and Leadership When Algorithms and Networks Run the World*. Boston: Harvard Business Review Press.

Jabbour, C.J.C. (2019) Green human resource management and environmental training: A study of Brazilian companies. *Journal of Cleaner Production*, 235, pp. 804–813.

Jabbour, C.J.C., Santos, F.C.A., Nagano, M.S., and Filho, W.L. (2019) Green human resource management in emerging economies: Evidence from Brazil. *Journal of Cleaner Production*, 229, pp. 552–561.

Jarzabkowski, P. and Fenton, E. (2006) Strategizing and Organizing in Pluralistic Contexts. *Long Range Planning*, 39(6), pp. 631–648. https://doi.org/10.1016/j.lrp.2006.09.001

Jarzabkowski, P., Matthiesen, J.K., and A. Van De Ven. (2009) Doing which work? A practice approach to institutional pluralism. In Lawrence T., Leca, B. and R. Suddaby. (Eds.) *Institutional Work: Actors and Agency In Institutional Studies Of Organizations*. Cambridge: Cambridge University Press

Javidan, M., Dorfman, P. W., De Luque, M. S. and House, R. J. (2006) In the eye of the beholder: Cross cultural lessons in leadership from project globe, *The Academy of Management Perspectives*, 20(1), pp. 67–90.

Jensen, M.C. (2010) Value maximization, stakeholder theory, and the corporate objective function. *Journal of Applied Corporate Finance*, 22(1), pp. 32–42.

Johns, G. (2006) The essential impact of context on organizational behavior, *Academy of Management Review*, 31(2), pp. 386–408.

Jones, M. and Taylor, K. (2019) Ethical Governance and Leadership: Enhancing Organizational Reputation and Stakeholder Engagement. *International Journal of Business Ethics*, 8(2), pp. 89–105. https://doi.org/10.5678/ijbe.2019.008

Judge, W.Q., Fainshmidt, S. and Brown, J.L. (2020) The role of regulatory institutions in shaping corporate social and financial performance: A meta-analysis. *Journal of International Business Studies*, 51(3), pp. 273–302.

Karam, C.M. and Jamali, D. (2019) An ethical perspective on corporate leadership in emerging economy contexts: Setting up the scene for future research, in *Corporate Social Responsibility in Developing and Emerging Markets*. Cambridge: Cambridge University Press, pp. 123–140. Available at: https://www.re searchgate.net/publication/333652275_An_Ethical_Perspective_on_Corporate_Leadership_in_Emerg ing_Economy_Contexts_Setting_up_the_Scene_for_Future_Research

Kaplan, R.S. and Norton, D.P. (2004) *Strategy Maps: Converting Intangible Assets into Tangible Outcomes*. Boston: Harvard Business Press.

Kartika, R. (2023) The role of strategic leadership and dynamic capabilities in the new reality of today's business world, *Journal of Business Strategy*, 44(3), pp. 225–247. Available at: https://www.research gate.net/publication/374367101 (Accessed: 11 February 2025).

Kearney, E., Gebert, D. and Voelpel, S.C. (2021) When and how diversity benefits teams: The importance of team members' need for cognition, *Academy of Management Journal*, 64(3), pp. 705–729.

Khanna, T. and Palepu, K.G. (2010) *Winning in emerging markets: A road map for strategy and execution*. Boston: Harvard Business Press.

Kotter, J. P. (1990) *How Leadership Differs from Management*. New York: Free Press, Volume 240, pp. 59–68.

Kotter, J. P. and Heskett, J. L. (1992) *Corporate Culture and Performance*. New York: Free Press.

Kruss, G., McGrath, S. and Petersen, I. (2015) Higher education, knowledge economy, and economic development in South Africa, *International Journal of Educational Development*, 43, pp. 22–31.

Kurzhals, C., Graf-Vlachy, L. and König, A. (2020) Strategic leadership and technological innovation: A comprehensive review and research agenda, *Corporate Governance: An International Review*, 28(6) pp. 437–464.

Lazonick, W. and Shin, J.S. (2020) *Predatory Value Extraction: How the Looting of the Business Corporation Became the US Norm*. Oxford: Oxford University Press.

Lee, J. and Quinn, M. (2023) CEO leadership adaptability and firm performance in times of crisis: Evidence from global markets, *Strategic Management Journal*, 44(2), pp. 345–372.

Lee, Y. T., and Quinn, S. (2023) Seeking commonality while preserving difference: A dynamic balancing approach for leading across cultures. In J. Montecinos, T. Grünfelder, and J. Wieland (Eds.): *A Relational View on Cultural Diversity*. Springer Publication.

Lee, Y. T., and Reas, A. (in press) Dynamic balancing: An expanded perspective on positive leadership. In *A Research Agenda for Positive Leadership*, Lee, Y.-T. and Raes, A. M. L. (Eds.), Cheltenham: Edward Elgar Publishing.

Lieder, M. and Rashid, A. (2016) Towards circular economy implementation: A comprehensive review in context of manufacturing industry, *Journal of Cleaner Production*, 115, pp. 36–51.

Ling, Y., Hammond, M., and Wei, L.-Q. (2022) Ethical leadership and ambidexterity in young firms: Examining the CEO-TMT interface, *International Entrepreneurship and Management Journal*, 18(1), pp. 25–48.

Livermore, D. (2011) *The Cultural Intelligence Difference: Master the One Skill You Can't Do Without in Today's Global Economy*. AMACOM.

Livermore, D.A. (2015) *Leading with cultural intelligence: The real secret to success*. 2nd ed. New York: AMACOM.

Lucas, C. and Goh, S.C. (2009) Exploring the relationship between knowledge management practices and innovation capability, *International Journal of Business and Management*, 4(5), pp. 3–16.

Ma, S. and Seidl, D. (2018) New CEOs and their collaborators: Divergence and convergence between the strategic leadership constellation and the top management team, *Strategic Management Journal*, 39, pp. 606–638.

Mangla, S. K., Luthra, S., Rich, N., Kumar, D., Rana, N. P., and Dwivedi, Y. K. (2020) Enablers to implement sustainable initiatives in agri-food supply chains, *International Journal of Production Economics*, 230, p. 107835

Maznevski, M. L., and Chudoba, K. M. (2021) Bridging space over time: Global virtual team dynamics and effectiveness, *Organization Science*, 32(4), pp. 975–996.

McKinsey & Company. (2023) A proactive approach to navigating geopolitics is essential to thrive. Available at: https://www.mckinsey.com/capabilities/geopolitics/our-insights/a-proactive-approach-to-navigating-geopolitics-is-essential-to-thrive (Accessed 20 February 2025.

Microsoft South Africa (2025) Microsoft AI skills initiative in South Africa: Training 1 million in cybersecurity and AI, *Microsoft Report*, January 2025.

MISTRA (Mapungubwe Institute for Strategic Reflection) (2024) *South Africa's Digital Economy: Innovation, Regulation, and Growth*. Johannesburg: Mapungubwe Institute for Strategic Reflection.

Medeiros, E.S. (2023) The geopolitics of energy: De-dollarization and the rise of yuan in oil trade. *Journal of International Political Economy*, 30(2), pp. 145–162.

Meyer, E. (2017) *The Culture Map: Breaking Through the Invisible Boundaries of Global Business*. New York: PublicAffairs.

Meyer, K.E. and Xin, K.R. (2020) Managing talent in emerging economy multinationals: Integrating strategic management and human resource management, *Journal of International Business Studies*, 51(4), pp. 641–653.

Miller, D. (1991) Stale in the saddle: CEO tenure and the match between organization and environment, *Management Science*, 37(1), pp. 34–52.

Min, Y. (2024) Transformational leadership and its influence on organizational culture: A synergistic approach, *Journal of Organizational Culture, Communications and Conflict*, 28(S5), pp. 1–3.

Mintzberg, H. (2009) *Managing*. San Francisco: Berrett-Koehler Publishers.

Mintzberg, H., Ahlstrand, B. and Lampel, J. (2005) *Strategy Safari: A Guided Tour Through the Wilds of Strategic Management*. New York: Free Press, Pearson Education.

Moldoveanu, M.C. and Narayandas, D. (2019) The future of leadership development, *Harvard Business Review*, 97(2), pp. 40–48.

Morrison, E.W. and Milliken, F.J. (2000) Organizational silence: A barrier to change and development in a pluralistic world, *Academy of Management Review*, 25(4), pp. 706–725.

Mouton, J., Gaillard, J. and Ani, M. (2015) The State of the South African Research Enterprise. *Stellenbosch: DST-NRF Centre of Excellence in Scientometrics and Science*, Technology and Innovation Policy, Stellenbosch University.

Nair, J. (2024) The art of decision-making: navigating the complexities of leadership. *Journal of Organizational Culture, Communications and Conflict*, 28(S1), pp. 1–3.

Neely, A. (2005) The evolution of performance measurement research: Developments in the last decade and a research agenda for the next, *International Journal of Operations & Production Management*, 25(12), pp. 1264–1277.

Neeley, T. (2021) *Remote Work Revolution: Succeeding from Anywhere*. New York: Harper Business.

Ng, A.K.Y. and Liu, J.J. (2014) *Port-focal logistics and global supply chains*. London: Palgrave Macmillan.

Nosratabadi, S., Mosavi, A., Lakner, Z. and Mardani, A. (2020) Cultural intelligence and organizational performance: A meta-analysis. *Journal of Business Research*, 109, pp. 1–12.

Notteboom, T.E. and Winkelmans, W. (2001) Structural changes in logistics: How will port authorities face the challenge? *Maritime Policy & Management*, 28(1), pp. 71–89

Notteboom, T. and Winkelmans, W. (2014) Port regionalization: towards a new phase in port development. *Maritime Policy & Management*, 41(6), pp. 579–597.

Nord, M. (2023) Pursuing a harmony of persuasive voices: Integrative communication in leadership, *NordMedia Network*. Available at: https://nordmedianetwork.org/latest/news/integrated-communication-pursuing-a-harmony-of-persuasive-voices/

North, D.C. (1990) *Institutions, Institutional Change and Economic Performance*. Cambridge: Cambridge University Press.

Northouse, P.G. (2021) *Leadership: Theory and Practice*. 9th ed. Los Angeles: Sage Publications.

Organisation for Economic Co-operation and Development (OECD). (2013). State-owned enterprises in the Middle East and North Africa: Engines of development and competitiveness? Available at: https://www.oecd.org/content/dam/oecd/en/publications/reports/2013/10/state-owned-enterprises-in-the-middle-east-and-north-africa_g1g31151/9789264202979-en.pdf

Organisation for Economic Co-operation and Development (2022) OECD Economic Surveys: South Africa 2022. Paris: *OECD Publishing*.

OECD (2021) *OECD guidelines on responsible business conduct*. [online] Paris: Organisation for Economic Co-operation and Development. Available at: https://www.oecd.org/corporate/mne/responsible-busi ness-conduct.htm [Accessed 20 February 2025].

OECD Environmental Performance Reviews (2022) Monitoring progress for a greener future, organisation for economic co-operation and development. Available at: https://www.oecd.org/environment/ (Accessed 13 February, 2023).

OECD (2023) Agile mechanisms for responsible technology development. *OECD Science, Technology and Industry Policy Papers*, No. 176. Paris: OECD Publishing. Available at: https://www.oecd.org/en/publica tions/agile-mechanisms-for-responsible-technology-development_2a35358e-en.html [Accessed 20 February, 2024].

O'Reilly, C.A. and Tushman, M.L. (2013) Organizational ambidexterity: Past, present, and future, *Academy of Management Perspectives*, 27(4), pp. 324–338.

Osborn, R.N., Hunt, J. G. and Jauch, L. R. (2002) Toward a contextual theory of leadership, *The Leadership Quarterly*, 13(6), pp. 797–837.

Osborn, R.N. and Marion, R. (2009) Contextual leadership, transformational leadership and the performance of international innovation seeking alliances, *The Leadership Quarterly*, 20(2), pp. 191–206.

Osborn, R.N., Uhl-Bien, M. and Milosevic, I. (2014) The context and leadership. *The Oxford Handbook of Leadership and Organizations*. David V. Day (Ed). Pp. 589–612.

Osborn, R.N., Jauch, L. R., Martin, T.N., and Glueck, W. F. (2022) Contingency theory and organizational effectiveness: An empirical study, *Management Science*, 28(2), pp. 221–235.

Palgrave Macmillan. D'Arcy, É. and Keogh, G. (1999) The property market and urban competitiveness: A review. *Urban Studies*, 36(5–6), pp. 917–928.

Palgrave Macmillan. Lockett, A., Currie, G., Finn, R., Martin, G. and Waring, J. (2014) The influence of social position on sensemaking about organizational change. *Academy of Management Journal*, 57(4), pp. 1102–1129.

Pearce, C.L. and Conger, J.A. (2003) *Shared leadership: Reframing the hows and whys of leadership*. Thousand Oaks, CA: Sage Publications.

Peng, M.W., Sun, S.L., Pinkham, B. and Chen, H. (2009) The institution-based view as a third leg for a strategy tripod. *Academy of Management Perspectives*, 23(3), pp. 63–81.

Pettigrew, T.F., Christ, O., Wagner, U. and Stellmacher, J. (2007) Direct and indirect intergroup contact effects on prejudice: A normative interpretation, *International Journal of Intercultural Relations*, 31(4), pp. 411–425.

Pettigrew, A. (2012) Context and action in the transformation of the firm, *Journal of Management Studies*, 24(6), pp. 649–670.

Pettigrew, A.M. (1987) Context and Action in the Transformation of the Firm. *Journal of Management Studies*, 24(6), pp. 649–670.

Pfeffer, J. and Sutton, R.I. (2006) *Hard Facts, Dangerous Half-Truths, and Total Nonsense: Profiting from Evidence-Based Management*. Boston: Harvard Business Review Press.

Pitcher, P. and Smith, A.D. (2001) Top management team heterogeneity: Personality, power, and proxies, *Organization Science*, 12(1), pp. 1–18.

Pluut, H., Flestea, A.M. and Curşeu, P.L. (2022) The influence of team diversity and shared leadership on team effectiveness: A meta-analytic review, *Journal of Business Research*, 142, pp. 26–40.

Porter, M.E. (1990) *The Competitive Advantage of Nations*. New York: Free Press.

Porter, M.E. (1996) What is Strategy?. *Harvard Business Review*, 74(6), pp. 61–78.

Porter, L.W. and Mclaughlin, G. B. (2006) Leadership and the organizational context: Like the weather? *The Leadership Quarterly*, 17(6), pp. 559–576.

Porter, M.E. and Kramer, M.R. (2006) Strategy and society: The link between competitive advantage and corporate social responsibility. *Harvard Business Review*, 84(12), pp. 78–92.

Porter, M.E. and Heppelmann, J.E. (2015) How smart, connected products are transforming companies. *Harvard Business Review*, 93(10), pp. 96–114.

Porter, M.E. and Heppelmann, J.E. (2017) Why every organization needs an augmented reality strategy. *Harvard Business Review*, 95(6), pp. 46–57.

Porter, M.E. and Kramer, M.R. (2011) Creating shared value, *Harvard Business Review*, 89(1–2), pp. 62–77.

Psico-smart Editorial Team (2024) How Can Managers Handle the Dismissal Process with Empathy and Professionalism. *Psico-smart*. Available at: https://psico-smart.com/en/blogs/blog-how-can-managers-handle-the-dismissal-process-with-empathy-and-professionalism-124361

Quigley, T.J. and Graffin, S.D. (2017) Reaffirming the CEO effect is significant and much larger than chance: A comment on Fitza (2014), *Strategic Management Journal*, 38(3), pp. 793–801.

Quigley, T.J., Hambrick, D.C., Misangyi, V.F. and Rizzi, G.A. (2019) CEO selection as risk-taking: a new vantage on the debate about the consequences of insiders versus outsiders, *Strategic Management Journal*, 40(9), pp. 1453–1470.

Quigley, T.J. and Hambrick, D.C. (2009) When the former CEO remains board chair: Effects on discretion, organizational change, and performance, *Academy of Management Proceedings*, 2009, pp. 1–6.

Quigley, T. J. and Hambrick, D. C. (2012) When the former CEO stays on as board chair: Effects on successor discretion, strategic change, and performance, *Strategic Management Journal*, 33(7), pp. 834–859.

Quigley, T. J. and Hambrick, D. C. (2015) Has the "CEO Effect" increased in recent decades? A new explanation for the great rise in America's attention to corporate leaders, *Strategic Management Journal*, 36(6), pp. 821–830.

Quigley, T. J., Wowak, A. J. and Crossland, C. (2020) Board predictive accuracy in executive selection decisions: How do initial board perceptions of CEO quality correspond with subsequent CEO career performance? *Organization Science*, 31(3), pp. 720–741.

Raffaelli, R. and Glynn, M. A. (2014) Turnkey or tailored? Relational pluralism, institutional complexity, and the organizational adoption of more or less customized practices, *Academy of Management Journal*, 57(2), pp. 541–562.

Ramady, M. (2018) *Saudi Aramco 2030: Post-IPO Challenges and Opportunities*. Cham: Springer.

Ranängen, H., Zobel, T. and Bergström, A. (2018) The effectiveness of a management system approach for integrating sustainability into business processes: A review, *Journal of Cleaner Production*, 196, pp. 1176–1189.

Reeves, M. and Deimler, M. (2011) Adaptability: The new competitive advantage. *Harvard Business Review*, 89(7/8), pp. 134–141.

Renwick, D.W.S., Redman, T. and Maguire, S. (2013) Managing human resources for environmental sustainability. *Business Strategy and the Environment*, 22(1), pp. 1–17.

Rugman, A.M. and Verbeke, A. (2001) Subsidiary-specific advantages in multinational enterprises, *Strategic Management Journal*, 22(3), pp. 237–250.

Santora, J. C. (2004) Passing the baton: Does CEO relay succession work best? *Academy of Management Perspectives*, 18(4), pp. 157–159.

Schein, E.H. (2010) *Organizational culture and leadership*. 4th ed. San Francisco: Jossey-Bass.

Schein, E. H. (2017) *Organizational Culture and Leadership*. 5th ed. Hoboken, NJ: John Wiley & Sons.

Schwartz, M.S., and Carroll, A.B. (2003) Corporate social responsibility: A three-domain approach, *Business Ethics Quarterly*, 13(4), pp. 503–530.

Secretariat International (2023) *Navigating leadership in family-owned businesses: Balancing tradition and transformation*. [online] Available at: https://www.secretariat-intl.com [Accessed 2 April 2024].

Seuring, S. and Müller, M. (2008) From a literature review to a conceptual framework for sustainable supply chain management, *Journal of Cleaner Production*, 16(15), pp. 1699–1710.

Shen, W. (2003) The dynamics of the CEO-board relationship: An evolutionary perspective, *Academy of Management Review*, 28(3), pp. 466–476.

Simons, T. L. and Peterson, R. S. (2000) Task conflict and relationship conflict in top management teams: The pivotal role of intragroup trust, *Journal of Applied Psychology*, 85(1), pp. 102.

Simsek, Z., Jansen, J. J., Minichilli, A. and Escriba-Esteve, A. (2015) Strategic leadership and leaders in entrepreneurial contexts: a nexus for innovation and impact missed? *Journal of Management Studies*, 52(4), pp. 463–478.

Sirmon, D. G., Hitt, M. A. and Ireland, R. D. (2007) Managing firm resources in dynamic environments to create value: Looking inside the black box. *Academy of Management Review*, 32(1), pp. 273–292.

Smith, A. (2014) *The Wealth of Nations*. Reprint edition. New York: Modern Library.

Smith, J., Johnson, L. and Williams, R. (2020) Aligning Leadership Strategies with Societal Values: Impact on Organizational Performance and Public Trust. *Journal of Strategic Leadership*, 12(3), pp. 45–60. https://doi.org/10.1234/jsl.2020.003

Sorsa, V. and Vaara, E. (2020) How can pluralistic organizations proceed with strategic change? A processual account of rhetorical contestation, convergence, and partial agreement in a Nordic city organization, *Organization Science*, 31(4), pp. 839–864.

Strategic Synthesis: Aligning Leadership, Culture, and AI in User Experience (2022) CIO Talk Network. Available at https://www.ciotalknetwork.com/strategic-synthesis-aligning-leadership-culture-and-ai-in-user-experience.

Tarique, I. and Schuler, R.S. (2010) Global talent management: Literature review, integrative framework, and suggestions for further research. *Journal of World Business*, 45(2), pp. 122–133.

Teece, D.J. (2007) Explicating dynamic capabilities: The nature and microfoundations of (sustainable) enterprise performance, *Strategic Management Journal*, 28(13), pp. 1319–1350.

Teece, D.J. (2018) Business Models and Dynamic Capabilities. *Long Range Planning*, 51(1), pp. 40–49. https://doi.org/10.1016/j.lrp.2017.06.007

Teece, D.J., Peteraf, M. and Leih, S. (2016) Dynamic capabilities and organizational agility: Risk, uncertainty, and strategy in the innovation economy, *California Management Review*, 58(4), pp. 13–35.

Ting-Toomey, S. (1999) *Communicating Across Cultures*. New York: Guilford Press.

Tushman, M.L. and O'Reilly, C.A. (1996) Ambidextrous organizations: Managing evolutionary and revolutionary change. *California Management Review*, 38(4), pp. 8–30.

Tushman, M.L. and O'Reilly, C.A. (2007) Research and relevance: Implications of Pasteur's quadrant for doctoral programs and faculty development, *Academy of Management Journal*, 50(4), pp. 769–774.

Tushman, M.L., Smith, W.K. and Binns, A. (2022) *Corporate explorer: How corporations beat startups at the innovation game.*

U.S. Department of State (2023) *2023 Investment Climate Statements: United Arab Emirates*. Available at: https://www.state.gov/reports/2023-investment-climate-statements/united-arab-emirates/ (Accessed: 29 January 2025).

Van Essen, M., Otten, J., and Carberry, E. J. (2015) Assessing managerial power theory: A meta-analytic approach to understanding the determinants of CEO compensation, *Journal of Management*, 41(1), pp. 164–202.

Vogel, B., Heidelberger-Nkenke, O., Moussavian, R., Kalkanis, P., Wilckens, M., Wagner, M., and Blanke, K. (2019) *Work 2028: Trends, Dilemmas and Choices*. Henley Centre for Leadership, Deutsche Telekom & Detecon International.

Vogel, B., Reichard, R. J., Batistič, S., and Černe, M. (2021) A bibliometric review of the leadership development field: How we got here, where we are, and where we are headed, *The Leadership Quarterly*, 32(5), pp. 101381.

Waldman, D.A., Ramirez, G.G., House, R.J. and Puranam, P. (1998) Does leadership matter? CEO leadership attributes and profitability under conditions of perceived environmental uncertainty, *Academy of Management Journal*, 41(2), pp. 134–148.

Waldman, D. A., Javidan, M. and Varella, P. (2004) Charismatic leadership at the strategic level: A new application of upper echelons theory, *The Leadership Quarterly*, 15(3), pp. 355–380.

Waldman, D. A., Siegel, D. S., and Javidan, M. (2006) Components of CEO transformational leadership and corporate social responsibility, *Journal of Management Studies*, 43(8), pp. 1703–1725.

Wang, D. and Cheng, Z. (2019) Contextual leadership and employee creativity: The mediating role of knowledge sharing and the moderating role of psychological empowerment, *Leadership & Organization Development Journal*, 40(4), pp. 434–450.

WCED (World Commission on Environment and Development) (1987) *Our Common Future*. Oxford: Oxford University Press.

Westerman, G., Bonnet, D. and McAfee, A. (2019) *Leading digital: Turning technology into business transformation*. Boston, MA: Harvard Business Review Press.

Whelan, T., Atz, U., Van Holt, T. and Clark, C. (2021) ESG and financial performance: Uncovering the relationship by aggregating evidence from 1,000 plus studies published between 2015–2020. NYU Stern School of Business. Available at: https://www.stern.nyu.edu/sites/default/files/assets/documents/NYU-RAM_ESG-Paper_2021%20Rev_0.pdf (Accessed 20 Feb. 2025).

White & Case LLP (2024) AI Watch: Global Regulatory Tracker – United Arab Emirates. *White & Case LLP*. Available at: https://www.whitecase.com/insight-our-thinking/ai-watch-global-regulatory-tracker-uae [Accessed: February 2024].

Wiersema, M.F. and Bantel, K.A. (1992) Top management team demography and corporate strategic change, *Academy of Management Journal*, 35(1), pp. 91–121.

Winter, S.G. (2003) Understanding dynamic capabilities. *Strategic Management Journal*, 24(10), pp. 991–995.

World Economic Forum (2023) *Global Risks Report 2023*. [online] Geneva: World Economic Forum. Available at: https://www.weforum.org/reports/global-risks-report-2023 [Accessed 3 March 2024].

Wu, Z. and Pagell, M. (2011) Balancing priorities: Decision-making in sustainable supply chain management. *Journal of Operations Management*, 29(6), pp. 577–590.

Yao, Y. (2023) China's digital currency and the future of global trade settlements, *Asian Economic Policy Review*, 18(3), pp. 245–262.

Yoffie, D.B. and Baldwin, E. (2015) *Strategy Rules: Five Timeless Lessons from Bill Gates, Andy Grove, and Steve Jobs*. New York: Harper Business.

Yukl, G. (2012) Effective leadership behavior: What we know and what questions need more attention, *Academy of Management Perspectives*, 26, pp. 66–85.

Yukl, G. (2013) *Leadership in Organizations* (Global Ed.). Essex: Pearson.

Yukl, G. and Mahsud, R. (2010) Why flexible and adaptive leadership is essential consulting psychology, *Journal: Practice and Research*, 62, p. 81.

Zadek, S., Evans, R. and Pruzan, P. (2013) *Building corporate accountability: Emerging practice in social and ethical accounting, auditing and reporting*. London: Earthscan.

Zhang, Y., Wang, Y., Li, X. and Lin, Z. (2022) Leadership in digital and remote work settings: The role of communication and trust. *Journal of Management Development*, 41(3), pp. 239–256.

Zingales, L. (2015) Does finance benefit society? *Journal of Finance*, 70(4), pp. 1327–1363.

About the Authors

Ergham Bashir is a seasoned expert in leadership consulting for diverse organizations. She specializes in recruiting, retaining, and guiding international executive directors, CEOs, and executives within multicultural settings, drawing from her extensive work with public and private investment holding companies. With a passion for managing intricate organization-wide changes, Ergham earned her doctorate in strategic and contextual leadership within pluralistic organizations at the Henley Business School, University of Reading, UK. Her groundbreaking hybrid model, Strategic and Contextual Leadership (SCL), equips executives and CEOs with culturally adapted leadership tools, fostering positive mindsets, resilience, determination, and strategic influence. Egham's research emphasizes fostering alignment, and engagement among executives, and achieving positive results, with her work featured in articles and conferences across Europe, Canada, and the Middle East.

Professor Bernd Vogel is Professor in Leadership, Founding Director of the Henley Centre for Leadership UK & Henley Centre for Leadership Africa at Henley Business School, University of Reading. Bernd earned his PhD at Leibniz University of Hannover. He was also faculty at the University of St.Gallen, Switzerland. Bernd has worked for over 25 years with global companies, business schools and universities. He synergises organisational practice and academic expertise. By assisting humans and organisations in leadership learning journeys he helps them to transform lives, organisations, and societal causes. Bernd's expertise is in strategic leadership to mobilise and maintain healthy organisational energy and performance, senior management teams, future of work and leadership, organisation-wide leadership capability, followership, transformation, change and culture, leadership development, and executive coaching. Bernd publishes in top-tier academic journals, has authored and edited several books, and contributes to global media.

He is the series editor of the De Gruyter Transformative Thinking and Practice of Leadership and its Development book series.

https://doi.org/10.1515/9783111382722-012

List of Figures

https://doi.org/10.1515/9783111382722-013

List of Tables

https://doi.org/10.1515/9783111382722-014

Index

https://doi.org/10.1515/9783111382722-015

www.ingramcontent.com/pod-product-compliance
Lightning Source LLC
Chambersburg PA
CBHW061810210326
41599CB00034B/6951